Themis
Bar Review

Multistate Practice Exams

How To Use This Book

Practice Exam One (45 Questions)

Practice Exam Two (55 Questions)

**Practice Exam Three:
Simulated MBE (200 Questions)**

Practice Exam Four (100 Questions)

How To Use This Book

OVERVIEW

This MBE Practice Exams Book is designed to work in tandem with the Themis Bar Review course. Contained within are four Practice Exams, including the 200-question Simulated MBE, that are assigned in your Directed Study schedule. To get the most out of these exams, ***do not attempt—or even view—these exams until they are assigned in your course calendar***.

There are two modes of learning with Themis Bar Review: Directed Study and Flex Study. In Directed Study mode, you will follow a structured, sequential daily task schedule. In Flex Study mode, you may choose to complete tasks in any order, at your own pace. You may alternate between these two modes of study; any work completed in Flex Study mode will be reflected in your Directed Study progress. However, we strongly recommend that you follow the steps below to optimize retention, recall, and success.

STEP 1: REVIEW FULL-LENGTH OUTLINES

- Full-length substantive outlines are located in your Multistate Outlines book and also online under the **Outlines** section of your course home page.
- If you have never been exposed to a subject, read the outline before proceeding. Otherwise, review the outline to refresh your memory of the subject and refer back to the outline when you need clarification or further discussion of a topic.

STEP 2: WATCH LECTURES

- Lectures are divided into 20-minute chapters. Select a chapter to begin the video and to download the corresponding handout (via the **Lecture Handout** link).
- After each chapter, thoughtfully complete the series of post-lecture assessment questions (via the **Assessments** link), which will reinforce the key concepts and assess whether you mastered that particular chapter.
- Refer back to the substantive outline and the lecture handout as you review the assessment questions you did not answer correctly.

STEP 3: PRACTICE QUESTIONS

- Your Dynamic Calendar will present you first with single-subject practice question sets, and later with mixed-subject sets. You can complete each practice question task in either Interactive Mode or Test Mode. Interactive Mode allows you to immediately view the answer and explanation for each question. Test Mode allows you to complete the entire session before issuing a score report and showing the answer explanations.
- Once the practice question task has been completed, access the task to see the questions you have completed and to thoroughly review each answer explanation. Make sure you understand why each incorrect answer choice is incorrect, and why the correct one is correct. Refer back to the outline, lecture handout, and your notes to understand the substantive law that you missed.

STEP 4: PRACTICE EXAMS ONE AND TWO

Practice Exam One is a 45-question test covering three MBE subjects; Practice Exam Two is made up of 55 questions covering the remaining four subjects. They are scheduled in your course calendar after you have watched the lectures and completed the practice question sets for the corresponding subjects, but will not be available online until their assigned dates.

- The day before the exam, review the MBE Final Review Outlines (found in the Multistate Outlines book) and your notes and lecture handouts for the tested subjects. Set aside the time indicated in the instructions for each exam, allowing 1.8 minutes per question.
- Access the Practice Exams by clicking on the **Practice Exams** link of your course home page. Or, use the enclosed paper version and bubble sheet to better mimic exam conditions.
- If you choose to take these exams using the enclosed paper versions, you will need to log in to the course to enter your answers and view the answer explanations. This allows you to compare your performance on the exam with other students taking Themis nationwide. This is an important check on where you stand so that you can make sure you are on track (or ahead of the curve)!
- After completing each Practice Exam, carefully review each answer explanation to understand your mistakes and to make sure you chose the correct answers for the correct reasons.

STEP 5: PRACTICE EXAM THREE: SIMULATED MBE

The 200-question Simulated MBE is the third Practice Exam you will be assigned.

- A few days before the exam, you should begin reviewing your notes for all seven MBE subjects so that the substantive law is fresh in your mind. You have six hours to complete the 200-question Simulated MBE, and you should take the entire exam in one day. Take three hours to complete the AM session in the morning, and after a one-hour break, take three hours to complete the PM session in the afternoon. Make sure you take the exam in a quiet place where you can concentrate and will not be distracted.
- Access this exam via the **Practice Exams** link. This simulated exam can be taken in the portal, or offline using the enclosed paper version. As with the first two Practice Exams, log your answers in the online version to view the explanations and comparison data.
- After you take the Simulated MBE, you will be assigned two full days of review. Take this time to carefully review the explanatory answers as presented in the MBE Analysis lecture series, which reviews and analyzes each of the 200 questions in depth.

STEP 6: PRACTICE EXAM FOUR

- After taking the Simulated MBE, continue to complete mixed-subject practice question sets as assigned in your Directed Study schedule, now armed with information from your careful review of the previous practice sessions and exams.
- Near the end of the course schedule, you will be assigned Practice Exam Four, which is comprised of 100 questions covering all seven MBE subjects. As with the previous Practice Exams, you may take this exam online or on paper. If you take it on paper, you will need to log in to your course to enter your answers and view the answer explanations.
- Good luck on the MBE!

Themis
Bar Review

Practice Exam One

Practice Exam One

Start Time:_____

End Time:_____

1. Ⓐ Ⓑ Ⓒ Ⓓ   26. Ⓐ Ⓑ Ⓒ Ⓓ
2. Ⓐ Ⓑ Ⓒ Ⓓ   27. Ⓐ Ⓑ Ⓒ Ⓓ
3. Ⓐ Ⓑ Ⓒ Ⓓ   28. Ⓐ Ⓑ Ⓒ Ⓓ
4. Ⓐ Ⓑ Ⓒ Ⓓ   29. Ⓐ Ⓑ Ⓒ Ⓓ
5. Ⓐ Ⓑ Ⓒ Ⓓ   30. Ⓐ Ⓑ Ⓒ Ⓓ
6. Ⓐ Ⓑ Ⓒ Ⓓ   31. Ⓐ Ⓑ Ⓒ Ⓓ
7. Ⓐ Ⓑ Ⓒ Ⓓ   32. Ⓐ Ⓑ Ⓒ Ⓓ
8. Ⓐ Ⓑ Ⓒ Ⓓ   33. Ⓐ Ⓑ Ⓒ Ⓓ
9. Ⓐ Ⓑ Ⓒ Ⓓ   34. Ⓐ Ⓑ Ⓒ Ⓓ
10. Ⓐ Ⓑ Ⓒ Ⓓ   35. Ⓐ Ⓑ Ⓒ Ⓓ
11. Ⓐ Ⓑ Ⓒ Ⓓ   36. Ⓐ Ⓑ Ⓒ Ⓓ
12. Ⓐ Ⓑ Ⓒ Ⓓ   37. Ⓐ Ⓑ Ⓒ Ⓓ
13. Ⓐ Ⓑ Ⓒ Ⓓ   38. Ⓐ Ⓑ Ⓒ Ⓓ
14. Ⓐ Ⓑ Ⓒ Ⓓ   39. Ⓐ Ⓑ Ⓒ Ⓓ
15. Ⓐ Ⓑ Ⓒ Ⓓ   40. Ⓐ Ⓑ Ⓒ Ⓓ
16. Ⓐ Ⓑ Ⓒ Ⓓ   41. Ⓐ Ⓑ Ⓒ Ⓓ
17. Ⓐ Ⓑ Ⓒ Ⓓ   42. Ⓐ Ⓑ Ⓒ Ⓓ
18. Ⓐ Ⓑ Ⓒ Ⓓ   43. Ⓐ Ⓑ Ⓒ Ⓓ
19. Ⓐ Ⓑ Ⓒ Ⓓ   44. Ⓐ Ⓑ Ⓒ Ⓓ
20. Ⓐ Ⓑ Ⓒ Ⓓ   45. Ⓐ Ⓑ Ⓒ Ⓓ
21. Ⓐ Ⓑ Ⓒ Ⓓ
22. Ⓐ Ⓑ Ⓒ Ⓓ
23. Ⓐ Ⓑ Ⓒ Ⓓ
24. Ⓐ Ⓑ Ⓒ Ⓓ
25. Ⓐ Ⓑ Ⓒ Ⓓ

Themis
Bar Review

PRACTICE EXAM ONE

TIME: 81 MINUTES

Welcome to Practice Exam One. This exam consists of 45 questions in the areas of Contracts, Real Property, and Torts. This exam will take approximately 81 minutes (an average of 1.8 minutes per question). After you have completed this exam, log in to your course to submit your answers, view detailed answer explanations, and compare your performance to other Themis students.

1. In need of money, the owner of a ring prepared an email one evening proposing to sell the ring to a friend for $500, but only if he responded within 24 hours. Unable to bring herself to send the email, the owner, who normally was a teetotaler, began drinking. When she was thoroughly intoxicated, she sent the email without realizing it. After the owner sobered up the following afternoon, she called her friend and said that she had never meant to send the email, but her friend informed her that he had already responded by email, agreeing to the transaction.

Does a valid contract exist?

- (A) Yes, because the friend accepted the owner's offer to sell the ring.
- (B) Yes, because the friend had 24 hours in which to respond.
- (C) No, because the owner lacked capacity at the time that she made the offer.
- (D) No, because the contract was executory.

2. A horticulturist grew many exotic indoor plants. At night, the horticulturist would open his floor-to-ceiling windows to provide the plants with fresh air. He would also turn on hundreds of fluorescent lights hanging from the ceiling over the plants. The horticulturist would leave the lights on all night to help the plants grow. The wall with the floor-to-ceiling windows abutted the bedroom window of his neighbor, an 85-year-old man. However, the man barely noticed the glaring light coming through the window because he had blurred vision due to cataracts. When the man's grandson visited him recently and noticed the lights, the grandson insisted that the man file a private nuisance action against the horticulturist.

If the man files suit, who will prevail?

- (A) The man, because he suffered harm that is different in kind from that suffered by other members of the community.
- (B) The man, because the glaring lights would be inconvenient and annoying to a normal, reasonable person in the community.
- (C) The horticulturist, because the glaring lights were not an unreasonable disturbance to any other neighbors.
- (D) The horticulturist, because the glaring lights did not substantially interfere with the man's use and enjoyment of his home.

3. An attorney was sued by a client for malpractice. The client obtained a judgment against the attorney and, by filing the judgment in the county in which the attorney rented an office, created a lien that was valid against any real property then owned or subsequently acquired by the attorney for up to 10 years. Three years later, the attorney purchased a residence in the same county. The attorney financed the purchase with a loan from a bank, which was secured by a mortgage on the residence. Two years later, the attorney failed to make the required mortgage payments. The bank initiated foreclosure proceedings, joining the client as a party. The jurisdiction has adopted the following statute: "No conveyance or mortgage of real property shall be good against subsequent purchasers for value and without notice unless the same be recorded according to law." In addition, the jurisdiction treats a mortgage as a lien against the real property.

Who has priority to the proceeds from the foreclosure sale?

(A) The client, because the lien was first in time.
(B) The client, because the lien was recorded first.
(C) The bank, because the lien is not affected by the foreclosure sale.
(D) The bank, because the mortgage was a purchase money mortgage.

4. Twenty years ago, a property owner deeded his house to a charitable organization. The warranty deed stated that the house was transferred to the organization "provided that the organization uses the premises as a halfway house for troubled teenagers; otherwise, the owner may reenter the property." Nine years after the property was transferred, the charitable organization ceased running a halfway house, and began using the house as its administrative office. Recently, upon the death of the property owner, all of his real property passed by will to his daughter. The time period for adverse possession in the state where the house is located is 10 years.

Does the charitable organization have a current possessory interest in the house?

(A) No, because the charitable organization ceased to use the house as a halfway house.
(B) No, because the owner devised his interest in the house to his daughter.
(C) Yes, because the charitable organization has outright ownership of the house through adverse possession.
(D) Yes, because the right of re-entry has not been exercised.

5. A homeowner devised her home to her best friend, "but if [the best friend] predeceases me, to her heirs." The best friend died shortly before the homeowner did. The best friend is survived by her daughter, and the homeowner is survived by her son. The best friend's daughter claims that she should take the home, while the homeowner's son claims that it should pass with the rest of the homeowner's estate.

The applicable jurisdiction has an anti-lapse statute. Who should receive the homeowner's home?

(A) The best friend's daughter, because of the anti-lapse statute.
(B) The best friend's daughter, because the homeowner left the home to the best friend and her heirs.
(C) The homeowner's son, because the gift lapsed.
(D) The homeowner's son, because the homeowner and the best friend were not related by blood.

6. A homeowner hired a roofer to install a new roof on his house. The homeowner scheduled the installation to take place during a week when he was to be on vacation. Although the contract specified that the color of the shingles was to be brown, the homeowner returned to find that the roofer instead had installed red shingles. Although the new roof was structurally sound, the homeowner refused the pay the roofer. The roofer sued the homeowner. The fact-finder determined that the roofer had materially breached the contract.

Under what theory of damages is the roofer most likely to recover?

(A) Expectancy damages
(B) Restitution damages
(C) Reliance damages
(D) None, because the roofer materially breached the contract.

7.   A woman built a water fountain in her backyard. The water fountain was located in the center of a flat, concrete surface, and the water from the fountain would drain through holes in the concrete surface. At night, the water falling from the fountain would change colors with the use of colored lights. Because the neighborhood children were enthralled by the fountain, but the concrete was very slippery, the woman erected a five-foot fence around her backyard with a locked gate that could only be opened with a passcode. In addition, she posted warning signs telling trespassers to keep out. One evening, a child saw the changing colors of the water over the fence. Unable to open the gate, the child got a ladder from his parent's yard and used it to climb over the fence. As he approached the fountain, the child slipped on the wet concrete surface, fell to the ground, and fractured his wrist. The parents of the child have filed a claim for damages against the woman.

Who will prevail?

  (A)   The child, because the fountain was
        an attractive nuisance.
  (B)   The child, because the slippery
        concrete surface posed an
        unreasonable risk of injury to
        children.
  (C)   The woman, because she does not
        owe a duty to the child since he is an
        unknown trespasser.
  (D)   The woman, because she exercised
        reasonable care to protect children
        from harm.

8.   A buyer agreed in writing to purchase sports memorabilia related to a legendary sports figure, which was on display at a museum, from the owner for $500,000. The agreement called for the payment to be made and the memorabilia handed over at the end of the display period, 60 days after the agreement was signed by both parties. Forty-five days later, a record held by the sports legend was broken and the fair market value of the memorabilia dropped to $275,000. The buyer repudiated the contract. The following week, before the owner could locate another buyer, the memorabilia, on loan for public display, was destroyed by no fault of either the buyer or the owner. The owner had only insured the memorabilia for $100,000.

How much is the owner likely to recover from the buyer?

  (A) $500,000.00
  (B) $400,000.00
  (C) $275,000.00
  (D) $225,000.00

9. In July, a toy store entered into a written agreement with a local supplier for 500 Halloween costumes at $25 per costume. Under the agreement, the costumes were to be delivered on or before October 1. On August 17, the supplier told the store that it would not under any circumstances be able to supply the costumes. The next day, the store contracted with a company to supply 500 similar Halloween costumes for $30 each for delivery on or before October 5. On September 1, the store filed a complaint against the local supplier for breach of contract. The supplier moves to dismiss the complaint.

How should the court rule on this motion?

(A) Deny it, because the complaint for breach was brought within 15 days of the supplier notifying the store it would not be able to supply the costumes.
(B) Deny it, because the supplier repudiated its contractual obligation.
(C) Grant it, because less than 30 days had expired since the supplier told the store it would not be able to supply the costumes before the store filed its complaint.
(D) Grant it, because the time for performance of the contract has not yet passed.

10. A homeowner borrowed money from a bank in order to install a deck at her residence. The bank loan, which was evidenced by a note that contained an acceleration clause, was secured by a five-year mortgage on the residence. The bank promptly recorded this mortgage. Two years later, the homeowner sold the residence to a buyer. The agreement between the homeowner and the buyer provided for the buyer to assume the mortgage. The bank was not a party to this agreement and did not provide any consideration to the buyer for entering into this agreement. Six months after the buyer took possession of the residence, the buyer stopped making payments on the loan. The bank initiated an action against the buyer for the outstanding balance due on the home improvement loan.

Is the buyer liable to the bank for the outstanding balance?

(A) Yes, because the buyer agreed to assume the homeowner's mortgage obligation.
(B) Yes, because the buyer is in possession of the residence.
(C) No, because the bank was not a party to the agreement between the homeowner and buyer.
(D) No, because the buyer did not receive consideration from the bank for agreeing to assume the loan obligation.

11. A hardware store owner observed a customer looking at a display of chain saws. The customer asked the owner which of two brands he would recommend. The owner said, "I swear by Brand X. In my opinion they make the best chain saws." In making this statement, the owner had no intent to offer the customer a warranty. The customer purchased a Brand X chain saw. On the customer's sales receipt, was printed, "All warrantees, express or implied, are hereby disclaimed." The chain saw malfunctioned, resulting in serious injury to the customer. The customer sued the store owner for breach of an express warranty.

Of the following, which would be the store owner's best defense?

(A) The store owner did not use the words "warranty" or "guarantee."
(B) The store owner did not intend to offer a warranty.
(C) Any express warranty was disclaimed by the sale receipt.
(D) The store owner's words constituted his opinion.

12. A tool distributor sold a retailer an assortment of tools on credit. Immediately prior to the sale, the distributor, concerned about the retailer's financial health, telephoned the retailer to ask if the retailer would be able to pay for the tools. The retailer assured the distributor that it was solvent, even though the retailer knew it might not be before it paid for the tools. Twelve days after the retailer received the tools, the distributor learned that the retailer was insolvent and immediately sought to reclaim the tools.

Can the distributor do so?

(A) No, because the retailer had retained the tools for twelve days.
(B) No, because the retailer had received the tools.
(C) Yes, because the retailer had falsely assured the distributor that it was solvent.
(D) Yes, because the distributor acted immediately upon learning that the retailer was insolvent.

13. A son went to visit his father, who was very ill. The father and son reminisced about hunting trips they had taken on property owned by the father. The father told the son that he wanted the son to have the property after the father died. The son did not know that the father had sold the property earlier that month to a farmer who owned and lived on adjacent property. Shortly after the father died, the son took a trip to hunt on the property. While the son was hunting, the farmer approached the son and correctly told him that the father had sold the land to the farmer. The son, bursting into tears, pointed his rifle at the farmer. The son told the farmer that he would shoot the farmer for telling lies about the father. The farmer's wife, who was watching the exchange, approached the son from behind and hit him over the head with a shovel. The son died from his injuries, and his estate has sued the farmer's wife.

Is the son's estate likely to succeed in a suit against the farmer's wife?

(A) No, because the farmer's wife is protected by the privilege of necessity.
(B) No, because the wife had a reasonable belief that the farmer would be entitled to use self-defense.
(C) Yes, because only the farmer would be entitled to use force against the son.
(D) Yes, because the son reasonably believed that the farmer was trespassing on the son's land.

14. An unscrupulous landowner sold undeveloped land to two different buyers and then disappeared with the proceeds. Each buyer paid fair market value for the land and neither buyer was aware of the landowner's transaction with the other buyer. Subsequently, the first buyer, upon learning of the second conveyance, recorded her deed. The second buyer did not record his deed.

The applicable recording act reads: "A conveyance of any interest in land shall not be valid against any subsequent purchaser for value, without notice thereof, unless the conveyance is recorded."

In action brought by the first buyer against the second buyer, who is entitled to ownership of the land?

(A) The first buyer, pursuant to the "first in time, first in right" rule, because the recording act does not apply since the second buyer did not record his deed.
(B) The first buyer, pursuant to the recording act, because she alone recorded her deed.
(C) The second buyer, pursuant to the recording act, because he paid fair market value for the land without notice of the first conveyance.
(D) The second buyer, pursuant to the recording act, because the first buyer knew of the second conveyance prior to recording her deed.

15.   A homeowner financed the purchase of his residence with a $200,000 loan from a bank. The loan, which was to be repaid over twenty years, was secured by a mortgage on the residence. The bank promptly recorded the mortgage. The following year, the homeowner borrowed $50,000 from a credit union to start a business. The credit union loan, which had a five-year term, was secured by a mortgage on the residence, which the credit union immediately recorded. The next year, the homeowner obtained a two-year loan from the bank for $25,000 to pay for his daughter's wedding. The homeowner agreed that the mortgage on the residence would also serve as security for this loan. The homeowner defaulted on all three loans. The bank initiated foreclosure proceedings to which the credit union was named as a party. The proceeds from the foreclosure sale were sufficient to repay the bank in full for its residential purchase loan and either the credit union's business loan or the bank's wedding loan, but not both.

Who should be paid in full?

(A)   The bank, because the bank's mortgage was recorded before the credit union's mortgage.
(B)   The bank, because the bank initiated the foreclosure proceedings.
(C)   The credit union, because its mortgage secured a commercial loan.
(D)   The credit union, because the bank's modification of its mortgage prejudiced the credit union.

16.   A customer at a bakery ordered a cake, which the bakery stated was made by an independent third party. The cake contained small shards of metal. The metal was not detected by the bakery, even though the bakery conducted a reasonable inspection of the cake and otherwise had no reason to suspect that the cake contained the metal. The customer ate the cake and immediately incurred serious injuries from eating the shards of metal. The customer brought suit against the bakery based on strict products liability for injuries suffered from eating the cake.

Who will prevail?

(A)   The customer, because the bakery was a commercial supplier of the dessert.
(B)   The customer, because the bakery failed to warn him of the presence of the metal in the dessert.
(C)   The bakery, because the bakery did not bake the cake.
(D)   The bakery, because the metal was not detectable by reasonable inspection.

17. Two farmers who own adjacent farms decided to construct a small road that straddles their common property line. They entered into a written agreement whereby each granted to the other a right of access over his property in accord with the dimensions and location of the road and each promised that he, his heirs, devisees, assignees, and successors would equally share the repair and maintenance of the road with the neighboring property owner. This agreement was promptly and properly recorded. After the road was built, one of the farmers sold his farm in fee simple absolute to a rancher. A year ago, the other farmer died. His property passed by intestacy to his son. Through an oral agreement, the son leased the inherited farm to another farmer for a one-year term. The son told the new farmer of the shared maintenance agreement with the rancher, but otherwise did not discuss the maintenance of the road with the new farmer. This past spring, due to heavy flooding, the maintenance of the road was costly. When the new farmer contacted the rancher, the rancher, noting that he rarely used the road and preferred the public highway that abutted his property, refused to reimburse the farmer for the maintenance expenditures.

Under which of the following theories can the new farmer successfully recover half of the costs for maintenance from the rancher?

(A) The agreement contains a covenant that runs with the land.
(B) Detrimental reliance on the son's revelation of the shared maintenance agreement.
(C) The agreement contains an easement.
(D) The agreement contains an equitable servitude.

18. A consumer purchased a ladder from a hardware store for use around the house. Due to a defect in the design of the ladder, the consumer fell from the ladder and was seriously injured. The manufacturer of the ladder had affixed a notice to the ladder that limited consequential damages from any defect in the ladder or from a breach of the implied warranty of merchantability. The consumer had read the notice prior to purchasing the ladder. The consumer brought an action based on both a products liability claim and breach of the implied warranty of merchantability claim against the manufacturer to recover damages for his personal injuries.

Can either claim support the consumer's recovery?

(A) No, as to either type of claim.
(B) Yes, as to the products liability claim, but no, as to the implied warranty of merchantability claim.
(C) Yes, as to the implied warranty of merchantability claim, but no, as to the products liability claim.
(D) Yes, as to both types of claims.

19. A child was playing mini-golf at a recreation center when she went into an artificial creek to retrieve a lost ball. A high fence with a childproof lock surrounded the creek, but the child's mother opened the lock to let her daughter into the creek area to quickly retrieve the ball. When the girl reached into the creek, she was electrically shocked by a live wire from a motorized windmill that had fallen in the creek. She suffered long-term disability because of the electric shock. The family of the child filed a claim against the recreation center. The recreation center filed a response claiming it was not liable for the accident because it posted warnings that the creek was dangerous and surrounded it with a high fence that could not be opened without the intervention of an adult.

Under the traditional approach, is the recreation center likely to be successful in defending the suit?

(A) Yes, because the child entered the prohibited area.
(B) Yes, because the creek was surrounded by a locked fence with warnings.
(C) No, because the creek was abnormally dangerous.
(D) No, because the creek was an attractive nuisance.

20. A university ordered scientific equipment from a manufacturer for prompt shipment. The manufacturer accepted the order. Several days later, prior to identification of the equipment, the manufacturer became insolvent. Upon learning of the manufacturer's insolvency, the university did not seek reasonable assurances of performance from the manufacturer. Although the university could have placed an order with another company for the same equipment, the university chose instead to tender the purchase price to the manufacturer. When the manufacturer refused to accept the tendered price and ship the equipment, the university filed an action to force the manufacturer to fill the order.

Is it likely that the university can compel the manufacturer to supply the scientific equipment?

(A) No, because the equipment was neither identified nor unique.
(B) No, because the university did not seek reasonable assurances of performance from the manufacturer.
(C) Yes, because the manufacturer is insolvent.
(D) Yes, because the university is a buyer and the manufacturer is in breach of the contract.

21. The plaintiff was driving on a city street when a car swerved in front of him, forcing the plaintiff to slam on his brakes to avoid a collision. The defendant was driving the car behind the plaintiff. Because the defendant was speeding, he was unable to slow down quickly enough to avoid hitting the plaintiff. The plaintiff sustained severe whiplash as a result of the collision. The plaintiff has sued the defendant. The evidence at trial shows that both the defendant and the driver of the car that swerved in front of the plaintiff were negligent, and that the negligence of each caused the plaintiff's injuries. The defendant has moved for a directed verdict, arguing that the plaintiff did not establish causation.

Is the court likely to grant the defendant's motion?

(A) No, because the defendant's conduct was the cause of the plaintiff's injury.
(B) No, because the plaintiff can prove proximate causation, even if he cannot prove actual causation.
(C) Yes, because a plaintiff may not recover against a single defendant when multiple individuals contributed to the plaintiff's injury.
(D) Yes, because the defendant can prove that his negligence would not have resulted in the plaintiff's injury had the other car not swerved.

22. A thief stole an expensive vase from the home of the vase's owner. The owner later acquired information that the vase was being stored in a warehouse on the other side of town. The owner went to the warehouse and broke a window to enter the premises. There, he encountered the thief, standing next to the vase. The owner brandished a gun, and said, "Hand over the vase, or else." The owner had no intention of actually firing a shot, but his finger slipped and pulled the trigger. The thief was hit by a bullet in the chest. While the thief writhed on the floor, the owner found and seized the vase, and exited the premises through the front door.

The thief survived the attack, and sued the owner for battery. Is he likely to prevail?

(A) Yes, because the thief suffered serious injury.
(B) Yes, because the owner intended to place the thief in fear.
(C) No, because the owner's conduct was privileged.
(D) No, because the shooting was accidental.

23. A homeowner mortgaged her home with a bank ten years ago and turned it into an inn. The bank recorded the mortgage at that time. She subsequently incurred obligations with a contractor for work on the inn to create two large, high-end suites for guests. This involved tearing down walls and thereby reducing the number of bedrooms at the inn.

A year later, she was forced to undergo a foreclosure action after failing to make six months of mortgage payments. She then realized that if she reinstated the walls and increased the number of bedrooms in the inn, she could turn a higher profit. She further hoped that making these improvements might negate the need to follow through with the foreclosure action. She therefore refinanced the mortgage with the bank to make these improvements after a family member helped her to get current with her mortgage obligations. The bank accordingly adjusted the existing mortgage so that its payments were decreased for three years but ballooned to a much higher interest rate if the homeowner missed more than three payments in a row.

Two years later, the inn had seen no profit, and the homeowner again defaulted on her mortgage for four months. After giving the homeowner an additional four months to catch up on her obligations, the bank again initiated a foreclosure action, which resulted in a sale of the home. At the time of the sale, the existing secured creditors included not only those associated with the foreclosure action but, by virtue of a lien that took effect prior to the refinancing, also the contractor who had performed the work on the two suites at the inn.

How did the refinance impact the bank's rights as a mortgagee?

(A)   The bank is not impacted by the action.
(B)   The bank subordinated its interest as to only the increased rate.
(C)   The bank subordinated its interest.
(D)   The bank will be treated as the most senior mortgagee at the increased rate.

24. A couple orally agreed that, after they were married, the husband would move into the wife's house, the husband would transfer $20,000 to the wife, and the house would be retitled under joint ownership. After the couple was married, the husband moved into the wife's house and transferred $20,000 to the wife's separate bank account, but before the wife had time to retitle the house under joint ownership, she died. Upon the wife's death, the husband petitioned the personal representative of his wife's estate to honor the couple's pre-marital agreement in determining the distribution of the wife's estate.

Of the following, which is best argument that the personal representative can advance to deny the husband's petition?

(A)   Marriage was a condition of the contract.
(B)   The agreement was not in writing.
(C)   The wife's death terminated her contractual obligation.
(D)   The wife had not breached her obligation to retitle the house under joint ownership.

25. Based on an honest belief, an employer terminated a bookkeeper for embezzlement. The employer also threatened to file a criminal complaint unless the bookkeeper agreed to repay the stolen funds. The bookkeeper, seeking to avoid criminal prosecution, agreed, and signed a promissory note payable to the employer in the amount of the embezzled funds. The bookkeeper subsequently admitted to having embezzled the money.

Can the bookkeeper avoid the promissory note?

(A) No, because the bookkeeper admitted to embezzling from her employer.

(B) No, because the employer's threat was based on an honest belief that the bookkeeper was an embezzler.

(C) Yes, because the bookkeeper signed the note under duress.

(D) Yes, because the employer terminated the bookkeeper.

26. The owner of a small parcel of undeveloped land conveyed the right to construct and use a road across the parcel to a corporation that owned a sizable tract of undeveloped adjacent land. The landowner was aware that the corporation intended to construct a factory on that tract of land and understood that the corporation intended to use the road to provide access to the factory. Before beginning construction of the factory, the corporation changed its plans and acquired additional contiguous property from a third party.

As a consequence, the corporation planned to build a factory that was slightly larger than the one originally planned on both this newly acquired property and the property the corporation originally owned. There would be a modest increase in the traffic using the road associated with this modification. Upon learning of the corporation's change in plans, the individual sued to enjoin the corporation from building and using the road to provide access to the factory.

Should the court grant the injunction?

(A) No, because the individual was aware of the purpose of the road.

(B) No, because the increase in usage of the road was modest.

(C) Yes, because there was no preexisting road on the parcel.

(D) Yes, because the easement would benefit property acquired after the easement was granted.

27. The owner of a new and unnamed store selling musical instruments was talking by telephone with a famous violinist who was known for her signature red violin. The owner asked whether the violinist would be able to perform at the store's opening and the violinist agreed. The next day, the owner and the violinist executed a valid written contract for the violinist to perform at the opening. The contract contained a clause stating that the contract was the complete and final agreement between the parties. When the violinist appeared at the store to perform, the owner refused to let her play. The violinist sued the owner for breach of contract. The owner moved to introduce evidence that during the telephone conversation, the owner had told the violinist that he would need her services only if he was able to secure the rights to use "theredviolin.com" as the domain name of the store; the violinist objected that the evidence was inadmissible. The contract contains no mention of this condition.

Is the court likely to admit evidence of the conversation regarding the domain name?

(A) Yes, because the conversation is evidence of a condition precedent to the existence of the contract.

(B) Yes, because this evidence does not contradict the written contract.

(C) No, because the parol evidence rule prohibits the introduction of prior extrinsic evidence.

(D) No, because the written contract was a complete integration of the parties' agreement.

28. A couple owned a home with a large backyard in which they hosted raucous parties, with extremely loud music and bright lights. These parties often occurred during weekdays and went until dawn. Despite multiple complaints, the couple continued to host these parties. The couple had the following three neighbors: an elderly woman who was abnormally sensitive to loud noises; a teacher who thought the parties were hilarious, as they reminded him of his fraternity days; and a mother who found the parties highly annoying and disruptive to her and her family but never addressed the issue with the couple.

Who would be barred from recovering from the couple in a nuisance action?

(A) The elderly woman, because she has special sensitivities.

(B) The teacher, because he is not offended by the actions.

(C) The mother, because she has not made the couple aware of the effect of their parties on her family.

(D) All of the above may recover.

29. An individual purchased a residence with the aid of a bank loan. In exchange, the individual signed a document giving the bank a security interest in the residence. A bank employee filed this mortgage document with the proper governmental entity, but did not file any of the other documents related to the loan, including the note that evidenced the individual's obligation to repay the loan. Subsequently, the individual sold the residence to a buyer who purchased the residence for its fair market value without actual knowledge of the mortgage. The buyer properly filed the deed. The individual later defaulted on the bank loan. A statute in the applicable jurisdiction provides, "No conveyance or mortgage of real property shall be good against subsequent purchasers for value unless the same be first recorded according to law."

Can the bank foreclose on its mortgage on the residence?

(A) No, because the buyer purchased the residence for its fair market value.

(B) No, because the bank did not record the other loan documents, including the note.

(C) Yes, because the buyer had record notice of the mortgage.

(D) Yes, because the bank recorded its mortgage before the buyer's purchase.

30. An attorney entered into a valid contract with a client to provide legal services for a set fee of $5,000. The contract provides that rather than paying the attorney, the client is to pay the fee to the attorney's daughter. The daughter, upon learning of the contract from her father, decided to donate this money to a local animal shelter. She told the manager of a local animal shelter that she planned to donate $5,000 to the shelter. The manager, relying on this, purchased $5,000 worth of pet supplies and medicine. The lawyer rendered the legal services, but the client ultimately failed to pay the daughter, who in turn did not donate the money to the shelter. The animal shelter files suit against the client for breach of contract.

Will the animal shelter prevail in its action against the client?

(A) Yes, because of the animal shelter's detrimental reliance.

(B) Yes, because the shelter is a donee beneficiary.

(C) No, because the attorney had no intention to benefit the animal shelter.

(D) No, because delegation of duties is not permitted under a services contract.

31. Two cousins received a residence as tenants in common when their grandmother left it to them in her will. The older cousin lived out of state, so the cousins both agreed that the younger cousin would live in the residence. While the younger cousin lived in residence, she paid the property taxes on the residence, an amount far less than the fair rental value of residence. She also paid for the maintenance of the residence, including substantial repairs to the plumbing after a pipe burst. The older cousin fell on hard times. He told his younger cousin that she owed him rent for the time she had been living in the residence. The younger cousin denied owing the older cousin any rent, and claimed that the older cousin owed her for reimbursement for taxes and repairs she had made on the residence throughout the years.

Neither cousin has requested a partition or an accounting. Do either of the cousins owe the other money with respect to the residence?

(A) The older cousin owes the younger cousin money for his share of the taxes and repairs, and the younger cousin owes the older cousin rent.

(B) The older cousin owes the younger cousin money for his share of the repairs, but the younger cousin does not owe the older cousin any money for rent.

(C) The younger cousin owes the older cousin money for rent, but the older cousin does not owe the younger cousin any money for his share of the taxes and repairs.

(D) The younger cousin does not owe the older cousin any money for rent, and the older cousin does not owe the younger cousin any money for his share of the taxes and repairs.

32. A manufacturer entered into a 30-year lease with the owner of a building zoned for commercial use. The lease contained a term that gave the manufacturer the right of first refusal if the owner ever decided to sell the building. Ten years later, the owner entered into a contract to sell the building to a third party. The owner has refused to honor the manufacturer's right of first refusal, contending that it violates the Rule Against Perpetuities. The jurisdiction recognizes the common-law Rule Against Perpetuities and its application to rights of first refusal.

Which of the following is the manufacturer's best argument that the Rule Against Perpetuities does not apply to the manufacturer's right of first refusal?

(A) The right of first refusal was granted in conjunction with a lease.

(B) The right of first refusal was granted as part of a commercial transaction.

(C) There is no life in being against which the right of first refusal is measured.

(D) The manufacturer exercised the right of first refusal before the expiration of the 21-year period.

33. Two individuals entered into a written contract for the sale of a moped for $475. The contract required delivery of the moped on July 1 and provided that oral modification of the contract was prohibited. On June 25, the seller called the buyer and asked if the seller could deliver the moped on July 2, explaining that the seller was overseas and could not return until July 2 due to work commitments that he could not change. The buyer agreed. On June 30 the buyer called the seller, informing him that he was disregarding the modification and demanding delivery of the moped on July 1. The seller delivered the moped on July 2, but the buyer refused to accept or pay for it.

Has the buyer breached the contract?

(A) Yes, because the buyer agreed to the modification.
(B) Yes, because the buyer waived the July 1 delivery requirement.
(C) No, because the buyer did not receive consideration for the modification.
(D) No, because the modification was not in writing.

34. Two brothers owned real property as joint tenants with the right of survivorship. The older brother obtained a loan from a credit union to start a business. He signed a note for the amount of the loan plus interest and received the loan proceeds. Both brothers executed a mortgage on the jointly owned property as security for the loan. The older brother operated the business without his younger brother's aid and retained all of the proceeds from the business. Approximately a year later, the older brother defaulted on the loan. The bank initiated foreclosure proceedings against the property. The applicable jurisdiction recognizes the lien theory with respect to the effect of a mortgage on a joint tenancy.

Can the bank enforce the mortgage against the younger brother's interest in the real property?

(A) Yes, because the applicable jurisdiction follows the lien theory.
(B) Yes, because the younger brother also executed the mortgage.
(C) No, because the real property was held in joint tenancy with the right of survivorship.
(D) No, because the younger brother did not receive an economic benefit from the loan.

35. A woman underwent gall bladder surgery, which was performed by the hospital's head surgeon. An intern observed the surgery and provided time updates to the surgical team, since the team had a limited time in which to complete the operation. The woman experienced significant pain following the surgery, and returned to her doctor. An x-ray revealed that a hemostat, which is an instrument typically used in gall bladder surgery, had been left in the woman's gall bladder. After the hemostat was removed, the woman continued to experience pain due to permanent injuries caused by the hemostat. The woman sued the head surgeon and the intern involved in her surgery. At trial, the woman did not provide any direct evidence that the surgeon or the intern had left the hemostat in her gall bladder. At the close of evidence, the intern moved for a directed verdict. The judge granted the motion.

What is the most likely reason that the judge granted the intern's motion?

(A) A negligence plaintiff must provide direct evidence of negligence.
(B) The doctrine of res ipsa loquitur is inapplicable to medical malpractice claims.
(C) The head surgeon was vicariously responsible for the intern's actions.
(D) The intern did not have exclusive control over the hemostat.

36. In response to a phone query by a manufacturer of fans, a supplier of motors offered to sell the manufacturer up to 10,000 motors at the price of $15 each. The supplier assured the manufacturer before ending the call that this price was good for 60 days. One month later, the manufacturer ordered 5,000 motors from the supplier. The supplier informed the manufacturer that the price was now $20 per motor.

Of the following, which is the manufacturer's weakest argument that the price is $15 per motor?

(A) The supplier's assurance of the $15 price was irrevocable for 60 days.
(B) A month is a reasonable time in which to accept the offer.
(C) The supplier could reasonably foresee that the manufacturer would rely on the supplier's offer.
(D) The supplier had not revoked its offer.

37. The owner of a building leased a portion of the ground floor for two years at a fixed monthly rent to a chef who opened a restaurant. Eight months later the chef, due to a souring of the local economy, informed the owner that she was closing the restaurant. She vacated the premises and stopped paying rent, which prior to that time she had timely paid. The owner unsuccessfully sought to rent the unoccupied space on behalf of the chef for the following four months before bringing suit against the chef for breach of the lease.

What is the maximum amount of rent to which the owner is entitled?

(A) Sixteen months' rent.
(B) Twelve months' rent.
(C) Four months' rent.
(D) Nothing.

38. A personal ad appeared in a pornographic magazine that was published and distributed nationwide. The ad stated that an individual was willing to perform various, specified deviant sexual acts. At the end of the ad, the individual was identified by her first and last name. As a consequence, the individual received lewd and offensive communications from strangers. The individual filed an action based on invasion of privacy due to the public disclosure of private facts and the publication of facts placing her in a false light, both recognized in the jurisdiction. In the complaint, the individual alleged that she had neither submitted the ad to the magazine publisher nor had any desire to perform such acts and that the publisher had published the ad with reckless disregard for its truthfulness. The publisher moved to dismiss the complaint.

How should the court rule on this motion?

(A) Grant the motion as to both counts.
(B) Grant the motion as to the public disclosure of private facts and deny it as to the publication of facts placing her in a false light.
(C) Grant the motion as to the publication of facts placing her in a false light and deny it as to the public disclosure of private facts.
(D) Deny the motion as to both counts.

39. At the beginning of the month, an aunt called her niece who lived in a distant city. During the conversation, the aunt promised to give a family heirloom worth $50,000 to her niece if the niece came to the aunt's home to retrieve it. The niece promised to come. The following day the niece bought an airline ticket to fly to the city where her aunt lived at the end of the month. The day before the niece was to make the trip, her aunt died. Under the terms of the aunt's will, the heirloom was left to someone else.

Can the niece acquire the heirloom by enforcing her aunt's promise against the aunt's estate?

(A) Yes, under the doctrine of promissory estoppel.
(B) Yes, because there was an exchange of promises.
(C) No, because the aunt's promise was oral.
(D) No, because the aunt promised to make a gift.

40. The owner of a tract of vacant land granted a power-line easement over the land to the electric company. The easement, which was granted in a properly executed written agreement, was never recorded. Several years later, the owner sold the tract of land. The buyer, who planned to sell hot air balloon rides on the property, bought the property sight unseen. After the buyer purchased the property, he discovered the power lines, which would make hot air balloon rides on the property prohibitively dangerous. The applicable jurisdiction has the following recording statute: "No conveyance or mortgage of real property shall be good against subsequent purchasers for value and without notice unless the same be recorded according to law."

Can the buyer successfully challenge the easement?

(A) Yes, because the buyer had no actual notice of the easement.
(B) Yes, because the easement was not recorded.
(C) No, because the buyer had inquiry notice of the easement.
(D) No, because with the easements, the land is not suited for the buyer's purpose.

41. As part of a fraternity dare, a college student stood in the middle of a road while drinking a beer. The driver of a car, tired of the fraternity pranks throughout the town, saw the student standing in the road, and reduced his speed but decided not to stop or swerve, saying to himself, "Well, he shouldn't be in the road anyway. He had better get out of the way, and if I hit him, it's his own fault." The intoxicated student could not get out of the way quickly enough, and the driver ran over his foot.

If the student sues the driver for negligence in a contributory-negligence jurisdiction, is the driver liable for the injuries that the student sustained to his foot?

(A) The driver would be liable only for part of the student's damages.
(B) The driver would not be liable for the student's damages due to the student's contributory negligence.
(C) The driver would be liable for all of the student's damages.
(D) The driver would be liable only if he intended to cause injury to the student.

42. At an auction without reserve, the auctioneer called for bids for an antique chair. The first bidder, a consumer without specialized knowledge about antique furniture, bid $10,000. Her bid was acknowledged by the auctioneer. The second bidder bid $11,000, which was also acknowledged by the auctioneer. Before the auctioneer announced the sale of the item to the second bidder, she withdrew her bid. The auctioneer then announced that the chair was sold to the first bidder for $10,000.

Can the first bidder successfully challenge this sale?

(A) Yes, because the first bidder was not a merchant.
(B) Yes, because the withdrawal of the highest bid did not reinstate the next lowest bid.
(C) No, because the auctioneer accepted the first bidder's bid.
(D) No, because the auction was without reserve.

43.   A client entered into a written contract with his lawyer for the lawyer to provide legal services with regard to the purchase of land. The contract specified that the lawyer was to be paid a flat fee of $2,000 for his services. Prior to completion of the purchase, the lawyer orally assigned his interest in the contract to a third-party landscaper, in exchange for services the landscaper had performed for the lawyer. The lawyer then rendered the legal services necessary for the completion of the purchase of the land.

Can the third-party landscaper collect the lawyer's fee from the client?

(A)   No, because the assignment was not in writing.

(B)   No, because the contract between the client and the lawyer was for services.

(C)   Yes, because the assignment was supported by consideration.

(D)   Yes, because the lawyer assigned his interest to the third party.

44.   A zookeeper adopted an injured orangutan from the zoo. Many years of living in the zoo had tamed the orangutan, and he had no known dangerous propensities, so the zookeeper allowed the orangutan to live inside his home. The orangutan was very intelligent, and had learned how to open doors and mimic other basic human behaviors. One day, while the zookeeper was in the shower, a salesman selling home insurance rang the doorbell. The orangutan heard the doorbell ring and opened the door. In fear for his life when he saw the orangutan open the door, the salesman collapsed from a non-lethal heart attack. The salesman filed a strict liability action against the zookeeper to recover damages. The jurisdiction applies the common-law rules for contributory negligence and assumption of the risk.

Is the salesman likely to succeed in his action against the zookeeper?

(A)   No, because the orangutan had no known dangerous propensities.

(B)   No, because the orangutan did not directly cause the salesman's injuries.

(C)   Yes, because the zookeeper failed to use reasonable care to restrain the orangutan.

(D)   Yes, because the zookeeper is liable for the salesman's fearful reaction to the orangutan.

45. A pharmaceutical company hired an experienced sales person. Their employment agreement stated that the sales person would be provided with a company car, and that the car could be used for both personal and business use. Prior to finalizing the agreement, the company checked the sales person's driving record and learned that he had no history of tickets or accidents. During his first week on the job, the sales person used his company car to attend a client meeting. After the meeting, the sales person met some friends at a bar, where he had several drinks. The sales person then drove his company car home. On the way, the sales person hit a pedestrian, breaking both the pedestrian's legs. The pedestrian has sued the sales person and the pharmaceutical company for negligence.

Is the company likely to be held liable on a theory of vicarious liability?

(A) No, because the company had no reason to know of the sales person's negligent propensities.
(B) No, because the sales person was not acting within the scope of his employment.
(C) Yes, because the company agreed to let the sales person use a company car for personal use.
(D) Yes, because the sales person was on his way home from a meeting with a client.

ANSWER KEY

Remember to log in to your course to submit your answers and view detailed answer explanations.

Question	Answer	Subject	Chapter	Section	ID
1	A	Contracts	Formation Of Contracts	Mutual Assent	3178
2	B	Torts	Harms to Personal Property and Land	Nuisance	6532
3	D	Real Property	Mortgages And Security Interests	Foreclosure	3144
4	D	Real Property	Ownership	Present Estates	4269
5	B	Real Property	Titles	Conveyance by Will, Trust, and Operation of Law	3113
6	B	Contracts	Conditions And Performance	Performance	2797
7	D	Torts	Negligence	The Standard of Care	6553
8	B	Contracts	Breach Of Contracts And Remedies	Remedies Under the UCC	3165
9	B	Contracts	Breach Of Contracts And Remedies	Anticipatory Repudiation	7603
10	A	Real Property	Mortgages And Security Interests	Transfer	3156
11	D	Contracts	Formation Of Contracts	Warranties in Sale-of-Goods Contracts	3162
12	A	Contracts	Breach Of Contracts And Remedies	Remedies Under the UCC	3189
13	B	Torts	Defenses To Intentional Torts Involving Personal Injury	Defense of Others	2970
14	C	Real Property	Titles	Delivery and Recording of Deed	3146
15	D	Real Property	Mortgages And Security Interests	Foreclosure	3152
16	A	Torts	Products Liability	Strict Products Liability	2844
17	A	Real Property	Disputes About The Use Of Land	Covenants Running with the Land	2018
18	D	Torts	Products Liability	Warranties	1352
19	B	Torts	Negligence	The Standard of Care	4305
20	A	Contracts	Breach Of Contract And Remedies	Remedies Under the UCC	3190
21	A	Torts	Negligence	Causation	2974
22	B	Torts	Intentional Torts Involving Personal Injury	Battery	1403
23	B	Real Property	Mortgages And Security Interests	Foreclosure	4268
24	B	Contracts	Statute Of Frauds	Types of Contracts Within the Statute of Frauds	3164
25	C	Contracts	Formation Of Contracts	Defenses to Formation	3167
26	D	Real Property	Disputes About The Use Of Land	Easements	4209
27	A	Contracts	Parol Evidence Rule	When the Parol Evidence Rule is Inapplicable	4376

Question	Answer	Subject	Chapter	Section	ID
28	D	Torts	Harms To Personal Property And Land	Nuisance	4259
29	D	Real Property	Titles	Delivery and Recording of Deed	4215
30	C	Contracts	Third-Party Beneficiary Contracts	Intended and Incidental Beneficiaries	4373
31	D	Real Property	Ownership	Concurrent Estates	3116
32	A	Real Property	The Land Sale Contract	Options and Rights of First Refusal	3132
33	D	Contracts	Formation Of Contracts	Consideration	3184
34	B	Real Property	Ownership	Concurrent Estates	4218
35	D	Torts	Negligence	Breach or Violation of Duty of Care	2977
36	A	Contracts	Formation Of Contracts	Mutual Assent	3173
37	C	Real Property	Landlord And Tenant	Duties of Tenant	3150
38	B	Torts	Defamation, Invasion Of Privacy, And Business Torts	Invasion of Privacy	1366
39	D	Contracts	Formation Of Contracts	Consideration	3193
40	C	Real Property	Titles	Delivery and Recording of Deed	3124
41	C	Torts	Negligence	Defenses to Negligence	2946
42	B	Contracts	Formation Of Contracts	Mutual Assent	3183
43	D	Contracts	Assignment Of Rights And Delegation Of Duties	Assignment of Rights	3192
44	D	Torts	Strict Liability	Animals	6559
45	B	Torts	Negligence	Vicarious Liability	2978

Themis
Bar Review

Practice Exam Two

Start Time:_____

End Time:_____

1. Ⓐ Ⓑ Ⓒ Ⓓ   26. Ⓐ Ⓑ Ⓒ Ⓓ   51. Ⓐ Ⓑ Ⓒ Ⓓ
2. Ⓐ Ⓑ Ⓒ Ⓓ   27. Ⓐ Ⓑ Ⓒ Ⓓ   52. Ⓐ Ⓑ Ⓒ Ⓓ
3. Ⓐ Ⓑ Ⓒ Ⓓ   28. Ⓐ Ⓑ Ⓒ Ⓓ   53. Ⓐ Ⓑ Ⓒ Ⓓ
4. Ⓐ Ⓑ Ⓒ Ⓓ   29. Ⓐ Ⓑ Ⓒ Ⓓ   54. Ⓐ Ⓑ Ⓒ Ⓓ
5. Ⓐ Ⓑ Ⓒ Ⓓ   30. Ⓐ Ⓑ Ⓒ Ⓓ   55. Ⓐ Ⓑ Ⓒ Ⓓ
6. Ⓐ Ⓑ Ⓒ Ⓓ   31. Ⓐ Ⓑ Ⓒ Ⓓ
7. Ⓐ Ⓑ Ⓒ Ⓓ   32. Ⓐ Ⓑ Ⓒ Ⓓ
8. Ⓐ Ⓑ Ⓒ Ⓓ   33. Ⓐ Ⓑ Ⓒ Ⓓ
9. Ⓐ Ⓑ Ⓒ Ⓓ   34. Ⓐ Ⓑ Ⓒ Ⓓ
10. Ⓐ Ⓑ Ⓒ Ⓓ   35. Ⓐ Ⓑ Ⓒ Ⓓ
11. Ⓐ Ⓑ Ⓒ Ⓓ   36. Ⓐ Ⓑ Ⓒ Ⓓ
12. Ⓐ Ⓑ Ⓒ Ⓓ   37. Ⓐ Ⓑ Ⓒ Ⓓ
13. Ⓐ Ⓑ Ⓒ Ⓓ   38. Ⓐ Ⓑ Ⓒ Ⓓ
14. Ⓐ Ⓑ Ⓒ Ⓓ   39. Ⓐ Ⓑ Ⓒ Ⓓ
15. Ⓐ Ⓑ Ⓒ Ⓓ   40. Ⓐ Ⓑ Ⓒ Ⓓ
16. Ⓐ Ⓑ Ⓒ Ⓓ   41. Ⓐ Ⓑ Ⓒ Ⓓ
17. Ⓐ Ⓑ Ⓒ Ⓓ   42. Ⓐ Ⓑ Ⓒ Ⓓ
18. Ⓐ Ⓑ Ⓒ Ⓓ   43. Ⓐ Ⓑ Ⓒ Ⓓ
19. Ⓐ Ⓑ Ⓒ Ⓓ   44. Ⓐ Ⓑ Ⓒ Ⓓ
20. Ⓐ Ⓑ Ⓒ Ⓓ   45. Ⓐ Ⓑ Ⓒ Ⓓ
21. Ⓐ Ⓑ Ⓒ Ⓓ   46. Ⓐ Ⓑ Ⓒ Ⓓ
22. Ⓐ Ⓑ Ⓒ Ⓓ   47. Ⓐ Ⓑ Ⓒ Ⓓ
23. Ⓐ Ⓑ Ⓒ Ⓓ   48. Ⓐ Ⓑ Ⓒ Ⓓ
24. Ⓐ Ⓑ Ⓒ Ⓓ   49. Ⓐ Ⓑ Ⓒ Ⓓ
25. Ⓐ Ⓑ Ⓒ Ⓓ   50. Ⓐ Ⓑ Ⓒ Ⓓ

Themis
Bar Review

PRACTICE EXAM TWO

TIME: 99 MINUTES

Welcome to Practice Exam Two. This exam consists of 55 questions in the areas of Civil Procedure, Constitutional Law, Criminal Law & Procedure, and Evidence. This exam will take approximately 99 minutes (an average of 1.8 minutes per question). After you have completed this exam, log in to your course to submit your answers, view detailed answer explanations, and compare your performance to other Themis students.

1.   The user of a power tool sued the tool's manufacturer in state court.   The action was based on a strict product liability claim that the manufacturer's failure to adequately warn the user of a defect in the power tool caused the user's injury.   The manufacturer properly removed the case to federal court.   The applicable law of the state that governs the existence of the strict product liability claim also recognizes a rebuttable heeding presumption. This presumption assumes that an injured plaintiff would have heeded an adequate warning if one had been given.   Under state law, this presumption does not shift the burden of persuasion on this issue to the manufacturer.

The manufacturer did not present evidence that the user would not have heeded a different warning had it been given.   The court instructed the jury that it must apply the presumption that the warning, if given, would have been heeded.

Is the court's instruction correct?

(A)   No, because the jury may, but is not required to, apply the presumption.
(B)   No, because state law presumptions are not recognized in a federal diversity action.
(C)   Yes, because the manufacturer failed to offer evidence to rebut the presumption.
(D)   Yes, because the Federal Rules of Evidence apply the bursting-bubble approach to presumptions.

2.   After a female politician is injured in a riot following a heated public debate, a state enacts the following statute: "Any words targeting women or minorities likely to produce violence or rioting are prohibited on any public property."

Is the statute constitutional?

(A)   No, because the statute punishes only speech targeting specific groups.
(B)   No, because the state cannot restrict speech in public forums.
(C)   Yes, because the state can prohibit fighting words.
(D)   Yes, because laws affecting women and minorities receive heightened scrutiny.

3. The defendant, a college student, attended a lecture for his history class regarding the first moon landing. The defendant, who had a history of mental illness, believed that the evidence of the moon landing was the result of a conspiracy by the U.S. government, and that a human had never set foot on the moon. Irate at the professor's lecture, the defendant started yelling his theories at the class. When the professor asked the defendant to leave the class, he became furious and hit the professor with his textbook. The defendant has been charged with battery and has pleaded not guilty by reason of insanity due to his history of mental illness. The evidence at trial shows that the defendant's mental illness caused him to hit the professor and that although he knew it was wrong, he could not resist the impulse to harm her. The jurisdiction follows the M'Naghten test regarding criminal insanity.

May the defendant be convicted of battery?

(A) Yes, because the defendant's loss of control was not sudden.
(B) Yes, because the defendant appreciated the wrongfulness of his actions.
(C) No, because the defendant lacked the capacity for self-control.
(D) No, because the defendant's unlawful act was the product of his mental defect.

4. A witness testified in a federal case on behalf of a criminal defendant. On cross-examination, the government sought to impeach the witness with a state court conviction for felony assault nine years prior. The witness had started a ministry for other prisoners during his short time in prison, and he became an active religious and community leader following his release. He has not had any arrests or convictions since being released from prison, and he was previously pardoned by the outgoing governor based on his efforts on behalf of the community. The defense has filed a motion to exclude evidence of the conviction. When presented with the motion, the judge noted that the conviction was probative of the veracity of the witness and would have little prejudicial effect.

Is the judge likely to allow evidence of the assault conviction to be admitted?

(A) Yes, because the conviction is less than 10 years old.
(B) Yes, because the probative value of the conviction is not outweighed by its prejudicial effect.
(C) No, because assault is not a crime of dishonesty or false statement.
(D) No, because the witness was pardoned and has not been convicted of another felony.

5. A retailer incorporated in State A sued the publisher of a newsletter for libel in a State C state court. The retailer's complaint sought $1 million in damages in good faith. The retailer, which had its headquarters in State B, did business throughout the United States but had its largest warehouse in State C, where it also operated more stores than any other state. The publisher of the newsletter, which had subscribers in every state, was an individual who lived most of the year abroad but continued to be domiciled in State C. The publisher timely filed a petition to remove the libel action to a State C federal district court.

Should the federal court deny this petition?

(A) No, because diversity jurisdiction exists.
(B) No, because the newsletter is published nationwide.
(C) Yes, because the retailer and publisher are citizens of the same state for diversity purposes.
(D) Yes, because the publisher is a citizen of the forum state.

6. Two gang members orchestrated a plan to scare a local priest who was organizing after-school programs to keep kids off the street. They planned to go into the priest's office with a gun, threaten him, and steal any money in the church offices. One gang member went into the office with the gun while the other stood outside as a lookout. When the priest approached the gang member with the gun in an attempt to reason with him, the gang member panicked and shot the priest, who died instantly. The prosecution charged both gang members with conspiracy and murder, but offered a deal to each in exchange for his testimony against the other. The shooter accepted the deal, while the defendant, who was the lookout, decided to proceed to trial.

Is the defendant likely to be convicted of murder?

(A) No, because the defendant did not conspire to murder the priest.
(B) No, because the defendant's co-conspirator will not be tried.
(C) Yes, because the Wharton Rule allows the defendant to be convicted without his co-conspirator.
(D) Yes, because the murder was committed in furtherance of the conspiracy.

7.   The defendant robbed an elderly woman at gunpoint. An off-duty police officer witnessed the incident from a distance while walking his dog. He chased down the defendant and placed him under arrest. After being informed of his Miranda rights, the defendant immediately invoked his right to counsel. The defendant was taken to the police station, and before the defendant's attorney arrived, the defendant was placed in a lineup. The defendant did not object to being placed in the lineup. The elderly woman immediately identified the defendant as the robber. The defendant's attorney moved to suppress the identification because it was conducted without the attorney present.

Is the defendant's motion likely to be granted?

(A) No, because the defendant waived his right to have counsel present.

(B) No, because the defendant was not entitled to the presence of counsel.

(C) Yes, because the defendant invoked his right to counsel.

(D) Yes, because the lineup was a corporeal identification.

8.   A supplier sued a commercial customer for nonpayment of its bill. The customer, contending that it had paid the supplier, produced and authenticated a printed version of a receipt purportedly prepared by the supplier showing a payment made by the customer. The receipt had been scanned by the customer into its computer databank. The customer had intentionally discarded the original receipt in the normal course of its business practice to reduce recordkeeping costs. Contending that the original receipt had been a forgery, the supplier objected to the admission of the printed version of the receipt into evidence. The judge ruled in favor of the supplier and prohibited the admission of the receipt. The customer then sought to call its employee to testify that he had personally sent the payment reflected in the receipt to the supplier.

Should the court, over the supplier's objection, permit the customer's employee to testify about the payment?

(A) No, because the supplier called into question the authenticity of the original receipt.

(B) No, because the customer had intentionally discarded the original receipt.

(C) Yes, because the printed version of the receipt constituted a duplicate.

(D) Yes, because the employee had personal knowledge of the payment.

9. An automobile dealer filed suit in federal court based on diversity jurisdiction against an automobile manufacturer for breach of contract, seeking damages in the amount of $500,000. After the manufacturer answered the dealer's complaint, both parties moved for summary judgment. The court granted the dealer's motion with regard to liability, but denied it as to the matter of damages. The court also denied the manufacturer's motion. The court determined that there was no just reason for delaying an appeal. Thirty-five days after the entry of the court order with regard to these motions, the manufacturer filed a notice of appeal of this order with the district court clerk.

Can the dealer successfully prevent this appeal?

(A) No, because the court determined that there was no just reason for delaying the appeal.
(B) No, because the court partially granted the dealer's summary judgment motion.
(C) Yes, because of the final judgment rule.
(D) Yes, because the manufacturer's notice of appeal was not timely filed.

10. An attorney filed a complaint in federal court, alleging that his client's property had been damaged through vandalism perpetrated by the defendant. The attorney was reasonably certain that evidence would support that the vandalism had been perpetrated by the defendant, but he did not have clear evidence at the time of the submission. He was confident that the discovery process would lead to the identification of the correct defendant and knew that if the defendant could not be identified, the claim would be unsuccessful. He did note on the pleading that he intended to learn such evidence during the discovery process.

Is the attorney subject to Rule 11 sanctions based on the filing?

(A) Yes, because he knew the factual allegations were inaccurate.
(B) Yes, because he is relying on discovery to establish an essential element of the claim.
(C) No, because he believed he would discover the correct defendant after discovery.
(D) No, because discovery had not yet commenced.

11. Congress passed a law allowing the Secretary of Transportation to designate speed limits on all interstate highways "at whatever speed prudent in the interests of both safety and efficiency." The Secretary of Transportation felt that each state was in the best position, based on their studies of their own highway systems, to determine the appropriate speed limit within that state, so he collaborated with each state's department of transportation to determine each state's limit. As a result of an increasing number of high-speed car accidents, one state decided to lower its speed limit. A driver was ticketed for driving over the state's newly lowered speed limit. The driver challenged the validity of the statute giving the Secretary of Transportation power to designate the speed limits.

Should the statute be found invalid or valid?

(A) Invalid, because Congress exceeded its authority to delegate this matter to the Secretary of Transportation.

(B) Invalid, because the legislation did not contain sufficiently intelligible standards by which to guide the Secretary of Transportation.

(C) Valid, because the legislation was a proper exercise of Congress's power to delegate to the executive branch.

(D) Valid, because the Secretary of Transportation consulted each state's department of transportation to guide his decision.

12. The State H federal district court chose a representative for a class of 67 patients who were allegedly injured by negligent medical care at a hospital in State H and collectively suffered damages of $3,000,000. After correctly asserting diversity jurisdiction, the court certified the class upon finding that the four basic requirements for a class action had been met and that prosecution of the claims through separate actions would impair the interests of other class members. The court posted on the courthouse bulletin board its certification order, which (1) described the action, the class, and the legal claims; and (2) informed class members that they may appear through an attorney and may request an exclusion, but otherwise are bound by the class judgment. Most members of the class never saw this notice, including one patient who suffered especially severe damages as a result of the hospital's negligence. After the class action trial was almost finished, the patient, who was unaware of the trial, filed a separate suit in the State H federal district court against the hospital.

Should the court allow that suit?

(A) Yes, because the contents of the notice did not meet the requirements of the federal class action rule.

(B) Yes, because the patient never received appropriate notice of the class action.

(C) No, because the Class Action Fairness Act prohibits such suits.

(D) No, because the court properly certified the class and was not required to provide notice of the class action.

13. While waiting at a bus stop after work, an office worker witnessed a man force a student to give him her backpack. Because no one else who witnessed the event reacted to it, the office worker gave chase, tackled the man, and held him until police arrived. The office worker has been charged with battery of the man.

Which of the following is the office worker's best defense to this charge?

(A) Defense of arrest
(B) Defense of property
(C) Defense of others
(D) Necessity

14. A witness was making a deposit at a local bank when the bank was robbed. The witness observed the robber closely and subsequently gave the police a detailed written description of the robber and the events that occurred in the bank. Following the robber's arrest and subsequent release on bail, the robber appeared at the witness's home, telling him to leave the state immediately and not appear at the trial or he would be killed. The witness telephoned the police to report the threat, but also told them that he was afraid for his life. At trial, the witness, who had left the state, did not appear and failed to respond to a subpoena. The prosecution now seeks to introduce the witness's written statement into evidence. The defendant objects to the introduction of the evidence.

Should the judge admit the written statement over the objection of the defendant?

(A) Yes, as a prior statement of identification.
(B) Yes, because the robber forfeited any right to object as a result of his threat against the witness.
(C) No, as it is hearsay not within any exception.
(D) No, because the witness's absence is voluntary and therefore does not constitute unavailability.

15. A plaintiff brought a products liability action against an out-of-state manufacturer seeking $125,000 in damages due to personal injuries received while using a tool made by the manufacturer. Pursuant to the permissive joinder rule, the plaintiff's spouse joined in the action, which was filed in federal court, seeking damages of $5,000 for loss of consortium.

Does the court have subject-matter jurisdiction over the spouse's claim?

(A) No, because the spouse's claim does not satisfy the amount-in-controversy requirement.
(B) No, because the court's jurisdiction over plaintiff's claim is not based on federal question jurisdiction.
(C) Yes, because the spouse's claim forms part of the same case or controversy as the plaintiff's claim.
(D) Yes, because the plaintiffs are related.

16. A woman sought to kill her husband. She developed an elaborate plan that involved cutting the brake lines on his automobile while his car sat in his office parking lot. On the morning of the planned killing, the woman walked with her husband to the garage. Watching as her husband began to pull his car out of the garage, the woman activated the switch to shut the garage door. The switch malfunctioned and as result the garage door came crashing down on the car and crushed the husband to death.

For which crime could the woman properly be found guilty?

(A) Murder.
(B) Voluntary manslaughter.
(C) Involuntary manslaughter.
(D) None of the above.

17. A plaintiff brought suit against a defendant for injuries she sustained in a car accident that she accused the defendant of negligently causing. Prior to filing suit, the plaintiff's attorney had the plaintiff visit a physician to determine the extent of her injuries for purposes of determining the damages to be claimed in the lawsuit. After the plaintiff's examination, while the attorney, plaintiff, and physician were discussing the extent of the plaintiff's injuries, the plaintiff admitted that she "may have had a few beers" right before the accident. At trial, the defendant's counsel sought to call the doctor to testify about the statement. The plaintiff properly objected to the introduction of this testimony.

How should the judge rule on the plaintiff's objection?

(A) Sustain the objection, as the attorney-client privilege is applicable.
(B) Sustain the objection, as the physician-patient privilege is applicable.
(C) Overrule the objection, as the statement was made by an opposing party.
(D) Overrule the objection, as the physician would constitute an expert witness.

18. A man borrowed his friend's truck in order to move to a new apartment and promised to return the truck two days later, following the completion of the move. After finishing the move, the man instead sold the truck to a used car dealer in order to pay off the back rent he owed to his landlord on his former apartment, which was his intention at the time he borrowed the truck.

With which of the following crimes should the man be charged?

(A) Larceny by trick.
(B) Embezzlement.
(C) False pretenses.
(D) No crime.

19. After violence against a specific religious minority becomes an epidemic in the United States, Congress enacts hate crime legislation pertaining to those of that religious faith and also establishes that no public entity may discriminate against this group unless such discrimination is the least restrictive means to achieve a compelling interest.

What is the most likely reason for the invalidity of this law?

(A) Congress is improperly creating hate crime legislation coupled with civil rights legislation.

(B) Congress is improperly creating new equal protection rights.

(C) The law should apply intermediate scrutiny to discrimination by a public entity to a group.

(D) Congress does not have a sufficiently compelling state interest in enacting the legislation.

20. An investor brought an action in federal district court for damages based on a violation of federal securities law. The defendant, a foreign corporation, received service of process by proper means in its country of incorporation. While the defendant's contacts with the state in which the forum court sits do not satisfy the "minimum contacts" test, the defendant's contacts with the entire United States satisfy this test.

Of the following, which additional fact must the investor establish in order for the court to exercise personal jurisdiction over the defendant?

(A) No state court could exercise jurisdiction over the foreign corporation.

(B) The district court is located in the state in which the investor is domiciled.

(C) The applicable federal securities law provides for nationwide service of process.

(D) The court has personal jurisdiction over the defendant under the long-arm statute of the forum state.

21. A defendant is on trial for soliciting a hit man to kill her father. During the investigation, the police visited the defendant's bank to demand any financial records maintained by the bank regarding the defendant's cash withdrawals. Even though the police did not have a warrant, the bank consented and provided the police with the requested information. The police discovered that the defendant made a large cash withdrawal an hour before meeting with the suspected hit man. At trial, the prosecution seeks to introduce the defendant's bank records, and the defendant moves to suppress the records under the exclusionary rule.

Should the court grant the defendant's motion to suppress this evidence?

(A) Yes, because the police did not have a warrant to seize the defendant's bank records.
(B) Yes, because the Fourth Amendment protects papers and effects in addition to places.
(C) No, because the defendant did not have a reasonable expectation of privacy in these records.
(D) No, because the bank consented to the seizure of the defendant's bank records.

22. Congress enacted a statute called the "Anti-Sweatshop Law" (ASL) making it a federal felony punishable by fines or imprisonment for an individual or private business to knowingly employ two or more workers and keep them in involuntary employment based on physical or legal threats made by the employer. The ASL's text and legislative history indicated that in enacting the ASL, Congress intended to regulate purely private behavior regardless of whether the behavior affected interstate commerce.

If the Supreme Court upholds the statute against a constitutional challenge, which of the following amendments, taken alone, would be sufficient to support the holding?

(A) The Twelfth Amendment.
(B) The Thirteenth Amendment.
(C) The Fourteenth Amendment.
(D) The Fifteenth Amendment.

23.   A plaintiff sued a defendant for damages resulting from an automobile accident. At trial, the defendant sought to offer into evidence a properly authenticated letter from the plaintiff to the defendant that stated, "I know I might have been partially at fault, so I am willing to accept half of my original request in order to avoid a lengthy trial."   The plaintiff objected to the introduction of the letter.

May the court admit the letter over the plaintiff's objection?

(A)   Yes, because it constitutes a statement against interest.

(B)   Yes, because it constitutes an admission by a party opponent.

(C)   No, because it was made as part of an offer to settle the dispute.

(D)   No, because it is hearsay not within any exception.

24.   As part of a divorce decree, a father was ordered to make monthly child support payments to his son's mother. The father failed to make such payments. At a criminal contempt hearing regarding the father's failure to comply with the child support order, the father's attorney presented evidence as to the father's inability to make such payments, which evidence was disputed by the mother. Under state law, there is a presumption that, with regard to enforcement of a child support order, the parent obligated to make child support payments has the ability to make such payments, since such ability was determined by the court at the time that the order was issued. In addition, the highest state court has ruled that, with regard to imposition of criminal contempt for a failure to make child support payments, the burden of proof as to the inability to make such payments is placed on the father. The court, finding that the father had not met this burden, held the father in criminal contempt and sentenced him to six months in prison. The father has appealed this decision as unconstitutional.

Which of the following is the father's best argument in support of his challenge to the constitutionality of this decision?

(A)   A presumption in a criminal trial violates the Due Process Clause of the Fourteenth Amendment.

(B)   The Due Process Clause of the Fourteenth Amendment does not permit the burden of proof to be placed on the person on whom the criminal penalty would be imposed.

(C)   The ability to make child support payments is an element of criminal contempt.

(D)   The father's right to trial by jury was violated.

25. On January 15, the plaintiff, a citizen of one state, sued the defendant, a citizen of another state, in the federal district court in the defendant's home state. The plaintiff's complaint credibly alleges that (1) the defendant breached a contract with the plaintiff that resulted in $150,000 in damages, and (2) the court has diversity jurisdiction. On April 1, the plaintiff served process on the defendant by sending the summons and complaint to the defendant's residence via Overnight Express Mail, a form of service authorized by the law of the forum state. The defendant moves to dismiss the complaint based on insufficient service of process.

Should the court grant this motion?

(A) Yes, because the Federal Rules authorize service only on a defendant personally, on a person of suitable age and discretion at defendant's usual abode, or on an agent authorized by a defendant or by law to receive service.
(B) Yes, because the service of process was not timely.
(C) No, because under the Erie doctrine, the federal court must apply state law.
(D) No, because the Federal Rules allow service that follows state law governing courts in the state where the federal district court is located.

26. A state enacts a statute prohibiting semi-truck drivers from using cellular phones while operating their vehicles. There is no general statute applying the same prohibition to regular drivers in the state. A truck driver in the state sues in federal court after he receives a citation for using his cellular phone while operating his vehicle. He claims he is being unfairly targeted.

Which of the following would govern the analysis of the driver's claim?

(A) Substantive Due Process.
(B) Privileges and Immunities Clause.
(C) Dormant Commerce Clause.
(D) Procedural Due Process.

27. The defendant was arrested for the murder of his wife. Following his arrest, the defendant was handcuffed and placed in a police car by two police officers. The officers did not provide the defendant with Miranda warnings. During the drive to the police station, the officers began questioning the defendant about his whereabouts the night of the murder. The defendant stated that he was home alone all night waiting for his wife, who never arrived home. At trial, the prosecution offered evidence showing that the wife was murdered in the home she shared with the defendant. The defendant took the stand in his own defense and testified that, on the night of the murder, he was at his brother's house watching a movie, and that he spent the night there. The prosecution seeks to introduce the defendant's earlier statement to the police that he was home alone.

Is the defendant's statement to the police admissible?

(A)   No, because the defendant was not advised of his Miranda rights.
(B)   Yes, but only to impeach the defendant's credibility.
(C)   Yes, but only to prove that the defendant was home on the night of the murder.
(D)   Yes, both to impeach the defendant's credibility and to prove that he was home on the night of the murder.

28. In a breach of contract action, the defendant denied that her signature appears on the contract. At trial, the plaintiff called the defendant's secretary as a witness to testify that, having worked for the defendant for several years, she had seen the defendant's signature many times and that the signature on the contract is the signature of the defendant. The defendant objected to the witness's testimony.

Should the court overrule the objection?

(A)   No, because the identification of handwriting requires expert testimony and the secretary has not been qualified as an expert.
(B)   No, because the jury must compare the signature in question with another signature of the defendant that has been proven to be genuine in order to authenticate it.
(C)   Yes, because a lay witness with prior personal knowledge of a person's handwriting may testify as to whether the document is in that person's handwriting.
(D)   Yes, because the secretary can be considered an expert with specific knowledge of her employer's handwriting and signature.

29. A defendant was prosecuted for embezzling money from his company. At trial, the defense seeks to introduce evidence regarding the defendant's reputation for honesty amongst his coworkers and friends.

Should the court admit the evidence?

(A) Yes, because the defendant's reputation for honesty is inconsistent with the crime of embezzlement.

(B) Yes, because the defendant can introduce any evidence of his good character.

(C) No, because the defendant cannot introduce evidence of his good character until the prosecution puts his character at issue.

(D) No, because proof of good character offered by the defendant can only be in the form of opinion testimony.

30. A consumer sued a lawn mower manufacturer in a federal district court sitting in diversity jurisdiction, alleging that the consumer suffered damages due to a defect in the manufacture of a lawn mower. Prior to commencing suit, the consumer consulted two experts, a design expert and a manufacturing expert, about the lawn mower that was the source of the consumer's injuries. After filing the complaint, the consumer, in making his required disclosures, identified the manufacturing expert as an expert expected to be called at trial. The design expert is not expected to testify. The manufacturer sent an interrogatory to the consumer requesting the identity of any other experts consulted with regard to the case.

Is the consumer required to identify the design expert in his answer to the interrogatory?

(A) No, because the design expert is not expected to testify at trial.

(B) No, because the information is protected by the work product doctrine.

(C) Yes, because the manufacturer has specifically requested the identity of all experts consulted by the plaintiff.

(D) Yes, because no privilege or other protection applies.

31.   A hotel developer was attempting to build a vacation resort upon a peninsula above sea level that was known for its landslides. The primary cause of these landslides was the erosive effect of the waves below it. The developer had already acquired a loan for the predicted cost of the development. In exchange for the necessary construction permits to build the resort on the peninsula, the city told the developer to build a concrete foundation at the foot of the peninsula below the planned resort where the erosion was taking place. The city had determined that a concrete foundation would reinforce the sedimentary rock below the resort, preventing future landslides along the entire peninsula. The cost of building the concrete foundation would add approximately 5% to the total cost of the planned development.   The developer has challenged the constitutionality of imposing this condition on the construction permits, calling the requirement an unconstitutional taking.

Is the city's requirement that the developer build this concrete foundation an unconstitutional taking?

(A)   No, because the condition has an essential nexus with a legitimate state interest of preventing landslides, and the burden is roughly proportional to its impact.

(B)   No, because the requirements for a regulatory taking have been met.

(C)   Yes, because the condition will result in the permanent physical occupation of the land by the required concrete foundation.

(D)   Yes, because this requirement increases the cost of the planned development, interfering with the developer's reasonable, investment-backed expectations regarding use of the property.

32.   Congress enacted immigration legislation that provided for special preferences for admitting into the United States an alien with a family member who is a United States citizen. In defining "family members" for this purpose, the statute included a natural mother and her illegitimate child, but made no similar provision for a natural father and his illegitimate child due to the greater administrative difficulty in ascertaining the existence of this relationship. A United States citizen who was the natural father of an illegitimate child filed an action in federal court challenging the constitutionality of the exclusion of a natural father and his illegitimate child from the definition of "family members."

Can the father successfully challenge this statute as unconstitutional?

(A)   No, because the father has not suffered an economic injury, and thus does not have standing.

(B)   No, because the exclusion is not arbitrary and unreasonable.

(C)   Yes, because the statute discriminates on the basis of gender.

(D)   Yes, because illegitimacy is a quasi-suspect classification.

33. A man overheard his co-worker make a pass at his wife at an office party. The man was furious and went outside to collect his thoughts. A few minutes later, he returned to the party and joined his wife and his co-worker in their conversation. When the man's co-worker excused himself to go to the restroom, the man followed him into the restroom and hit him over the head with a beer bottle. Although the man did not intend to kill his co-worker, the co-worker fell into a coma and died a week later.

What is the most serious crime, listed in order of increasing seriousness, for which the man could properly be convicted?

(A) Aggravated battery.
(B) Involuntary manslaughter.
(C) Voluntary manslaughter.
(D) Murder.

34. A plaintiff secured a default judgment for breach of contract against a defendant in a diversity action brought in federal district court in State X. The defendant, a natural person, was not domiciled in State X, but had sufficient contacts with the state to satisfy the minimum contacts test. The defendant was properly served with process but elected not to contest the action. The plaintiff has, pursuant to statute, registered the judgment with a federal district court located in State Y. The defendant has a bank account in State Y, but otherwise has no property or contacts with the state. The plaintiff has sought a court order permitting a levy against the defendant's bank account to satisfy the judgment. The defendant has challenged this order on grounds that the federal district court in State Y lacks personal jurisdiction over the defendant.

How should the court rule on the defendant's challenge?

(A) Uphold the challenge, because the defendant did not litigate the matter in the federal district court in State X.
(B) Uphold the challenge, because the defendant lacks minimum contacts with State Y.
(C) Deny the challenge, because of the Full Faith and Credit Clause in Article IV of the U.S. Constitution.
(D) Deny the challenge, because the minimum contacts test does not apply.

35. A police officer saw a man who was a convicted drug dealer walking down the street. The officer temporarily detained the man based on a reasonable suspicion that the man was illegally carrying a weapon. The officer conducted a pat-down of the man and felt an indeterminate lump in the man's jacket pocket. The officer removed the object, which turned out to be a pocket Bible. Protruding from the Bible was a plastic bag containing a white powder. The officer recognized the powder as heroin, and immediately arrested the man. Later tests confirmed that the powder was heroin. At trial, the man's attorney moved to exclude evidence of the heroin.

How should the judge rule?

(A) Deny the motion, because the evidence was discovered during a valid Terry stop.

(B) Deny the motion, because the officer had reasonable suspicion that the man was carrying a weapon.

(C) Grant the motion, because the pocket Bible did not immediately resemble a weapon or contraband.

(D) Grant the motion, because the officer did not have probable cause to stop the man and conduct a pat-down.

36. A state government official was murdered by the defendant. In response to the murder, the state legislature passed and the governor signed into law a statute that made it a crime to use a handgun to inflict serious bodily injury or death on a state government official. Subsequently, the defendant was arrested, prosecuted, and convicted of common-law murder and violation of the handgun statute. The defendant was sentenced to 20 years in prison for the murder and five years in prison for the handgun offense, to be served concurrently. On appeal, the defendant argued that his conviction for the handgun offense was unconstitutional. This argument had been rejected by the trial court.

Should the appellate court affirm the defendant's conviction for this offense?

(A) No, because it constitutes a bill of attainder in violation of Article 1, section 10.

(B) No, because it constitutes an ex post facto law in violation of Article 1, section 10.

(C) Yes, because the defendant's sentence for the handgun offense ran concurrently with his sentence for common-law murder.

(D) Yes, because the law was in existence before the defendant's arrest.

37. In a negligence action in a jurisdiction that had adopted comparative negligence, a jury rendered a verdict that the plaintiff suffered $90,000 in damages and was 10 percent at fault. The plaintiff's attorney had presented evidence and argued in his closing argument that the plaintiff's damages were $100,000. Immediately after the verdict, the plaintiff, with permission from the court, discussed the case with all six of the jurors together before they left the courtroom. The plaintiff discovered that each of the jurors thought, contrary to the court's instructions, that the damage amount was the amount that the plaintiff would receive, rather than the amount from which 10 percent would be deducted. The plaintiff seeks to offer testimony from each juror to that effect in order to increase the amount of the verdict to $100,000.

Is the testimony of the jurors admissible?

(A) Yes, because a mistake was made by the jury in rendering its verdict.
(B) Yes, because the jury misunderstanding was related to the applicable law, rather than the facts.
(C) No, because a juror cannot be questioned about a verdict in the presence of the other jurors.
(D) No, because a juror cannot testify as to any juror's mental processes concerning a verdict.

38. A federal statute makes it a crime to distribute or possess with the intent to distribute an illegal drug within 1000 feet of a public or private elementary or secondary school. Various other federal laws make it a crime to buy, sell, grow, manufacture, or possess illegal drugs.

Through which of the following constitutional provisions may this statute be most easily justified?

(A) The Commerce Clause of Article I, Section 8 of the U.S. Constitution
(B) The General Welfare Clause of Article I, Section 8 of the U.S. Constitution
(C) The Enabling Clause, Section 5 of the Fourteenth Amendment
(D) The Dormant Commerce Clause

39. A driver and bus driver were involved in a serious car accident. The driver properly brought an action against the bus driver for negligence in federal district court based on diversity jurisdiction. In her complaint, the driver alleged that the bus driver was texting on his cellular phone at the time of the accident. The bus driver intends to call a passenger on the bus, who was sitting in the front row, to testify that the bus driver was not using his cellular phone and that the passenger did not see him use the phone during the entire trip.

When must the bus driver disclose her intention to call the passenger as a witness?

(A) At or within 14 days of the discovery conference.
(B) At or within 30 days of the discovery conference.
(C) At least 30 days before the date set for trial.
(D) At least 90 days before the date set for trial.

40. A plaintiff brought an injunctive action in federal court under the federal Clean Water Act, based on alleged pollution of a stream. The stream is located in a state in which both parties are citizens. The complaint also contained a nuisance claim based on state law arising from the same set of circumstances as the federal claim. The plaintiff sought injunctive relief only with respect to the nuisance claim. The defendant has filed a motion to dismiss the nuisance claim for lack of subject-matter jurisdiction.

Must the court grant this motion?

(A) Yes, because the defendant did not seek monetary damages.
(B) Yes, because there is no diversity of citizenship between the parties.
(C) No, because the court may exercise supplemental jurisdiction over this claim.
(D) No, because the court has general equity jurisdiction to issue an injunction.

41. A prosecutor convened a grand jury to bring criminal charges against a pharmaceutical corporation. The charges were related to a new drug that was linked to several deaths. The prosecutor served a subpoena on a corporate employee who oversaw the testing of new drugs and kept the records related to such testing, requiring the production of all records related to testing done on the new drug. The employee refused to produce the records on Fifth Amendment grounds, asserting that the production of the records might incriminate him personally.

Is the employee likely to be required to produce the records?

(A) No, because the Fifth Amendment privilege applies to corporations.
(B) No, because the production of the records would incriminate the employee personally.
(C) Yes, because the Fifth Amendment privilege does not apply in grand jury proceedings.
(D) Yes, because the Fifth Amendment privilege does not extend to the custodian of corporate records.

42. After the defendant murdered his neighbor, the victim's family members lined the street when the defendant was taken away by police and screamed, "Murderer! Murderer!" At the trial for wrongful death, the plaintiffs' attorney sought to have the evidence of the family's statements admitted to show the initial impact the crime had on these family members, who had always been quiet and private members of the community. He intended to provide even more evidence to demonstrate increasing the damages suffered by the victim's family.

Is the evidence admissible for these purposes?

(A) Yes, because the statements are not being used to establish that the defendant murdered the neighbor.
(B) Yes, because the statements are relevant to the plaintiffs' argument.
(C) Yes, because the statements are being used in a civil trial.
(D) No, because the statements are hearsay.

43. A state law authorizes the state department of education to conduct an audit and to assign ratings to all public schools in the state based on graduation rates, test scores, and teacher attrition. The law also prohibits students from transferring to another school until at least the following school year in order to maintain the accuracy of statistics related to each school. The only exception allows the transfer of students whose families relocate to communities in other school districts, but requires that even students who relocate to other communities must continue to attend a public school in the new district. Three students in a single family relocated to another public school district; the public schools in that district were known to be struggling with high dropout rates and low test scores. The parents of these students applied to a local parochial school, and their children were accepted by the school, but the school was forced to deny the children admission based on the state law. The school then filed suit in federal court and asserted that the students have a right to attend the parochial school. Neither the students nor their parents were joined as plaintiffs in the suit.

How should the court proceed?

(A) Hear the merits of the case and rule in favor of the state.
(B) Hear the merits of the case and rule in favor of the school.
(C) Dismiss the case, because the school does not have standing to sue.
(D) Dismiss the case, because only the students would have standing to sue.

44. A security guard was charged with criminal battery of a student. The prosecution alleged that the security guard used excessive force when he removed the student from a campus event after the student became disruptive. The security guard's only argument in his defense was that he exerted lawful force to remove the disruptive student from the event pursuant to his duties as a security guard. The security guard testified that the student had a reputation on campus for disrupting campus events by starting physical fights with other students.

Is the security guard's testimony regarding the student's reputation admissible?

(A) No, because the prosecution has not presented evidence of the security guard's bad character.
(B) No, because the security guard has not asserted a theory of self-defense.
(C) Yes, because the security guard has personal knowledge of the student's reputation for violence.
(D) Yes, because the student's reputation for violence is relevant to whether the student was the initial aggressor.

45. On August 1, the plaintiff properly filed a complaint in federal court against the defendant for violating federal water pollution laws in a way that damaged the plaintiff's waterfront property. The defendant did not waive service of process. On August 7, the plaintiff properly served the defendant with the summons and complaint. On August 16, the plaintiff amended her complaint to add a claim under state nuisance law and, that same day, properly served the amended complaint on the defendant.

When is the latest date that the defendant can submit his answer?

(A) 21 days after the complaint was filed (August 22).
(B) 21 days after the complaint and summons were served (August 28).
(C) 14 days after the amended complaint was served (August 30).
(D) 21 days after the amended complaint was served (September 6).

46. Two siblings own real property located in State A as tenants in common. The brother was a citizen of State B; his sister was a citizen of Canada who was domiciled in State C. The oil and mineral rights to the property had been leased to a citizen of State C. The siblings initiated a breach-of-lease action against the lessee in a State A federal district court. In the complaint, each sibling asserted in good faith that damages suffered individually as a lessor of a half-interest in the mineral rights equaled $40,000. Shortly after the case was filed, the brother died. His property interests passed by will to his son who was a citizen of State C. Upon receiving title to the property and prior to trial, the son's motion to substitute himself as a party was granted. At trial, the defendant-lessee moved to dismiss the case for lack of subject-matter jurisdiction.

For which of the following reasons should the court grant the defendant's motion?

(A) Diversity jurisdiction does not exist because the amount-in-controversy requirement has not been met.
(B) Diversity jurisdiction does not exist because an alien cannot bring a federal action against an American citizen.
(C) Diversity jurisdiction does not exist because the sister and the lessee are both domiciled in State C.
(D) Diversity jurisdiction does not exist because the son and the lessee are both citizens of State C.

47. During a period of exceptionally high unemployment, a group of students in a major city began protesting the salary of some of the highest paid businessmen in the country. Coincidentally, many of those businessmen reside in the city where the students intend to protest. The students organized peacefully on the sidewalks in front of the homes of the individual businessmen for two hours each morning during the workweek. They held signs, chanted quietly, and left without much fanfare, though they did create a substantial amount of traffic, media interest, and disruption to the daily routines of the businessmen. The students were subsequently arrested under a state statute that bans picketing in front of individual residences.

Is the state statute prohibiting this speech constitutional as applied to the students' actions?

(A) No, but only because their demonstration is not inciting any lawless action.
(B) No, because the sidewalk constitutes a public forum.
(C) Yes, but only because the regulation is content-neutral.
(D) Yes, because they are focusing the protests on particular residences.

48. A state statute required that all students engaged in contact sports must have a minimum level of hearing in order to ensure the safety of themselves and others. The statute allowed the use of hearing aids to attain this requisite level of hearing. A new student at a public high school who was hard of hearing wanted to join the girl's field hockey team, but had no hearing aid and could not meet the level of hearing required by the statute without one. The public school had been granted federal funds to assist students who are hard of hearing. Accordingly, the school administration offered to pay for a top-of-the-line hearing aid that would satisfy the statute's hearing requirement. However, the student refused to wear the hearing aid because it was against her religious beliefs to receive or use any type of medical treatment or medical device. As a result, the school would not let her play on the field hockey team.

If the student's parents challenge the constitutionality of the statute as a violation of the Equal Protection Clause, which of the following is the most appropriate standard of review?

(A) The rational basis test, because disparate impact alone does not trigger a higher level of review.
(B) The intermediate scrutiny test, because disability is a quasi-suspect classification.
(C) The strict scrutiny test, because the student is a member of a suspect class.
(D) The strict scrutiny test, because the student has a fundamental privacy right to refuse medical treatment.

49. A property owner constructed a fence along what he thought was the boundary to his property. A year later, a neighbor who was selling adjoining property had a survey conducted. As a consequence of the survey, the neighbor brought an action against the property owner seeking removal of the fence. At trial, the neighbor testified that he had orally objected to the property owner about the placement of the fence at the time it was constructed. After the neighbor left the witness stand, the property owner sought to introduce into evidence a certified copy of the official judgment and conviction of the neighbor for perjury. The neighbor was convicted 11 years ago and released from prison nine years ago. The property owner had not asked the neighbor about the conviction while the neighbor was on the stand.

Should the court permit the introduction of the judgment for the purpose of impeaching the neighbor's testimony?

(A) No, because the neighbor was convicted of perjury more than 10 years ago.

(B) No, because the neighbor was not questioned about the conviction while the neighbor was on the witness stand.

(C) Yes, because a conviction used to impeach a witness's character for truthfulness may be proved by extrinsic evidence.

(D) Yes, because a witness in a civil case may not be impeached with a previous conviction.

50. On March 1, the plaintiff sued the defendant, a citizen of a different state, in the appropriate federal court and credibly alleged that the defendant negligently injured her in a car accident, requested $100,000 in damages, and invoked diversity jurisdiction. The plaintiff did not demand a jury trial, and she properly served the defendant on March 1. On March 20, the defendant served his answer, making a general denial. On April 1, the defendant served the plaintiff with a demand for jury trial.

Should the court grant the defendant's demand?

(A) Yes, because the defendant has made a timely demand for a jury trial.

(B) Yes, because there is a constitutional right to a jury trial in any legal action for damages in excess of $75,000.

(C) No, because there is no right to a jury trial in a civil action.

(D) No, because only a plaintiff has the right to demand a jury trial.

51. Three plaintiffs sued as representatives of a class of 75 individuals allegedly injured by a defectively designed product in federal district court. The three plaintiffs asserted product liability claims under state law, and alleged that they each suffered injuries resulting from the defectively designed product. Two of the named plaintiffs, as well as the unnamed plaintiffs, suffered relatively minor injuries, and asserted damages ranging from $10,000 to $25,000. The third named plaintiff, who suffered severe physical injuries, sought damages of $200,000. None of the named plaintiffs are domiciled in the state where the manufacturer is incorporated and has its principal place of business. The defendant manufacturer has asserted that the federal district court lacks subject-matter jurisdiction.

What is the plaintiffs' best argument that the court may exercise jurisdiction over their claims?

(A) As long as one plaintiff in a putative class asserts a good-faith claim over $75,000, a court may exercise supplemental jurisdiction over the remaining claims.

(B) The amount-in-controversy requirement for diversity jurisdiction is satisfied for all claims of a putative class if any putative class member asserts a good-faith claim over $75,000.

(C) The claims of the putative class members may be aggregated to satisfy the amount-in-controversy requirement for diversity jurisdiction.

(D) There is no amount-in-controversy requirement for class actions if there is complete diversity between the parties.

52. In state court, an employee was tried and convicted of embezzling funds from her employer. Pursuant to the criminal statute, the employee was ordered to make restitution of the embezzled funds, but not otherwise subjected to imprisonment or a fine for her conduct, even though both were statutorily permitted. The employee successfully appealed her conviction due to improperly admitted evidence. Upon retrial, the employee was again found guilty. In addition to ordering the defendant to make restitution, the judge, commenting that she had wasted valuable judicial resources by appealing her prior conviction, also fined her $50,000. On appeal, the employee contends that her punishment was unconstitutional.

Should the appellate court vacate her sentence?

(A) Yes, because the constitutional prohibition against double jeopardy prevents the imposition of a harsher sentence upon retrial of defendant after a successful appeal of a conviction.

(B) Yes, because the imposition of a fine violated the Due Process Clause of the Fourteenth Amendment.

(C) No, because the constitutional prohibition against double jeopardy does not apply to fines, but only to imprisonment.

(D) No, because a defendant may be retried after an appeal results in the defendant's conviction being overturned due to trial errors.

53. The defendant, the owner of a paving company, paid the mayor of a city $5,000. The defendant made this payment with the purpose of securing the mayor's agreement to award the defendant's paving company a lucrative city contract. A state statute makes it a felony for a public official to receive anything of value in return for being influenced in the performance of any official act. The mayor was charged with violating this statute and the paving company owner was charged as an accomplice. The mayor was tried first and found guilty.

If the defendant is found not guilty at his subsequent trial, which of the following is the most likely reason?

(A) The defendant was not tried first.
(B) The defendant lacked the requisite mental state required for the crime.
(C) The crime required the defendant's participation.
(D) The defendant was a member of a protected class.

54. A secretary was angry at her boss for not granting her a raise. The secretary decided to "teach the boss a lesson," by breaking into the boss's house and stealing the boss's personal computer. That evening, the secretary waited until she was sure the boss had gone to sleep and then used a key the boss had given her to the house for emergencies in order to enter the house. She took the personal computer and then left the house.

The secretary is subsequently arrested and charged with burglary in a jurisdiction that follows the common law. Should the woman be convicted?

(A) No, because she did not break into the house.
(B) No, because she did not intend to commit a felony in the house.
(C) Yes, because the boss was in the house at the time the secretary entered.
(D) Yes, because she entered the house that evening during a non-emergency situation to steal the computer.

55. A state enacted a statute requiring that prior to voting in a local primary election, a resident must reside within the state for six months. The intent behind the statute is to prohibit transient residents from affecting the long-term affairs of the state. A resident of the state has been a registered voter in another state for many years but has only lived and worked in the state for 90 days. On the day of the primary, the resident tried to vote at a polling station but was banned from doing so by an elections official citing the above statute. The resident then filed suit in federal district court to challenge the constitutionality of the statute.

Which of the following reflects the proper burden of persuasion in this suit?

- (A) The resident must demonstrate that the statute is not necessary to achieve an important state interest.
- (B) The resident must demonstrate that the statute is not rationally related to a legitimate state interest.
- (C) The state must demonstrate that the statute is the least restrictive means of achieving a compelling state interest.
- (D) The state must demonstrate that the statute is rationally related to a legitimate state interest.

ANSWER KEY

Remember to log in to your course to submit your answers and view detailed answer explanations.

Question	Answer	Subject	Chapter	Section	ID
1	C	Evidence	Presentation Of Evidence	Burdens and Presumptions	3000
2	A	Constitutional Law	Freedom Of Expression And Association	Regulation of Content	3199
3	B	Criminal Law	General Principles	Responsibility	3089
4	D	Evidence	Witnesses	Impeachment	2993
5	D	Civil Procedure	Subject Matter Jurisdiction	Removal Jurisdiction	4906
6	D	Criminal Law	Inchoate Crimes	Conspiracy	3094
7	B	Criminal Procedure	Pretrial Procedures	Eyewitness Identification Procedures	3097
8	D	Evidence	Tangible Evidence	Best Evidence Rule	4187
9	C	Civil Procedure	Post-Trial Procedure	Appeals	6457
10	C	Civil Procedure	Pleadings	Rule 11	5039
11	C	Constitutional Law	Federal Interbranch Relationships	Delegation of Legislative Power	3212
12	D	Civil Procedure	Multiple Parties And Claims	Class Actions	4977
13	A	Criminal Law	Defenses	Specific Defenses	7563
14	B	Evidence	Hearsay Exceptions	Declarant Unavailable as a Witness	3049
15	C	Civil Procedure	Subject Matter Jurisdiction	Supplemental Jurisdiction	4919
16	D	Criminal Law	General Principles	Mens Rea- State of Mind	3066
17	A	Evidence	Privileges And Other Policy Exclusions	Privileges	3048
18	A	Criminal Law	Other Crimes	Crimes Against Property	3062

Question	Answer	Subject	Chapter	Section	ID
19	B	Constitutional Law	The Powers Of Congress	Power to Enforce the Thirteenth, Fourteenth, and Fifteenth Amendments	3222
20	A	Civil Procedure	Personal Jurisdiction	In General	4981
21	C	Criminal Procedure	Fourth Amendment: Application To Arrest	Search and Seizure	7310
22	B	Constitutional Law	The Powers Of Congress	Commerce	4180
23	C	Evidence	Privileges And Other Policy Exclusions	Public Policy Exclusions	3038
24	C	Criminal Procedure	Trial	Due Process	388
25	D	Civil Procedure	Pleadings	Service of Process	4973
26	A	Constitutional Law	Substantive Due Process	Standard of Review	3200
27	B	Criminal Procedure	Fifth Amendment Rights And Privileges	Fifth Amendment in Police Interrogation Context	3102
28	C	Evidence	Tangible Evidence	Authentication	3044
29	A	Evidence	Relevance	Character Evidence	6977
30	A	Civil Procedure	Pretrial Procedure And Discovery	Discovery Scope and Limits	4930
31	A	Constitutional Law	Takings Clause	Types of Takings	7062
32	C	Constitutional Law	Equal Protection	Suspect Classifications	3241
33	D	Criminal Law	Homicide	Types of Homicide	3092
34	D	Civil Procedure	Personal Jurisdiction	In Personam Jurisdiction	4985
35	C	Criminal Procedure	Fourth Amendment: Application To Arrest, Search And Seizure	Search and Seizure	4348
36	B	Constitutional Law	Prohibited Legislation	Ex Post Facto Laws	3267
37	D	Evidence	Witnesses	Competence	3036

Question	Answer	Subject	Chapter	Section	ID
38	A	Constitutional Law	The Powers of Congress	Commerce	6278
39	C	Civil Procedure	Pretrial Procedure and Discovery	Mandatory Disclosures	5755
40	C	Civil Procedure	Subject Matter Jurisdiction	Supplemental Jurisdiction	4914
41	D	Criminal Procedure	Fifth Amendment Rights And Privileges	The Privilege Against Compulsory Self-Incrimination	4329
42	A	Evidence	Hearsay	What is Hearsay	4314
43	B	Constitutional Law	Judicial Power	Judicial Review in Operation	3216
44	B	Evidence	Relevance	Character Evidence	7194
45	C	Civil Procedure	Pleadings	Amendments and Supplemental Pleadings	4974
46	C	Civil Procedure	Subject Matter Jurisdiction	Diversity Jurisdiction	4896
47	D	Constitutional Law	Freedom Of Expression And Association	Regulation of Time, Place, and Manner of Association	3195
48	A	Constitutional Law	Equal Protection	General Considerations	7175
49	C	Evidence	Witnesses	Impeachment	2991
50	A	Civil Procedure	Trial Procedure	Jury Trial	4979
51	A	Civil Procedure	Subject Matter Jurisdiction	Diversity Jurisdiction	4902
52	B	Criminal Procedure	Post-Trial Considerations	Double Jeopardy	393
53	C	Criminal Law	General Principles	Parties to a Crime	6237
54	D	Criminal Law	Other Crimes	Crimes Against Property	3073
55	C	Constitutional Law	Substantive Due Process	Fundamental Rights	3205

Themis
Bar Review

Practice Exam Three

Simulated MBE: AM Session

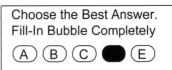

Choose the Best Answer.
Fill-In Bubble Completely
Ⓐ Ⓑ Ⓒ ⬤ Ⓔ

Start Time:_____

End Time:_____

1. Ⓐ Ⓑ Ⓒ Ⓓ
2. Ⓐ Ⓑ Ⓒ Ⓓ
3. Ⓐ Ⓑ Ⓒ Ⓓ
4. Ⓐ Ⓑ Ⓒ Ⓓ
5. Ⓐ Ⓑ Ⓒ Ⓓ
6. Ⓐ Ⓑ Ⓒ Ⓓ
7. Ⓐ Ⓑ Ⓒ Ⓓ
8. Ⓐ Ⓑ Ⓒ Ⓓ
9. Ⓐ Ⓑ Ⓒ Ⓓ
10. Ⓐ Ⓑ Ⓒ Ⓓ
11. Ⓐ Ⓑ Ⓒ Ⓓ
12. Ⓐ Ⓑ Ⓒ Ⓓ
13. Ⓐ Ⓑ Ⓒ Ⓓ
14. Ⓐ Ⓑ Ⓒ Ⓓ
15. Ⓐ Ⓑ Ⓒ Ⓓ
16. Ⓐ Ⓑ Ⓒ Ⓓ
17. Ⓐ Ⓑ Ⓒ Ⓓ
18. Ⓐ Ⓑ Ⓒ Ⓓ
19. Ⓐ Ⓑ Ⓒ Ⓓ
20. Ⓐ Ⓑ Ⓒ Ⓓ
21. Ⓐ Ⓑ Ⓒ Ⓓ
22. Ⓐ Ⓑ Ⓒ Ⓓ
23. Ⓐ Ⓑ Ⓒ Ⓓ
24. Ⓐ Ⓑ Ⓒ Ⓓ
25. Ⓐ Ⓑ Ⓒ Ⓓ

26. Ⓐ Ⓑ Ⓒ Ⓓ
27. Ⓐ Ⓑ Ⓒ Ⓓ
28. Ⓐ Ⓑ Ⓒ Ⓓ
29. Ⓐ Ⓑ Ⓒ Ⓓ
30. Ⓐ Ⓑ Ⓒ Ⓓ
31. Ⓐ Ⓑ Ⓒ Ⓓ
32. Ⓐ Ⓑ Ⓒ Ⓓ
33. Ⓐ Ⓑ Ⓒ Ⓓ
34. Ⓐ Ⓑ Ⓒ Ⓓ
35. Ⓐ Ⓑ Ⓒ Ⓓ
36. Ⓐ Ⓑ Ⓒ Ⓓ
37. Ⓐ Ⓑ Ⓒ Ⓓ
38. Ⓐ Ⓑ Ⓒ Ⓓ
39. Ⓐ Ⓑ Ⓒ Ⓓ
40. Ⓐ Ⓑ Ⓒ Ⓓ
41. Ⓐ Ⓑ Ⓒ Ⓓ
42. Ⓐ Ⓑ Ⓒ Ⓓ
43. Ⓐ Ⓑ Ⓒ Ⓓ
44. Ⓐ Ⓑ Ⓒ Ⓓ
45. Ⓐ Ⓑ Ⓒ Ⓓ
46. Ⓐ Ⓑ Ⓒ Ⓓ
47. Ⓐ Ⓑ Ⓒ Ⓓ
48. Ⓐ Ⓑ Ⓒ Ⓓ
49. Ⓐ Ⓑ Ⓒ Ⓓ
50. Ⓐ Ⓑ Ⓒ Ⓓ

51. Ⓐ Ⓑ Ⓒ Ⓓ
52. Ⓐ Ⓑ Ⓒ Ⓓ
53. Ⓐ Ⓑ Ⓒ Ⓓ
54. Ⓐ Ⓑ Ⓒ Ⓓ
55. Ⓐ Ⓑ Ⓒ Ⓓ
56. Ⓐ Ⓑ Ⓒ Ⓓ
57. Ⓐ Ⓑ Ⓒ Ⓓ
58. Ⓐ Ⓑ Ⓒ Ⓓ
59. Ⓐ Ⓑ Ⓒ Ⓓ
60. Ⓐ Ⓑ Ⓒ Ⓓ
61. Ⓐ Ⓑ Ⓒ Ⓓ
62. Ⓐ Ⓑ Ⓒ Ⓓ
63. Ⓐ Ⓑ Ⓒ Ⓓ
64. Ⓐ Ⓑ Ⓒ Ⓓ
65. Ⓐ Ⓑ Ⓒ Ⓓ
66. Ⓐ Ⓑ Ⓒ Ⓓ
67. Ⓐ Ⓑ Ⓒ Ⓓ
68. Ⓐ Ⓑ Ⓒ Ⓓ
69. Ⓐ Ⓑ Ⓒ Ⓓ
70. Ⓐ Ⓑ Ⓒ Ⓓ
71. Ⓐ Ⓑ Ⓒ Ⓓ
72. Ⓐ Ⓑ Ⓒ Ⓓ
73. Ⓐ Ⓑ Ⓒ Ⓓ
74. Ⓐ Ⓑ Ⓒ Ⓓ
75. Ⓐ Ⓑ Ⓒ Ⓓ

76. Ⓐ Ⓑ Ⓒ Ⓓ
77. Ⓐ Ⓑ Ⓒ Ⓓ
78. Ⓐ Ⓑ Ⓒ Ⓓ
79. Ⓐ Ⓑ Ⓒ Ⓓ
80. Ⓐ Ⓑ Ⓒ Ⓓ
81. Ⓐ Ⓑ Ⓒ Ⓓ
82. Ⓐ Ⓑ Ⓒ Ⓓ
83. Ⓐ Ⓑ Ⓒ Ⓓ
84. Ⓐ Ⓑ Ⓒ Ⓓ
85. Ⓐ Ⓑ Ⓒ Ⓓ
86. Ⓐ Ⓑ Ⓒ Ⓓ
87. Ⓐ Ⓑ Ⓒ Ⓓ
88. Ⓐ Ⓑ Ⓒ Ⓓ
89. Ⓐ Ⓑ Ⓒ Ⓓ
90. Ⓐ Ⓑ Ⓒ Ⓓ
91. Ⓐ Ⓑ Ⓒ Ⓓ
92. Ⓐ Ⓑ Ⓒ Ⓓ
93. Ⓐ Ⓑ Ⓒ Ⓓ
94. Ⓐ Ⓑ Ⓒ Ⓓ
95. Ⓐ Ⓑ Ⓒ Ⓓ
96. Ⓐ Ⓑ Ⓒ Ⓓ
97. Ⓐ Ⓑ Ⓒ Ⓓ
98. Ⓐ Ⓑ Ⓒ Ⓓ
99. Ⓐ Ⓑ Ⓒ Ⓓ
100. Ⓐ Ⓑ Ⓒ Ⓓ

Themis
BarReview

Practice Exam Three

Simulated MBE: PM Session

 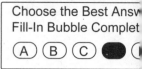

Start Time:_____

End Time:_____

101. Ⓐ Ⓑ Ⓒ Ⓓ	126. Ⓐ Ⓑ Ⓒ Ⓓ	151. Ⓐ Ⓑ Ⓒ Ⓓ	176. Ⓐ Ⓑ Ⓒ Ⓓ
102. Ⓐ Ⓑ Ⓒ Ⓓ	127. Ⓐ Ⓑ Ⓒ Ⓓ	152. Ⓐ Ⓑ Ⓒ Ⓓ	177. Ⓐ Ⓑ Ⓒ Ⓓ
103. Ⓐ Ⓑ Ⓒ Ⓓ	128. Ⓐ Ⓑ Ⓒ Ⓓ	153. Ⓐ Ⓑ Ⓒ Ⓓ	178. Ⓐ Ⓑ Ⓒ Ⓓ
104. Ⓐ Ⓑ Ⓒ Ⓓ	129. Ⓐ Ⓑ Ⓒ Ⓓ	154. Ⓐ Ⓑ Ⓒ Ⓓ	179. Ⓐ Ⓑ Ⓒ Ⓓ
105. Ⓐ Ⓑ Ⓒ Ⓓ	130. Ⓐ Ⓑ Ⓒ Ⓓ	155. Ⓐ Ⓑ Ⓒ Ⓓ	180. Ⓐ Ⓑ Ⓒ Ⓓ
106. Ⓐ Ⓑ Ⓒ Ⓓ	131. Ⓐ Ⓑ Ⓒ Ⓓ	156. Ⓐ Ⓑ Ⓒ Ⓓ	181. Ⓐ Ⓑ Ⓒ Ⓓ
107. Ⓐ Ⓑ Ⓒ Ⓓ	132. Ⓐ Ⓑ Ⓒ Ⓓ	157. Ⓐ Ⓑ Ⓒ Ⓓ	182. Ⓐ Ⓑ Ⓒ Ⓓ
108. Ⓐ Ⓑ Ⓒ Ⓓ	133. Ⓐ Ⓑ Ⓒ Ⓓ	158. Ⓐ Ⓑ Ⓒ Ⓓ	183. Ⓐ Ⓑ Ⓒ Ⓓ
109. Ⓐ Ⓑ Ⓒ Ⓓ	134. Ⓐ Ⓑ Ⓒ Ⓓ	159. Ⓐ Ⓑ Ⓒ Ⓓ	184. Ⓐ Ⓑ Ⓒ Ⓓ
110. Ⓐ Ⓑ Ⓒ Ⓓ	135. Ⓐ Ⓑ Ⓒ Ⓓ	160. Ⓐ Ⓑ Ⓒ Ⓓ	185. Ⓐ Ⓑ Ⓒ Ⓓ
111. Ⓐ Ⓑ Ⓒ Ⓓ	136. Ⓐ Ⓑ Ⓒ Ⓓ	161. Ⓐ Ⓑ Ⓒ Ⓓ	186. Ⓐ Ⓑ Ⓒ Ⓓ
112. Ⓐ Ⓑ Ⓒ Ⓓ	137. Ⓐ Ⓑ Ⓒ Ⓓ	162. Ⓐ Ⓑ Ⓒ Ⓓ	187. Ⓐ Ⓑ Ⓒ Ⓓ
113. Ⓐ Ⓑ Ⓒ Ⓓ	138. Ⓐ Ⓑ Ⓒ Ⓓ	163. Ⓐ Ⓑ Ⓒ Ⓓ	188. Ⓐ Ⓑ Ⓒ Ⓓ
114. Ⓐ Ⓑ Ⓒ Ⓓ	139. Ⓐ Ⓑ Ⓒ Ⓓ	164. Ⓐ Ⓑ Ⓒ Ⓓ	189. Ⓐ Ⓑ Ⓒ Ⓓ
115. Ⓐ Ⓑ Ⓒ Ⓓ	140. Ⓐ Ⓑ Ⓒ Ⓓ	165. Ⓐ Ⓑ Ⓒ Ⓓ	190. Ⓐ Ⓑ Ⓒ Ⓓ
116. Ⓐ Ⓑ Ⓒ Ⓓ	141. Ⓐ Ⓑ Ⓒ Ⓓ	166. Ⓐ Ⓑ Ⓒ Ⓓ	191. Ⓐ Ⓑ Ⓒ Ⓓ
117. Ⓐ Ⓑ Ⓒ Ⓓ	142. Ⓐ Ⓑ Ⓒ Ⓓ	167. Ⓐ Ⓑ Ⓒ Ⓓ	192. Ⓐ Ⓑ Ⓒ Ⓓ
118. Ⓐ Ⓑ Ⓒ Ⓓ	143. Ⓐ Ⓑ Ⓒ Ⓓ	168. Ⓐ Ⓑ Ⓒ Ⓓ	193. Ⓐ Ⓑ Ⓒ Ⓓ
119. Ⓐ Ⓑ Ⓒ Ⓓ	144. Ⓐ Ⓑ Ⓒ Ⓓ	169. Ⓐ Ⓑ Ⓒ Ⓓ	194. Ⓐ Ⓑ Ⓒ Ⓓ
120. Ⓐ Ⓑ Ⓒ Ⓓ	145. Ⓐ Ⓑ Ⓒ Ⓓ	170. Ⓐ Ⓑ Ⓒ Ⓓ	195. Ⓐ Ⓑ Ⓒ Ⓓ
121. Ⓐ Ⓑ Ⓒ Ⓓ	146. Ⓐ Ⓑ Ⓒ Ⓓ	171. Ⓐ Ⓑ Ⓒ Ⓓ	196. Ⓐ Ⓑ Ⓒ Ⓓ
122. Ⓐ Ⓑ Ⓒ Ⓓ	147. Ⓐ Ⓑ Ⓒ Ⓓ	172. Ⓐ Ⓑ Ⓒ Ⓓ	197. Ⓐ Ⓑ Ⓒ Ⓓ
123. Ⓐ Ⓑ Ⓒ Ⓓ	148. Ⓐ Ⓑ Ⓒ Ⓓ	173. Ⓐ Ⓑ Ⓒ Ⓓ	198. Ⓐ Ⓑ Ⓒ Ⓓ
124. Ⓐ Ⓑ Ⓒ Ⓓ	149. Ⓐ Ⓑ Ⓒ Ⓓ	174. Ⓐ Ⓑ Ⓒ Ⓓ	199. Ⓐ Ⓑ Ⓒ Ⓓ
125. Ⓐ Ⓑ Ⓒ Ⓓ	150. Ⓐ Ⓑ Ⓒ Ⓓ	175. Ⓐ Ⓑ Ⓒ Ⓓ	200. Ⓐ Ⓑ Ⓒ Ⓓ

Themis
Bar Review

PRACTICE EXAM THREE:
SIMULATED MULTISTATE BAR EXAMINATION

TIME: SIX HOURS

This simulated Multistate Bar Exam (MBE) is presented in the same format that the MBE will appear when you take it. We recommend that you take this exam under actual exam conditions. That is, you should schedule two consecutive **uninterrupted** 3-hour blocks of time (with an hour-long break in between) in which to complete this exam.

During the actual exam, your score will be based on the number of questions you answer correctly. It is therefore to your advantage to try to answer as many questions as you can. Use your time effectively. Do not hurry, but work steadily and as quickly as you can without sacrificing your accuracy. If a question seems too difficult, go on to the next one. Give only one answer to each question; multiple answers will not be counted.

After you have completed this simulated exam, you may grade your work using the answer key provided. In order to fully understand each question and answer, we recommend that you review the explanatory answers in your online course materials, as well as view the Simulated MBE Analysis lectures, which discuss each question and answer in detail.

Please do not take this exam until it has been assigned in your course. (Flex study students: Be sure you have completed all MBE lectures and practice sessions, as well as the first two Practice Exams, before beginning this exam.)

AM Session

3 hours

Directions: Each of the questions or incomplete statements below is followed by four suggested answers or completions. You are to choose the best of the stated alternatives. Answer all questions according to the generally accepted view, except where otherwise noted.

For the purposes of this test, you are to assume the application of (1) the Federal Rules of Civil Procedure as currently in effect; and (2) the sections of Title 28 to the U.S. Code pertaining to jurisdiction, venue, and transfer. The terms "Constitution," "constitutional," and "unconstitutional" refer to the federal Constitution unless indicated otherwise. Assume also that Article 2 and Revised Article 1 of the Uniform Commercial Code have been adopted and are applicable when appropriate. All Evidence questions should be answered according to the Federal Rules of Evidence, as currently in effect. Finally, with respect to Torts questions, assume that there is no applicable statute unless otherwise specified; however, survival actions and claims for wrongful death should be assumed to be available where applicable. You should assume that joint and several liability, with pure comparative negligence, is the relevant rule unless otherwise indicated.

1. A collector owned a painting that needed professional restoration. The collector brought the painting to a restorer and, after examining the painting, the restorer quoted the collector a price for the restoration. The restorer told the collector that since she was going on a vacation and would be unreachable, the collector had a month to make his decision. Two days later, the collector mailed a letter to the restorer accepting the restorer's price. Through no fault of the collector, this letter was lost in the mail and never delivered. The next day, the collector learned of another person who would do the restoration for a lower price and would begin immediately. The collector mailed a second letter to the restorer that stated that he did not require her services. On arriving home from her vacation, the restorer received the collector's second letter. As a consequence, she contacted another art owner and began restoration work for that owner. In the meantime, the collector became dissatisfied with the work of the second restorer. He contacted the original restorer and demanded that she begin the restoration work on his painting, which she refused to do. The collector is suing the restorer for breach of contract in a jurisdiction that follows the mailbox rule.

Will the collector prevail?

(A) No, because the restorer relied on the collector's rejection.
(B) No, because the restorer never received the collector's acceptance.
(C) Yes, because the collector had timely accepted the restorer's offer.
(D) Yes, because the "mailbox rule" does not apply when both a rejection and an acceptance are sent.

2. An employee sued her former employer after she was fired. At trial, the employee argued that when she was hired she had signed an employment contract that stated that she could be fired only for cause. The employer argued that the parties had never signed an employment contract, and that the employee was an at-will employee. The employer stipulated that there was not cause to discharge the employee, because she performed her job in a satisfactory manner. Rather, the CEO testified that, as part of a downsizing effort, he had approved the discharge of all at-will employees in the department where the employee worked. At trial, the employee sought to question the CEO about a conversation in which the CEO told the employee that he was happy with her performance. The employer objected to admission of the testimony.

Is the CEO's testimony likely to be admitted?

(A) No, because the testimony is hearsay not within any exception.
(B) No, because the evidence is not probative and material.
(C) Yes, because the evidence does not constitute hearsay.
(D) Yes, because the probative value outweighs any danger of unfair prejudice.

3. A company owned and operated a private golf course. One of the fairways on the course ran parallel to a navigable body of water. The company was aware that golfers frequently but unintentionally hit golf balls into the water when playing that hole because there were no barriers to prevent the balls from going into the water. A 12-year-old child, while sailing on the water, was struck by one such ball and suffered a serious physical injury. The injured child's parent has filed a public nuisance action against the company, on behalf of his child, to recover for his injuries.

Is the plaintiff precluded from recovering?

(A) No, because the child was seriously injured while on navigable water due to the company's negligence.
(B) No, because of the attractive nuisance doctrine.
(C) Yes, because the child did not have an ownership interest in land.
(D) Yes, because the golfer's action was unintentional.

4. A plaintiff brought a negligence action in federal court to recover damages for injuries suffered as an audience member at an event held by the defendant. The defendant was a citizen of the forum state; the plaintiff was a citizen of the neighboring state in which the event was held. Under the forum state's choice-of-law rules, the negligence law of the neighboring state applied to this action. Under the negligence law of the neighboring state, the defendant owed a duty to the plaintiff. Under the negligence law of the forum state, the defendant did not owe a duty to the plaintiff.

Which law should the court apply in deciding this action?

(A) The negligence law of the forum state, because that is the law of the state in which the federal court sits.
(B) The negligence law of the forum state, because choice-of-law rules are procedural rules.
(C) The negligence law of the neighboring state, because of the forum state's choice-of-law rules.
(D) The negligence law of the neighboring state, because the plaintiff is a citizen of this state.

5. A testator who was estranged from her immediate family properly executed a will. Under the terms of the will, the testator devised various items of personal property to her daughter. The terms of the will left the remainder of the testator's estate to an unrelated friend who was living at that time. At the time of the testator's death, the friend had died intestate, but the friend's wife and their only child, a son, were alive. The testator was unmarried at the time of her death, survived solely by her only child, a daughter.

The applicable jurisdiction has the following two statutes:

If a devisee related by blood to the testator in any degree of kinship is dead at the time of execution of the will, fails to survive the testator, or is treated as if the devisee predeceased the testator, the issue of the deceased devisee who survive the testator take in place of the deceased devisee.

When a decedent dies without a will or possesses property that is not devised under the terms of the decedent's will, and the decedent is survived by a spouse and any child, the spouse shall share the decedent's property equally with the children. If the decedent is not survived by a spouse but is survived by any child, each surviving child shall share equally the decedent's property.

The testator died owning her residence in fee simple absolute. Who is entitled to her residence?

(A) Both the friend's wife and son, under the intestacy statute.
(B) The friend's son only, under the anti-lapse statute.
(C) The testator's daughter, because the testator's will did not specifically devise the residence to anyone.
(D) The testator's daughter, under the intestacy statute.

6. During a trial for injuries a plaintiff sustained in a car accident with the defendant, the plaintiff's attorney called a witness to the stand to testify that the witness, a 25-year-old woman, saw the defendant run a stop sign and crash into the plaintiff's car. The witness was not associated with the defendant in any way. The plaintiff's attorney questioned the witness in an attempt to get her to testify that she saw the defendant run the stop sign, but she would not do so, and seemed to be deliberately avoiding the topic. Finally, the plaintiff's attorney asked that the witness be treated as hostile, and asked her, "Did you see the defendant run the stop sign on the day in question?" The defendant's attorney objected to the form of the question.

How is the court likely to rule on the defendant's objection?

(A) Overrule it, because a party may generally ask leading questions of his own witnesses.
(B) Overrule it, because a leading question was necessary to develop the witness's testimol
(C) Sustain it, because a party may not treat his own witness as hostile.
(D) Sustain it, because leading questions are not appropriate for this witness.

7. A husband and his friend agreed to kill the husband's wife and split the insurance proceeds the man received following the wife's death. The friend helped the husband obtain a handgun to commit the murder, but on the night of the planned murder, the friend decided that she could not go through with it. Afraid that the husband would kill her if she went to the police, she did not contact them. Instead, she called the husband and told him that she could not go through with the crime and urged him not to kill his wife. The husband ignored her and went through with the killing. The husband and friend were subsequently arrested and the friend was charged with conspiracy to commit murder.

Should the friend be convicted?

(A) No, because she successfully withdrew from the conspiracy.
(B) No, because at the time of the murder, the friend lacked the intent for the wife to be killed.
(C) Yes, because the friend committed an overt act in furtherance of the conspiracy.
(D) Yes, because withdrawal is not a valid defense to conspiracy.

8. A state feared abuse of its statute providing for welfare benefits, which was administered by its department of public assistance. The department believed that a particular man who had been receiving welfare payments for the past year was not eligible for them because he had adequate means of support. The department informed the man in writing of its decision to terminate his welfare benefits, effective immediately. The department also informed the man that he could schedule an administrative hearing, which would be held in approximately one month, to contest that decision and to present any evidence on his own behalf.

If the man challenges this termination on constitutional grounds, will he likely be successful?

(A) Yes, because the man had a Due Process right to notice and a hearing before his welfare benefits were terminated.
(B) Yes, because the department of public assistance has impaired the obligations of i contract with the man in violation of the Contracts Clause.
(C) No, because the department has provided the man with notice and a hearing sufficient to satisfy the Due Process Clause.
(D) No, because a state can establish the procedures for terminating an interest that the state itself has created, as distinguished from a purely private interest.

9. A retail furniture store ordered ten sofas from a manufacturer at $1,000 each, plus shipping, to be delivered and paid for in five equal monthly installments. With the first shipment of two sofas, the manufacturer sent an invoice to the retailer, billing the retailer $2,000 plus shipping. The invoice also noted that the manufacturer retained a security interest in all sofas shipped until the purchase price for all sofas ordered was paid in full.

Not happy with the security interest term, the retailer immediately notified the manufacturer that this term was unacceptable. After sending payment for the first two sofas, the retailer told the manufacturer not to send any more sofas. The manufacturer sued the retailer for breach of contract.

In the breach of contract action by the manufacturer against the retailer, what will be the result?

(A) The manufacturer will prevail, because both parties are merchants.
(B) The manufacturer will prevail, but can only enforce the terms of the original offer.
(C) The retailer will prevail, because the knock-out rule voids the contract.
(D) The retailer will prevail, because the additional terms materially affected the bargain.

10. A developer purchased a 60-acre parcel of wooded land and divided the parcel into 20 three-acre lots. The developer advertised the rustic character of the lots and the intent to sell the lots for development as single-family residences. This was in conformity with the zoning restrictions on the land, which required that the land be used for residential purposes and that the size of each lot not be less than two acres. Over a period of several years, the developer sold 15 of the lots.

The deed for each of these lots contained the following provision:

This deed is subject to the condition that the property may only be used for residential purposes and may not be subdivided but must be sold in its entirety. This condition shall be a covenant running with the land and shall be binding on all owners, their heirs, devisees, successors, and assignees.

The deed for each lot was promptly and properly recorded.

The developer, facing financial difficulty, sold the remaining five lots to a land speculator. The deeds to these lots did not contain the character and size provision that the developer had inserted into the other deeds, nor did the speculator have actual knowledge of the developer's advertising related to the character and size of the lots. The land speculator, acting in response to a zoning change that reduced the minimum permissible size of a lot to only one acre, has obtained governmental approval to divide each of the five remaining lots in thirds and is now offering the 15 lots for sale.

An owner of one of the three-acre lots has brought suit against the speculator seeking an injunction to prevent him from selling the lots in less than three-acre parcels. Can the speculator successfully defend against this lawsuit?

(A) Yes, because the speculator's deeds did not contain the character and size provision.
(B) Yes, because the speculator has obtained governmental approval to subdivide the lot
(C) No, because the lots purchased by the speculator are subject to an implied servitude.
(D) No, because the speculator purchased the lots for commercial rather than residential purposes.

11. For an agreed upon fee, a pest control company properly treated a residence for termites. In addition, the company entered into an agreement with the homeowner that, in exchange for an additional annual fee, the company would repair any damage to the residence caused by termites for four years. The day after the homeowner paid the final annual fee at the beginning of the fourth year of the agreement, he discovered a termite infestation in the home while changing a light bulb in his basement. The homeowner took no action until the final month of the agreement, when he notified the pest control company of the infestation. The pest control company refused to repair the termite damage. The homeowner then hired a contractor to repair the termite damage at a cost of $25,000. Had the homeowner notified the pest control company when he first discovered the termite infestation, the cost to repair the termite damage to the residence would have been $3,000.

The homeowner sued the pest control company for breach of their annual repair agreement. What damages should the court award to the homeowner?

(A) $25,000, because this was the cost to repair the termite damage to the residence that occurred within the four-year term of the contract.
(B) $3,000, because the homeowner failed to timely notify the company of the termite infestation.
(C) $3,000, because the company was entitled to damages of $22,000 due to the homeowner's breach of his duty to mitigate damages.
(D) Nothing, because the contractor performed the repairs, relieving the company of its duty to perform.

12. Congress passed the Equality in Employment Act ("EEA"), which was co-sponsored by both senators from a particular state and enjoyed the support of all of that state's federal representatives. Section 1 of the EEA required every state, within 18 months of passage, to enact legislation prohibiting employment discrimination based on sexual orientation. Section 2 of the EEA provided that any state that enacted such legislation before the deadline would receive $20 million in federal funding for programs designed to eliminate employment discrimination against gays and lesbians. Two years after passage of the act, the state had not enacted a statute prohibiting such discrimination.

If the United States sues the state for violating this act, what would be the most likely decision by the Supreme Court with regard to these two sections?

(A) Strike down Section 1 as exceeding Congress's power under the Commerce Clause, but uphold Section 2 as a proper exercise of the Spending Power.
(B) Strike down Section 1 as a "commandeering of state legislatures to enact laws, but uphold Section 2 as a proper exercise of the Spending Power.
(C) Uphold Section 1 as a proper exercise of Congress's power under the Commerce Clause, but strike down Section 2 as an improper exercise of the Spending Power.
(D) Uphold Sections 1 and 2 against any federalism-based challenge because the state's own congressional delegation supported the EEA and thus consented to any possible infringement on the state's sovereignty.

13.   A plaintiff brought an action in federal court based on diversity jurisdiction to rescind a contract to transfer real property to the defendant. The plaintiff contended that the defendant's conduct with regard to the contract constituted duress. Upon the death of the plaintiff, the personal representative of the plaintiff's estate continued the action.

The applicable state law, which otherwise follows the Federal Rules of Evidence, contains a Dead Man's statute, which reads:

> In any civil proceeding, where any party to a contract in action is dead and his right thereto has passed to a party who represents his interest in the subject in controversy, any surviving party to the contract shall not be a competent witness to any matter occurring before the death of said party.

As part of the case-in-chief, the personal representative introduced an email written by the defendant and sent to the decedent that was relevant to the issue of duress. Immediately thereafter, the defendant, noting that the email was written in response to a letter written by the decedent to the defendant, sought to introduce that letter into evidence. The personal representative objected.

Which of the following is the strongest ground upon which the personal representative can base this objection?

(A) The introduction of the letter violates the state's Dead Man's statute.
(B) The letter constitutes inadmissible hearsay.
(C) The rule of completeness does not apply because the letter was a separate writing.
(D) Fairness does not require introduction of the letter during the presentation of the personal representative's case-in-chief.

14.   A witness who was not a defendant invoked his Fifth Amendment right to remain silent during a federal criminal trial for insider trading. After being given derivative-use immunity, the witness testified. Several weeks later, the witness was a defendant in a state-law civil fraud proceeding based on his previous testimony in the federal trial. He moved to dismiss the case on the grounds that the previous grant of immunity protected him against a future action against him.

Will the defendant's motion be granted?

(A) Yes, because a grant of immunity can be given to a witness who is not a defendant.
(B) Yes, because the defendant was given derivative-use immunity.
(C) No, because the defendant's immunity was limited to federal prosecution.
(D) No, because the defendant's immunity does not extend to a subsequent civil trial.

15.   A law makes it a crime to "knowingly sell, distribute, or barter a sexually explicit film featuring actors younger than the age of majority." The owner of an adult video store sold explicit videos in her store that featured 18-year-old actors, but she took reasonable steps to ensure that no videos featuring younger actors were sold in her store. The video store owner, however, incorrectly believed that the age of majority in the jurisdiction was 18; in fact, the age of majority was 19 years old.

The owner was arrested and charged with violating the statute in a jurisdiction that has adopted the Model Penal Code. The prosecution does not contest that her error was made honestly. Should she nonetheless be convicted?

(A) Yes, because the owner's error was a mistake of law, which is not a valid defense.
(B) Yes, because the owner knowingly sold the illegal videos.
(C) No, because the owner's error negated the requisite mens rea.
(D) No, because the owner's conscious objective was not to engage in selling the illicit videos.

16.   A patient, a citizen of state A, had a severe allergic reaction to a prescription drug approved by the federal Food & Drug Administration (FDA). The patient was hospitalized for many days and missed a number of days of work. She filed suit in the U.S. District Court in the city of her residence against the manufacturer of the drug. The manufacturer is incorporated in State B, but has its principal place of business in State A. The patient claims that the manufacturer violated both State A tort law and the federal Safe Drug Act (SDA), which provides that "persons who reasonably believe that they may have been injured by a prescription drug have a cause of action in the appropriate U.S. District Court."

State A law is unsettled on the issue of whether obtaining FDA approval shields a drug manufacturer from tort liability. The patient requests damages of $40,000 for medical expenses, $20,000 for lost pay, and $15,000 for pain and suffering.

Should the U.S. District Court exercise jurisdiction?

(A) Yes, because the court has federal-question jurisdiction.
(B) Yes, because the court has diversity jurisdiction.
(C) No, because the federal court should abstain from exercising jurisdiction until the State A courts decide the unsettled issue of state law.
(D) No, because by adding an uncertain state-law cause of action, the patient did not present a well-pleaded complaint.

17. The maker of a prescription drug provides physicians who prescribe the drug with detailed instructions regarding its use. The instructions include a warning about the possibility of an allergic reaction that could result in serious physical harm if the drug is taken with a common over-the-counter medication. However, the allergic reaction is only likely to occur in a very small portion of the population, so the drug maker does not provide this warning to consumers of the drug in the instructions that accompany the drug.

A physician who had received the detailed instructions from the drug maker prescribed the drug for a patient. The physician did not warn the patient about the possible allergic reaction. The patient experienced an allergic reaction from taking the drug in combination with the over-the-counter medication and suffered a debilitating injury.

The patient brought a strict products liability action against the drug maker based on its failure to warn the patient of the possibility of an allergic reaction. Who will prevail?

(A) The patient, because the drug maker failed to warn the patient of the allergic reaction.
(B) The patient, because the drug maker, as a commercial supplier, is liable for harm done by the drug.
(C) The drug maker, because it warned the prescribing physician of the allergic reaction.
(D) The drug maker, because the number of persons at risk was very limited.

18. A plaintiff filed a complaint in federal district court in the state where the plaintiff was domiciled. The plaintiff asserted that the defendant, who lived in a neighboring state, was liable for damages the plaintiff sustained in a car accident that took place in the neighboring state. The plaintiff had the defendant personally served by a process server while the defendant was traveling through the forum state, which was his only contact with the forum state.

Nineteen days after being served with the complaint, the defendant served an answer in which he denied that he was responsible for the car accident. The next day, the defendant filed a motion to dismiss, arguing that the court lacked personal jurisdiction over him.

Is the court likely to grant the defendant's motion?

(A) Yes, because the defendant raised the issue of personal jurisdiction within 21 days of being served with the complaint.
(B) Yes, because the defendant did not have sufficient minimum contacts with the forum state.
(C) No, because the defendant waived any objection to personal jurisdiction.
(D) No, because the defendant was personally served with process while in the forum state.

19. The owner of a chain of retail stores built a warehouse that was financed by a loan from a bank. In exchange for the loan, the bank took a mortgage on the warehouse.

Several years later, a thief broke into the warehouse by cutting a hole in the roof. The owner hired a contractor to repair the roof but, due to the contractor's shoddy work, the roof leaks whenever it rains, making a large portion of the warehouse unusable. Due to a contraction in the owner's business, the remaining usable space of the warehouse is sufficient for the owner's needs, but the unusable space impairs the bank's security interest.

Learning of the condition of the warehouse, the bank requested that the owner repair the warehouse roof. The owner refused. The bank brought an action to compel the owner to properly repair the roof.

The mortgage provides that it was made with recourse to the personal liability of the owner. Neither the mortgage nor the deed contains a covenant requiring the owner to maintain or repair the premises. The owner is not in default with respect to the mortgage payments. The jurisdiction follows a lien theory with regard to ownership of a mortgage and does not have an anti-deficiency statute.

Will the bank succeed?

(A) No, because the owner is not liable for waste.
(B) No, because the owner is not in default wit respect to the required mortgage payment:
(C) Yes, because the mortgaged property is not residential.
(D) Yes, because the condition of the roof impairs the bank's security interest.

20. A large clothing retailer contracted with a firm that specialized in custom printing to print the logo of a major sporting event onto 5,000 jerseys. The logo was coupled with an identifying landmark of the city in which the event was to take place. The retailer planned to sell the jerseys as souvenirs at the event. As called for in the contract, the retailer supplied the firm with the jerseys and paid half the contract price. Shortly before the event and before any shirts had been printed, the stadium where the game was to be held was damaged by an earthquake. As a consequence, the event was moved to another city.

The retailer demanded the return of its payment and the jerseys. The supplier, claiming that it was entitled to the benefit of its bargain, kept its anticipated profit of $2,000 but returned the jerseys and the remainder of the payment to the retailer. The retailer filed a lawsuit seeking rescission of the contract and return of the $2,000.

What is the retailer's best argument in support of its suit?

(A) Performance of the contract has become impracticable because the relocation of the sporting event was an unforeseeable occurrence.
(B) The relocation of the sporting event has made enforcement of the contract on its original terms unconscionable.
(C) The contract is void due to mutual mistake, as both parties were mistaken as to an essential element of the contract.
(D) The retailer's contractual duties are discharged because the game's relocation frustrated the purpose of the contract.

21.   On a winter day, a youth, seeking refuge from the cold, entered a small neighborhood grocery store without the knowledge of the store's owner, who was standing at the cash register. Shortly thereafter, the only other person in the store approached the register and requested an item located on a shelf behind the owner.   As the owner turned to retrieve the requested item, the individual drew a gun and commanded the owner to give him the money in the register. As the owner turned back toward the customer, the customer fired the gun at her and missed.   The owner grappled with the customer and succeeded in knocking the gun out of the customer's hand.   As the customer retrieved his gun, the owner grabbed her own gun, for which she had a valid license. They fired at each other, each missing the other. Although the owner's actions did not create an unreasonable risk of harm to the youth, the bullet from the owner's gun nevertheless struck and killed the youth. The estate of the youth filed a wrongful death action against the store owner.

Who will prevail?

(A) The store owner, because the owner acted in self-defense.
(B) The store owner, because the owner's shooting of the youth was not negligent.
(C) The estate of the youth, because the youth was an invitee.
(D) The estate of the youth, because the youth was not a co-conspirator with the robber.

22.   An organization against drunk driving sought permission from the owner of a mall to pass out leaflets in favor of tougher drunk driving laws in front of a liquor store. The mall owner denied the organization permission.   The organization, filing an action in an appropriate court, sought an injunction permitting the organization to pass out its leaflets in accord with its free speech rights.

The state's highest court, interpreting the state constitution, permits the exercise of free speech rights on private property that is regularly held open to the public. Of the following reasons, which is the best argument for granting the injunction?

(A) Leafleting is a form of speech that is protected by the First Amendment of the United States Constitution.
(B) The reason for leafleting was related to the place where the organization sought to leaflet.
(C) The leafleting was permitted by the state constitution.
(D) By admitting members of the general public, the mall constituted a limited public forum.

23. The plaintiff attended a professional baseball game, where he was hit by a foul ball. He was rushed to a hospital and diagnosed with a head bruise. The injury was minor, and the plaintiff's pain went away after three days. However, such a blow to the head, in one out of every 500,000 cases, can lead to serious brain injuries many years later. The plaintiff sued the defendant baseball team for negligence and requested $1,000,000 in damages. The federal court properly exercised diversity jurisdiction. The jury's verdict was that the defendant was liable for negligence, based on evidence that the ball that hit the plaintiff went through a hole in protective netting that the team failed to repair. The jury awarded the plaintiff $15,000 for medical expenses and three days of lost wages, plus $985,000 for "pain and suffering," primarily for the mental anguish of not knowing whether a brain injury would develop later. In similar cases, the highest award for pain and suffering was $50,000. The defendant moved for a new trial. The court concluded that the damages awarded were excessive and ordered a new trial limited to the issue of damages. The plaintiff properly appealed the court's order.

Should the appellate court rule in his favor?

(A) Yes, because the district court should have ordered a new trial on all the issues, not on the issue of damages alone.
(B) Yes, because the district court failed to give the plaintiff the option of remittitur instead a new trial.
(C) No, because a district court with diversity jurisdiction is required to order a new trial whenever the "pain and suffering" component of a damages award is more than ten times the plaintiff's tangible losses.
(D) No, because the district court had discretion to order a new trial on the issue of damages.

24. A plaintiff brought an action against a defendant for damages to her vehicle resulting from a car accident. To prove her damages, the plaintiff introduced a dated and authenticated invoice from the mechanic who repaired her car after the accident. After the invoice was admitted into evidence, the woman sought to enter into evidence a printout of a digital photograph of her vehicle at the scene of the accident. If admitted, she plans to testify that she called her brother immediately after the accident so he could meet her at the scene and take photographs. She will also testify that her brother took this photograph the day of the accident, and that the photograph fairly and accurately represents the condition of her vehicle and its position in the intersection after colliding with the defendant's vehicle.

Should the court rule that the photograph is admissible?

(A) No, because the photograph is needlessly cumulative following the admission of the invoice.
(B) No, because the plaintiff must call her brotl to authenticate the photograph.
(C) Yes, because a digital photograph is self-authenticating.
(D) Yes, because the plaintiff has personal knowledge of the accuracy of the photograph.

25. A man whose terminally ill aunt had promised to devise an undeveloped parcel of land to him sold the parcel to a friend. The friend purchased the property based on the nephew's false assertion that he owned the parcel; the friend was unaware of the aunt's ownership of the parcel. The friend did not perform a title search and did not record the deed, which was a general warranty deed. Subsequently, the aunt died. As promised, she devised the parcel to her nephew. The personal representative of the estate executed and recorded a deed transferring title to the parcel to the nephew. After the aunt's death, no one paid the property taxes on the parcel. Eventually, the state seized the parcel and sold it through a tax sale. Before expiration of the redemption period that is statutorily permitted to the owner of the real property, the friend learned of the sale of the parcel for delinquent taxes. Claiming ownership of the parcel, the friend sought to pay the delinquent taxes and other costs and fees associated with the sale and thereby redeem the parcel. The buyer of the parcel at the tax sale, who had no prior knowledge of the friend's claim with respect to the parcel, objected.

In an action to determine ownership of the parcel, if the court finds for the friend, what is the likely reason?

(A) The friend was record owner of the parcel.
(B) The friend purchased the parcel for value a without notice.
(C) Under the doctrine of equitable conversion, the friend is the owner of the parcel.
(D) Title to the parcel vested in the friend upon the nephew's acquisition of the parcel.

26. A defendant was charged with the sale of narcotics. At his trial, the prosecution planned on calling as witnesses the police officer who investigated the crime, an eyewitness to the crime, a desk officer to testify regarding chain of custody, and a former co-defendant who had reached a plea agreement with the prosecution. The defendant demanded, as a matter of right, that each of these individuals be excluded from the courtroom to prevent them from hearing the testimony of the other witnesses. The prosecution objected to removing any of these individuals from the courtroom.

Which of the following individuals should the judge order be removed from the courtroom?

(A) The eyewitness only.
(B) The eyewitness and the former co-defenda only.
(C) The eyewitness, the former co-defendant, and the desk officer, but not the investigating officer.
(D) The eyewitness, the former co-defendant, the desk officer, and the investigating officer.

27. In a bicycle race with a $5,000 prize for the winner, a cyclist was leading by a significant margin. A spectator at the race was married to the second place rider. Sensing that her husband would not win unless she took action, the spectator drove to a point two miles ahead on the course, scattered several nails in the middle of the course, and then left the area. Soon thereafter, the cyclist approached the area and noticed the nails. He attempted to swerve around the obstruction but a nail punctured his tire. He fell off his bike, suffered significant physical injuries, and was unable to complete the race.

If the cyclist sues the spectator, under what theory is the cyclist least likely to recover maximum punitive damages?

(A) Assault
(B) Intentional infliction of emotional distress
(C) Trespass to chattels
(D) Battery

28. An artist who had designed a sculpture to be made out of steel went to the website of a merchant that sold specialized tools. Using the chat feature, the artist explained to an employee of the merchant that the artist wanted to purchase a tool that could cut through steel. The employee suggested that the artist purchase a particular saw. The employee, pointing out that the website's description of the saw indicated that it could cut through most metals, added that the saw "should cut through steel with no problem." The artist purchased the saw from the merchant's website for a total cost of $450. Conspicuously appearing on the page where the artist had to indicate his consent in order to purchase the saw was the following: "There are no implied warranties provided with this product other than the general warranty of merchantability." The tool failed to cut through the steel that the artist intended to use for his sculpture. The artist sued the merchant for damages attributable to breach of the implied warranty of fitness for a particular purpose.

Which party is likely to prevail?

(A) The merchant, because the merchant disclaimed the warranty of fitness for a particular purpose.
(B) The merchant, because warranties do not apply to goods valued under $500.
(C) The artist, because the merchant's employee knew that the artist wanted a saw that would cut steel and relied on his judgment that the saw would do so.
(D) The artist, because the implied warranty of fitness for a particular purpose cannot be disclaimed by a merchant.

29. A 15-year-old male was being tried in state court as an adult for murder. At voir dire, the prosecutor exercised all of his peremptory challenges to exclude persons under the age of 30 from the jury. The defendant's attorney timely raised the issue as to whether the prosecutor had utilized his peremptory challenges in an unconstitutional manner. In response to questioning by the court, the prosecutor stated that it was his intent to exclude persons who, because of their age, would be sympathetic to the defendant. The judge found that the prosecutor's reason was genuine and not pretextual.

Should the judge sustain the defendant's objection?

(A) Yes, because the prosecutor's use of peremptory challenges violates the defendant's Sixth Amendment right to trial by an impartial jury.
(B) Yes, because the defendant was a member the affected class.
(C) No, because the prosecutor is permitted to exercise peremptory challenges for any rational reason.
(D) No, because the prosecutor's use of peremptory challenges does not violate the Equal Protection Clause.

30. Concerned with protecting the use of federal funds from the deleterious effects of bribery, Congress enacted a statute criminalizing the acceptance of a bribe by a state or local official where the state or local government received at least $10,000 in federal funds.

A county government, in exchange for its agreement to permit the housing of federal prisoners in the county's jail, received a payment of federal funds for each prisoner. The total amount received by the county government for housing federal prisoners exceeded $100,000 annually. A federal prisoner housed in the county jail agreed to transfer title to a pickup truck to a prison guard in exchange for the guard permitting the prisoner to receive illegal conjugal visits. The prison guard was charged with violating the statute. Is the application of the statute to the guard's taking title to the prisoner's truck constitutional?

(A) No, because the bribe did not directly relate to the federal funds.
(B) No, because a federal statute that criminalizes noneconomic behavior must have a significant impact on interstate commerce.
(C) Yes, because the statute was a valid congressional exercise, pursuant to the Necessary and Proper Clause, of ensuring that its power to appropriate money for the general welfare was not thwarted.
(D) Yes, because the statute was a valid congressional exercise of its inherent police powers.

31. A contractor decided to purchase a house to renovate and then sell. The contractor entered into a written contract with a homeowner for the purchase of the homeowner's house. The contract, signed by both parties, set forth the agreed upon price of $100,000 and a description of the property, as well as the terms of payment. No other information was included in the contract. After the contract was executed, the contractor received notice that another house he was interested in renovating had become available to purchase for $65,000. Realizing that he would be able to obtain a significantly higher profit from the newly available house, the contractor called the homeowner to inform him that he was backing out of their contract and would not purchase the house. When the homeowner stated that he would try to enforce the contract in court, the contractor argued that the contract was unenforceable because it did not set forth the closing date. The homeowner subsequently brought an action against the contractor for specific performance of the contract.

Will the homeowner prevail?

(A) Yes, because the contract is enforceable under the Statute of Frauds.
(B) Yes, because the homeowner detrimentally relied on the contract.
(C) No, because a seller cannot seek specific performance of a land sales contract.
(D) No, because the contract did not contain all of the essential terms.

32. Engrossed in a cell phone conversation, a pedestrian in a rural area failed to look out for traffic while crossing a road. The driver of an oncoming car noticed the pedestrian and began to brake, which caused a cake sitting on the front passenger seat to slide off the seat and onto the floor of the car. Distracted by the cake, the driver, who was 17 years old and properly licensed to operate the car without supervision, momentarily forgot about the pedestrian. When the driver's attention returned to the road, the driver did not have sufficient time to avoid striking the pedestrian, who suffered serious physical injuries as a result.

The applicable jurisdiction has adopted a modified comparative negligence statute.

The pedestrian brings a negligence action against the driver for damages stemming from the pedestrian's physical injuries, which total $200,000. The jury determines that the driver was 80% at fault and the pedestrian was 20% at fault.

How much will the pedestrian be permitted to recover?

(A) Nothing, because the pedestrian was negligent.
(B) $160,000, because the pedestrian's damag are reduced by the percentage that the pedestrian was at fault.
(C) $200,000, because the driver had the last clear chance to avoid the accident.
(D) $200,000, because the driver was engaged in an adult activity.

33.   The owner of a residence in an older residential community entered into a contract to sell the residence. The contract was silent on whether the owner was required to deliver marketable title. In researching the title to the residence, the buyer found that residences in the community were subject to a restrictive covenant that prohibits property owners from selling their residences to members of a particular religious sect.

Which of the following is the best reason for a court to compel the buyer to purchase the property?

(A) The buyer is not a member of the religious sect and therefore is not subject to this restrictive covenant.
(B) The covenant is only a promissory restraint on alienation, not a disabling restraint.
(C) A private restrictive covenant does not constitute a title defect for purposes of the implied covenant of marketable title.
(D) The restriction is patently unenforceable.

34.   A car dealership sued a car manufacturer in the federal court for State A for breach of contract, alleging that the cars provided by the manufacturer to the dealership were defective. The car dealership is incorporated in State A where its principal place of business is located. The car manufacturer is incorporated in State B where its principal place of business is located. The federal court for State A has personal jurisdiction over the car manufacturer. The contract that formed the basis of the action contains a forum-selection provision that designated the federal court for State B as the only appropriate venue in which litigation of disputes arising under the contract could be pursued. The car manufacturer has moved to dismiss this action for improper venue.

Under the law of State A, a forum selection clause is unenforceable.

How should the court rule on this motion?

(A) Grant this motion, because of the forum selection clause.
(B) Grant this motion, because, under federal law, a forum selection clause generally is enforceable.
(C) Deny this motion, because the federal court for State A had personal jurisdiction over the car manufacturer.
(D) Deny the motion, because a forum selection clause is unenforceable under the law of the forum state.

35. A man decided to master the art of throwing knives. He practiced for several years, until he had perfected his skills and was able to hit a spot no larger than a dime with confidence. After demonstrating his prowess to a friend, the man convinced the friend to stand against a wall while the man threw knives at her. The man threw three knives extremely close to the friend, but the fourth knife struck the friend, injuring her slightly. Although the friend's injury was minor, unbeknownst to the man, she had a rare blood disorder that caused her to bleed to death.

The crimes below are listed in ascending order of seriousness. What is the most serious common law crime for which the man can be convicted?

(A) Battery
(B) Involuntary manslaughter
(C) Voluntary manslaughter
(D) Murder

36. A pregnant mother and a soccer coach of the mother's young child were involved in a serious verbal altercation. The argument continued escalating until the coach suddenly punched the mother in the face and pushed her to the ground. The coach immediately fled the area. The mother did not suffer serious physical injury. Nonetheless, the incident greatly traumatized her. In the weeks following the attack, she had many sleepless nights and suffered several panic attacks.

The mother brought suit against the coach for intentional infliction of emotional distress. The coach filed a motion for summary judgment. How should the court rule on the motion?

(A) Grant the motion, because the coach did not intend to cause severe emotional distress.
(B) Grant the motion, because the mother did not suffer a significant physical injury.
(C) Deny the motion, because a jury could find that the coach was reckless as to the risk of causing emotional distress.
(D) Deny the motion, because the doctrine of transferred intent applies.

37.   A plaintiff sued the owner of a small clothing store for injuries she sustained when she slipped and fell while shopping in the defendant's store.   The defendant wants to introduce into evidence a written record of the event made by one of his employees.   The record detailed the fact that the plaintiff slipped on her own drink that she had spilled without reporting to anyone. It also included the plaintiff's threat to sue the store, and the store owner's instructions to the employee to immediately write a report, so that there was a record of what happened in the event that the plaintiff sued.   The employee is unavailable to testify. The plaintiff objects to the introduction of the document.

Should the court sustain the plaintiff's objection to the introduction of the document?

(A) Yes, because the document violates the best evidence rule.
(B) Yes, because the document is hearsay not within any exception.
(C) No, because the document is a business record.
(D) No, because the employee is unavailable to authenticate the record.

38.   A college student entered the back yard of a zoology professor to attend a social gathering for students that was to be held there.   The professor was cleaning out the cage of his pet porcupine and had carelessly allowed the porcupine to roam free.   The porcupine, well camouflaged in a pile of leaves, was sunning itself.   The student didn't see the porcupine, tripped over it, and broke his hand.   The applicable jurisdiction permits the keeping of a porcupine as a pet.

In a strict liability action by the student against the professor, who will prevail?

(A) The student, because the professor possessed a wild animal.
(B) The student, because the professor, aware that students were coming to a social gathering, failed to act with reasonable car
(C) The professor, because the student was only a licensee, not an invitee.
(D) The professor, because the student was not injured as a consequence of a dangerous propensity of the animal.

39. The defendant declined to enter into a contract to sell her house for $200,000 to the plaintiff. The next day, the defendant executed a contract to sell her house to another individual for $201,000. The plaintiff sued the defendant in the appropriate federal court and claimed that the defendant's decision was based on the plaintiff's ethnicity and thus violated a federal statute. The court granted summary judgment for the defendant. The plaintiff then sued in the same federal court, claiming that the defendant's decision was based on the plaintiff's disability, in violation of another federal statute.

Can the plaintiff pursue this action if challenged by the defendant?

(A) Yes, because the second claim of disability discrimination was based on a different federal statute than the first claim.

(B) Yes, because the court decided the prior claim of discrimination based on ethnicity through summary judgment, rather than upon a full consideration of the merits.

(C) No, because the doctrine of collateral estoppel precludes the second case.

(D) No, because the claim of disability discrimination was precluded, as it arose out of the same transaction as the prior claim of discrimination based on ethnicity.

40. A publishing company entered into a contract to purchase a newspaper company. The contract specified that "it shall be a condition precedent to buyer's obligation to pay that the newspaper shall have 200,000 subscribers by December 31 of this year." In anticipation of the purchase, the publishing company purchased $200,000 of new equipment to be used in printing the newspaper; the newspaper was aware of the investment.

At the end of the business day on December 31, the newspaper had only 199,750 subscribers, and had no justification for the shortfall. The publishing company immediately redirected $100,000 of the new equipment to print one of its magazines, but the other $100,000 of equipment was custom-made for the newspaper and could not be used elsewhere. The publishing company refused to go through with the sale, and then sued the newspaper company for $100,000.

Is the publishing company likely to prevail?

(A) Yes, because the newspaper company did not comply with the condition precedent.

(B) Yes, because the publishing company mitigated its damages to the maximum extent reasonably possible.

(C) No, because the newspaper company substantially complied with the condition precedent.

(D) No, because failure of a condition precedent does not give rise to damages.

41. An attorney represents a corporation in a federal securities case. As the attorney reviewed her files before court, she discovered that—despite her diligence—a memo marked "PRIVILEGED AND CONFIDENTIAL" had inadvertently been included in a folder containing public financial documents. The attorney knew that she had copied this folder and produced it in its entirety to opposing counsel during discovery. However, the memo is detrimental to her client's case. The attorney immediately contacted opposing counsel and requested that the memo be returned to her, that all copies be destroyed, and that the information within the memo not be used at trial; she included the judge on this correspondence. Opposing counsel refused to return the memo, and informed the attorney that they did plan to use it at trial. The memo in question was from the corporation's chief executive officer to the attorney, and contained the chief financial officer's thoughts and questions regarding the attorney's trial strategy.

Should the court allow opposing counsel to introduce the memo into evidence at trial?

(A) Yes, because the attorney waived the privilege when she disclosed the memo to opposing counsel.
(B) Yes, because the memo was not privileged begin with.
(C) No, because the attorney did not waive the privilege.
(D) No, because all documents from clients to attorneys are privileged.

42. A buyer purchased a newly constructed house from a builder for use as a residence. The buyer did not perform an inspection of the house prior to the purchase. Neither the contract nor the deed contained any warranties as to the condition of the house.

Six months later, during a heavy downpour, the basement flooded. Since that time, whenever there has been a substantial rain, there has been water in the basement. The source of the problem has been identified as several cracks in the foundation wall that surrounds the basement. An expert hired by the buyer has opined that the cracks formed due to settling after the home was built and could have been prevented by adherence to proper construction methods. The builder has repeatedly refused to address the problem.

Just before the first anniversary of the purchase, the buyer filed suit against the builder for the defective foundation wall and the resulting damages. There are no applicable state statutes that address the issue. Who will prevail?

(A) The builder, because the builder did not give the buyer a written warranty as to the condition of the house.
(B) The builder, because the buyer failed to conduct a home inspection.
(C) The buyer, because the builder of a residence is liable for any material defects in the house.
(D) The buyer, because the builder breached the implied warranty of fitness or suitability.

43. A significant number of colleges were located in a small state. Local police departments constantly received complaints about the conduct of college students, especially those who lived together off-campus. Due to constant pressure from citizens of the college towns, the state legislature enacted a statute preventing more than four unrelated men under the age of 25 from living together in any privately owned house, apartment, or condominium. A group of five unrelated men between the ages of 18 and 23 attempted to lease a house together but were refused on the basis of this law. The men have challenged the constitutionality of the law in court.

Which of the following is the group's best argument for declaring the statute unconstitutional?

(A) The statute is not rationally related to a legitimate state interest.
(B) The statute unconstitutionally discriminates against the men based on their gender.
(C) The statute unconstitutionally discriminates against the men based on their age.
(D) The statute denies the group the fundamental right to live together.

44. During a severe storm, a horse came onto a rancher's property. The rancher discovered the horse the next morning, and saw a serious wound on one of its legs. The rancher paid a veterinarian to examine and treat the horse, and the rancher then provided the horse with food and shelter. Two weeks later, the horse's owner arrived at the rancher's home and asked for the return of his horse. The rancher returned the horse to its owner, and asked the owner for reimbursement for the veterinary visit and for the expenses incurred in feeding and sheltering the horse. The horse's owner refused to pay.

The rancher sued the horse's owner for the costs of veterinary care, food, and shelter. Is he likely to prevail?

(A) Yes, because the rancher's conduct created an implied-in-fact contract.
(B) Yes, because the horse's owner would be unjustly enriched if he is not forced to pay the rancher's expenses.
(C) No, because a valid contract was never formed between the rancher and the horse's owner.
(D) No, because the horse's owner never engaged in any conduct to signify that he assented to the rancher's expenditures.

45. A plaintiff sued a defendant for injuries sustained when the defendant ran a red light and struck the plaintiff as she crossed the street. The defendant denies that he ran the red light. The intersection where the accident took place features a camera that automatically captures a series of images of vehicles passing through the intersection when the light is red. During discovery, the plaintiff's attorney subpoenaed the city for copies of the photographs. The city printed two sets of the requested photographs directly from the camera, and sent one set to the plaintiff's counsel and the other set to the defendant's counsel. After laying a proper foundation, the plaintiff's attorney plans to introduce her set of the pictures into evidence. The defense attorney objects.

Is the plaintiff's set of photographs taken by the camera admissible?

(A) Yes, because the set of photographs is relevant and not excluded by a specific rule or law.
(B) Yes, because photographic evidence is alwa admissible.
(C) No, because of the best evidence rule.
(D) No, because there is no photographer to testify.

46. The United States Supreme Court, overruling *Roe v. Wade* and *Planned Parenthood v. Casey*, held that women do not have a constitutional right to abortion. Congress responded by passing the Abortion Rights Restoration Act (ARRA), which restored the essential holdings of Roe and Casey by prohibiting any government from unduly burdening a woman's exercise of the constitutional right to abortion.

In a constitutional challenge to the validity of ARRA, is a federal court likely to strike down the act?

(A) No, because Congress had a rational basis for concluding that abortions are a commercial activity that, considered in the aggregate, substantially affect interstate commerce.
(B) No, because Congress is defining constitutional rights more expansively than the Supreme Court, not restricting them.
(C) Yes, because Congress is not remedying the violation of a judicially recognized constitutional right, but rather is attempting to create a new constitutional right.
(D) Yes, because it violates the constitutional principle of federalism.

47. Police officers have a reasonable suspicion, but not probable cause, that the defendant committed a robbery. The police officers, acting without a warrant, went to the defendant's home and requested that he come to the stationhouse for fingerprinting. The defendant refused until the police officers threatened him with arrest. The defendant, reasonably believing that he was not free to deny the officers' request, accompanied the police officers to the stationhouse, where he was fingerprinted. His fingerprints matched those taken from the scene of the crime. Consequently, the defendant was arrested and charged with the robbery.

At his trial, the defendant moved to suppress the fingerprint evidence. Should the judge grant this motion?

(A) Yes, because the police officers' action constituted an unlawful seizure and evidence seized as a consequence must be excluded.
(B) Yes, because the procedure violated the defendant's Fifth Amendment privilege against self-incrimination.
(C) No, because fingerprinting is a reliable form of scientific evidence that would assist the trier of fact.
(D) No, because the police officers' reasonable suspicions justified the defendant's warrantless detention for the purpose of fingerprinting.

48. A buyer purchased a residence from an individual seller. Within the buyer's deed, which was not recorded, was a provision that the buyer, his heirs, assignees, and successors promised to adhere to the community association guidelines and to recognize the association's right to enforce those guidelines. Among the guidelines issued by the community association was the following: "No fence greater than six feet in height shall be installed or maintained by the homeowner." The community association has rigorously enforced this guideline. The buyer subsequently died and devised the residence to her husband for life and then to her son. The husband, without actual knowledge of the guidelines or their contents, installed an eight-foot-high fence. The local zoning ordinance permits fences no greater than eight feet in height to be constructed in the residential neighborhood. The community association has sought an injunction against the husband to compel him to remove the fence.

Who will prevail?

(A) The community association, because the provision in the buyer's deed creates an equitable servitude.
(B) The community association, because the fence constitutes waste.
(C) The husband, because he only possesses a life estate.
(D) The husband, because neither he nor his wife acquired the residence from the community association.

49. A buyer who was not a merchant entered into a written contract to purchase a new car from a dealer at a cost of $35,000. Since the buyer desired a particular combination of features on the car and the dealer did not have a car with such features in its inventory, the dealer ordered the car from the manufacturer. When the car arrived, the dealer discovered that the manufacturer had increased the dealer's price for the car by five percent. Acting in good faith, the dealer sought to increase the buyer's price of the new car by a similar percentage. Reluctantly, the buyer orally agreed to the price increase, then had a change of heart and refused to complete the purchase. The car dealer eventually sold the car to another customer for $35,000. The dealer sued the buyer to recover damages for breach of contract.

Will the dealer be entitled to damages?

(A) No, because the dealer had a preexisting duty to sell the car for the original contract price.
(B) No, because the price increase was not in writing.
(C) Yes, because the dealer sought the price increase in good faith.
(D) Yes, because the car was specially manufactured for the buyer.

50. A small restaurant utilized the same beverage supplier for many years. The owner of the restaurant had developed a very strong working relationship with the supplier's employees. The contract between the supplier and the restaurant only obligated the supplier to provide beverages, but the supplier's employees frequently performed repairs on the restaurant's soda dispensers, and were available to fill emergency orders even late at night and on weekends. Furthermore, the restaurant received a commission for each beverage sold at its restaurants, which the beverage supplier, unlike many other suppliers, paid in cash. The restaurant received lucrative offers to switch to other distributors, but repeatedly chose to stay with its supplier because of the personalized service.

The beverage supplier decided that it would be advantageous to concentrate its business solely on larger accounts. Without obtaining approval from the restaurant, the supplier "assigned all rights and delegated all duties" arising under its contract with the restaurant to a second beverage distributor. The second distributor did not pay any consideration for this transfer. While there was no anti-assignment clause in its contract with the original supplier, the restaurant was not pleased with the assignment, and refused service from the new distributor.

The new distributor filed suit against the restaurant, claiming breach of contract. What is the restaurant's strongest argument in defense?

(A) While rights under a contract may normally be assigned, delegations of contractual duties are generally not permitted.
(B) The new distributor's failure to pay any consideration to the original supplier makes the assignment unenforceable.
(C) The failure to seek the restaurant's approval of the transfer of contractual rights and duties means that the restaurant is not bound by the transfer.
(D) The restaurant has a substantial interest in having the original beverage supplier perform the contract.

51. An employee at a toy store intervened in a dispute between two unrelated customers, a mother and a grandfather, over who was entitled to a particular hard-to-come-by doll, which was the only remaining one at the store. The employee arbitrarily determined that the mother had possession of the doll first and awarded her the right to purchase the doll. When the grandfather protested the employee's decision, the mother threatened to inflict physical harm on the grandfather and raised her arm to strike him. Fearful that the mother would do so, the grandfather looked to the employee for help. The employee, who because of his size could easily have forestalled the mother's attack, simply shrugged his shoulders. Before the mother made contact with the grandfather, he crumpled to floor, the victim of a stroke caused by the mother's threat. The grandfather initiates a lawsuit against the mother, the employee, and the owner of the store on the grounds of assault for damages attributable to his stroke.

The owner of the store moves to dismiss the complaint against herself for failure to state a cause of action. How should the court rule?

(A) Deny the motion, because the grandfather was reasonably apprehensive of an immediate battery.
(B) Deny the motion, because the employee failed to act to protect the grandfather.
(C) Grant the motion, because the owner is not vicariously liable for assault by one customer upon another.
(D) Grant the motion, because respondeat superior does not apply to an employee's intentional torts.

52. The plaintiff and the defendant were involved in a physical altercation, and the plaintiff sustained serious injuries to his hand. Several weeks later, the defendant inherited a valuable piece of real estate from a distant relative in a state several thousand miles away. The defendant had never been to the state where the property was located. The plaintiff heard about the defendant's inheritance, and filed suit against the defendant in the state where the property was located. In his complaint, the plaintiff asserted a claim of battery against the defendant, alleging $100,000 in damages. Before filing a responsive pleading, the defendant, who was properly served, filed a motion to dismiss, arguing that the court lacked jurisdiction over both parties. The forum state has adopted a long-arm statute that extends jurisdiction up to the constitutional limits.

Is the court likely to grant the motion to dismiss?

(A) Yes, because personal jurisdiction is improper over both parties.
(B) Yes, because personal jurisdiction is improp over the defendant.
(C) No, because personal jurisdiction is proper under the doctrine of in rem jurisdiction.
(D) No, because personal jurisdiction is proper under the doctrine of attachment jurisdiction.

53. A city often required persons seeking building permits to agree to aesthetic and environmental conditions in order to obtain such permits.

A company applied for a permit to construct a 300,000 square foot warehouse on its land in the city. The city conditioned the permit on the company's agreement to plant 45 trees on the property and to limit the building's height to 70 feet. The city had imposed similar conditions on other property owners. The effect of these conditions was to reduce the value of the company's property by three percent, but they did not prevent the construction of a warehouse on the land.

The company sued, claiming that the imposition of these conditions violated its constitutional rights. Would a court be likely to strike down these conditions?

(A) Yes, because they constitute an unconstitutional taking of private property for public use.
(B) Yes, because they are not substantially related to an important governmental interest.
(C) No, because, under the Takings Clause, they advance a legitimate government interest and do not deny the company the economically viable use of its land.
(D) No, because, under the Takings Clause, they are valid restrictions, but the court should require the city to compensate the company for the three percent reduction in its property value.

54. A party properly filed suit in federal district court in State A against a corporation that was incorporated in State B. The corporation successfully transferred the action to a federal district court in State B under the venue rules of 28 U.S.C. Â§ 1404 for the convenience of the parties and witnesses.

Which state's conflict-of-law rules should the district court in State B apply?

(A) The laws of State A, because it is the transferor court.
(B) The laws of State B, because it is the transferee court.
(C) The court may use its discretion to determine which laws to apply.
(D) The parties may agree to use the law of either state.

55. An individual acquired a newly constructed house with a purchase money mortgage. Although the deed was recorded, through an oversight by the mortgagee, the mortgage was not. Several years later, the individual sold the house at its fair market value to a couple who obtained a purchase money mortgage through another mortgagee. Both the deed and the mortgage were recorded. Neither the couple nor the second mortgagee was aware of the prior mortgage. Shortly thereafter, the couple was killed in an accident, survived by their two young children. The couple did not leave a will. Under the law of intestate succession, the young children are the rightful heirs of their parents. The children's financial guardian, having been contacted by both mortgagees, has filed an appropriate action to determine ownership of the house. The jurisdiction is a lien state with regard to mortgages. In addition, the applicable recording act reads, "No conveyance or mortgage of real property shall be good against subsequent purchasers for value and without notice unless the same be recorded according to law."

Who is entitled to priority with respect to the house?

(A) First mortgagee, second mortgagee, children
(B) Second mortgagee, first mortgagee, childre
(C) Second mortgagee, children, first mortgagee
(D) First mortgagee, children, second mortgagee

56. Many state agricultural agencies conduct random discretionary inspections of meat processing facilities in their states. Relying only on its authority under the Commerce Clause, Congress passed a statute forbidding any state agricultural agency from considering whether a meat processing facility is licensed as "organic" when deciding when and where to conduct these inspections. The statute also provided that if a facility believed that the state agricultural agency was not following this statute in good faith, the facility could sue the state agency in federal court for damages. An organic meat processing facility in State A, believing that the State A agricultural agency conducted more random inspections of its facility than of non-organic facilities in the state, brought an action against the agency in federal court for damages. State A moved to dismiss the suit on the ground that it was immune under the Eleventh Amendment.

Should the court dismiss the action on these grounds?

(A) No, because the Eleventh Amendment only provides immunity for a state, not a state agency.
(B) No, because Congress has unlimited authoi to authorize private actions for damages against a state.
(C) Yes, because a state may only be sued for damages if it consents to the suit.
(D) Yes, because Congress cannot abrogate state immunity by exercising its Article I powers.

57. A defendant got into a physical altercation with a third party after the third party insulted his honor. At the defendant's battery trial, the prosecutor called a witness of the altercation, believing he would testify that the defendant was the initial aggressor. The witness behaved in a hostile manner to the prosecutor, refusing to testify that the defendant was the initial aggressor in the altercation at issue. The prosecutor decided to call a second witness to minimize any damage done by the first witness's testimony. This second witness, who was the first witness's sister, testified that in her opinion, her brother was too easily provoked by insults and had poor judgment regarding who should be considered the initial aggressor in a fight. She also testified that just before the trial, her brother had been goaded into a fight similar to the one he had witnessed between the defendant and the third party. The defendant's attorney objects to the sister's testimony.

Should the prosecutor be allowed to ask the sister about the witness's fight just before trial?

(A) Yes, because the credibility of a witness may be attacked by reputation or opinion evidence.
(B) Yes, because the first witness put his character at issue by testifying.
(C) No, because the prosecutor cannot impeach his own witness.
(D) No, because the altercations have no bearing on the first witness's character for untruthfulness.

58. Seeking to protect its small wine industry, a state passes a law prohibiting a large out-of-state corporation that engaged in the wine business in the state from entering into any new business deals within the state. The corporation sues in an appropriate federal court to enjoin state officials from enforcing this law.

On which of the following grounds would the court hold that the state's law is unconstitutional?

(A) The Dormant Commerce Clause of Article I, Section 8
(B) The Privileges and Immunities Clause of Article IV, Section 2
(C) The Privileges or Immunities Clause of the Fourteenth Amendment
(D) The Contracts Clause of Article I, Section 10

59.   One summer night, a man attended a party at one of the most lavish homes in town. Midway through the party, the man asked the host if he could use the restroom, and the host directed him to a restroom on the second floor of the house. After using the restroom, the man became curious about the other rooms upstairs, and wondered if they were as beautiful as the rest of the house. His curiosity got the best of him, and he turned the handle and opened a door, which turned out to be the master bedroom. He stepped inside the room and immediately saw a large pearl necklace on the vanity table. He walked over to the table, grabbed the pearls, put them in his pocket, left the room, and went downstairs. Later in the evening, the party host saw the pearls slip out of the man's pocket. She immediately confronted the man and called the police.

If the man is later charged with common-law burglary, what is the man's best defense to the charge?

(A) The man did not break and enter the home.

(B) The man did not intend to steal anything when he entered the room.

(C) The man did not use any force to enter the bedroom.

(D) The man did not leave the premises with the pearls.

60.   A surgeon was operating on a patient using a new device she invented. Unfortunately, the patient died. The patient's husband has filed a wrongful death lawsuit against the surgeon in federal court. The husband retained an expert witness who will testify at trial that the device used by the surgeon was defective and the cause of the patient's death. The husband disclosed the identity of this expert witness and provided the expert's report to the surgeon 30 days before the date set for trial, although the husband could have made the disclosure several months earlier. At that time, the surgeon had already hired her own expert witness to testify as to the safety of the new device. The disclosure of the husband's expert witness had no impact on the surgeon's pre-trial preparation.

Can the husband's expert testify at trial?

(A) Yes, because the disclosures related to this expert were made in a timely manner.

(B) Yes, because the failure to timely make the expert disclosures was harmless.

(C) No, because the disclosures related to this expert were not made in a timely manner.

(D) No, because the timing of the disclosures was not substantially justified.

61. A defendant was charged with fraud in a state-law civil proceeding. During cross-examination, he was asked to state whether a note being entered into evidence was in his handwriting. Since the note contained a material false statement on which the plaintiff had relied, the defendant invoked his Fifth Amendment privilege against self-incrimination to avoid answering the question. The judge upheld the defendant's assertion of the privilege.

Was the judge correct in permitting the defendant to invoke his Fifth Amendment privilege against self-incrimination?

(A) Yes, because handwriting evidence is always testimonial in nature.
(B) Yes, because the defendant's answer is testimonial evidence.
(C) No, because the defendant may not invoke his Fifth Amendment privilege in a civil proceeding.
(D) No, because the Fifth Amendment privilege against self-incrimination is not applicable in state-law proceedings.

62. An expert witness was called by the defendant to testify in a murder trial. The expert was to testify that the defendant was not responsible for his actions due to a specific mental defect. On cross-examination, the prosecutor brought to the expert witness's attention an authoritative book on psychological conditions, judicially noted to be a reliable authority in the field. The book described the symptoms of the mental defect at issue differently than the expert witness had described them, and the prosecutor read the book's description into evidence. The prosecutor wanted the jury to be able to consider the book's description as substantive evidence, but the defendant objected that the description could be used for impeachment purposes only, and not as substantive evidence. The prosecutor further wanted to introduce the book itself into evidence; the defendant objected to this as well.

Should the court allow the jury to consider the description in the book as substantive evidence, and should the book itself be introduced as evidence?

(A) The description should be considered for impeachment purposes only, and the book should not be introduced into evidence.
(B) The description should be considered as substantive evidence, and the book should not be introduced into evidence.
(C) The description should be considered as substantive evidence, and the book should be introduced into evidence.
(D) The book should be introduced into evidence, though the description may be used only for impeachment purposes.

63. The owner of a ring advertised its sale over the internet. A buyer purchased the ring from the owner, paying by check. The check was dishonored by the bank upon its presentment by the owner. The buyer sold the ring to a third party who purchased the ring in good faith for cash. The owner, unable to recover damages from the buyer due to the buyer's insolvency, learned of the third party's possession of the ring and sought its return from the third party. When the third party refused, the owner filed an action to recover the ring from the third party. None of the parties was a merchant.

Will the owner prevail?

(A) Yes, because the buyer did not give value for the ring since the check was dishonored by the bank.
(B) Yes, because the buyer was not a merchan to whom the owner had entrusted the ring.
(C) No, because the third party was a good faith purchaser of the ring.
(D) No, because the third party was not a merchant.

64. A high school teacher played on a hockey team in a local recreational league. During a league game, the teacher was involved in a fight with another hockey player. That player sued the teacher in a battery action to recover for injuries inflicted during the fight. The teacher contended that he had acted in self-defense. The teacher called his principal to testify that the teacher had a reputation within the school community for peacefulness. The plaintiff, who had not introduced evidence of the teacher's character for violence, objected to this testimony.

Should the court admit this testimony?

(A) Yes, because the defendant is entitled to introduce evidence of a pertinent good character trait.
(B) Yes, because character evidence may be introduced through reputation testimony.
(C) No, because the plaintiff had not introduced evidence of the teacher's character for violence.
(D) No, because such evidence is not admissible in a civil action.

65. A landowner subdivided his land into two parcels, retaining the parcel on which his residence was located and selling the other parcel to a stranger. In the deed, the landowner retained the right to use a path that accessed a river running through the parcel sold to the stranger. The stranger recorded the deed. After the sale, the landowner regularly made use of the path and maintained it as a path.

Several years later, the landowner's daughter, over her father's objections, purchased the parcel from the stranger. Upon the landowner's death shortly thereafter, the parcel retained by the landowner passed by will to his daughter. Within a year, she gave this parcel to her son and sold the other parcel to a third party. The deeds conveying the parcels were recorded but made no reference to the right of access.

After the father's death, no one made use of the path for four years. Recently, the son, remembering hikes to the river with his grandfather, cleared and began using the path again. Upon learning of the son's actions, the third party objected to the son's use of the path.

The son has consulted a lawyer as to his use of the path. Should the lawyer advise the son that he has the right to use the path?

(A) No, because the right of access had been abandoned.
(B) No, because the right of access had been lost through merger.
(C) Yes, because the right of access was an express easement.
(D) Yes, because the right of access was an implied easement.

66. A manufacturer of hot water heaters contacted a supplier of plastic resin about using the resin in the manufacturing of a heater. The supplier gave the manufacturer technical advice about how to mold the resin into a hot water tank. The supplier told the manufacturer that, in order to withstand the temperatures specified by the manufacturer, the resin would need to be at least one inch thick. The manufacturer ordered the resin from the supplier. The manufacturer designed and made the tank for its hot water heaters three-quarters of an inch thick using the supplier's resin.

A homeowner purchased a hot water heater made by the manufacturer from a local plumbing supply store. Due solely to the walls of the tank being too thin, the tank melted when used by the homeowner. The homeowner did not suffer physical injury, but experienced substantial property damage as a consequence of the melted tank.

The homeowner initiated a strict products liability action against the plastic supplier for damages suffered as a consequence of the melted hot water tank. Who will prevail?

(A) The homeowner, because the supplier was a commercial seller of the plastic resin.
(B) The homeowner, because the melting of th material provided by the supplier caused th homeowner's harm.
(C) The supplier, because the homeowner did not suffer a physical injury.
(D) The supplier, because the defect in the hot water heater was not attributable to the supplier.

67. A series of burglaries was committed while the inhabitants were away from their homes. A police officer, relying in good faith on a valid search warrant for evidence related to these burglaries, knocked on the door of the residence specified in the warrant but did not identify himself as a police officer. Without waiting for the door to be opened by the inhabitants, the officer pried it open with a crowbar, even though he had no specific reason to believe that evidence would be destroyed or that he was in danger. The officer did not find any evidence related to the burglaries, but did find a cache of illegal drugs in plain view.

The applicable statute provides that an officer can break into a house "if, after notice of his authority and purpose, he is refused admittance."

Prior to the trial of the homeowner for possession of the illegal drugs found during the search, the homeowner moved to exclude the drugs as evidence. Should the court grant this motion?

(A) No, because the officer relied in good faith on the search warrant.
(B) No, because the officer had a valid search warrant and the drugs were in plain view.
(C) Yes, because the drugs were not covered by the search warrant.
(D) Yes, because the search was illegal.

68. A manufacturer entered into a contract with a forklift supplier to purchase 10 new forklifts for use in the manufacturer's warehouse. The contract specified that the forklifts were to be delivered within 45 days of the execution of the contract.

The day after entering into the contract, the supplier was told by a reliable source that the manufacturer was in a precarious financial position. That day the supplier, reasonably relying on the information, which was in error, sent a written notice to the manufacturer demanding assurance of the manufacturer's ability to pay.

Thirty-five days after receiving the notice, the manufacturer sent the supplier its most recent financial statements, which adequately demonstrated that the manufacturer was not in a precarious financial position and had the funds to pay for the forklifts, along with a statement of its willingness to receive the shipment of the forklifts. Immediately upon receiving the manufacturer's correspondence the following day, the supplier called the manufacturer's CEO and demanded his personal guarantee of payment for the forklifts before the supplier would deliver the forklifts. When the manufacturer's CEO declined, the supplier refused to deliver the forklifts. The manufacturer then purchased forklifts from another distributor at a higher price.

The manufacturer sued the forklift supplier for breach of contract. Should the manufacturer prevail?

(A) Yes, because the supplier breached the contract by failing to deliver the forklifts.
(B) Yes, because the supplier's information regarding the manufacturer's financial position was in error.
(C) No, because the manufacturer failed to provide adequate assurances in a timely manner.
(D) No, because the manufacturer's CEO refused to guarantee payment of the forklifts.

69. A widower owned a residence in fee simple absolute. He contracted to sell it to a couple. The couple did not record the contract. The contract did not require either party to acquire or maintain casualty insurance on the premises, and neither party did so. After the parties entered into the contract, the widower continued to occupy the residence. A week before closing, the residence was completely destroyed by a fire caused by a lightning strike.

On whom does the risk of loss fall?

(A) The couple, because they failed to record the contract.
(B) The couple, because of the doctrine of equitable conversion.
(C) The widower, because he, as possessor of the residence, had a duty to insure it.
(D) The widower, because he retained possession of the residence.

70. The driver of a pickup truck, through no fault of his own, struck a pedestrian who darted into the street in front of the driver's vehicle. The pedestrian was thrown up into the air and died instantly when her head struck the pavement of the street. The driver, panicked by the event, stepped on the accelerator pedal. The body of the pedestrian became lodged underneath the truck. The driver drove for a city block before abandoning the truck and fleeing on foot. Under state law, fleeing the scene of an accident is a felony.

Can the driver be charged with involuntary manslaughter?

(A) No, because the driver acted in the heat of the moment without malice.
(B) No, because the pedestrian died when her head struck the pavement.
(C) Yes, because the driver was criminally negligent in driving for a city block after the striking the pedestrian.
(D) Yes, because the driver was guilty of a felony.

71. An engineer and a corporation entered into a contract. After the engineer failed to perform as required under the contract, the corporation filed a complaint for breach of contract in federal district court based on diversity jurisdiction. The corporation was incorporated and had its principal place of business in the forum state. The contract had been executed and performance was required to have taken place in a neighboring state of which the engineer was a lifelong resident. Instead of answering the complaint, the engineer served a motion to dismiss based on a lack of personal jurisdiction.

Prior to the court ruling on the engineer's motion to dismiss, can the corporation dismiss the action without the engineer's agreement or the approval of the court?

(A) No, because it is likely that the court lacked personal jurisdiction over the engineer.
(B) No, because the engineer failed to perform required under the contract.
(C) Yes, because a plaintiff is free to dismiss an action until it is set for trial.
(D) Yes, because the engineer had not served an answer or summary judgment motion.

72. A man played in a recreational ice hockey league that had a well-known reputation for aggressive play. The games often became quite physical, and injuries were common. In one game, the man scored the winning goal as time expired in the game. After the referee had blown his whistle, ending play, the man launched into a particularly exuberant celebration. An opposing player, angered by the celebration, hit the man on the forearm with a hockey stick, but did not intend to cause serious injury. The man collapsed in pain; tests later revealed that he suffered a severe forearm fracture as a result of the incident.

If the man sues the opposing player for battery, will the man prevail?

(A) Yes, because the opposing player's conduct was willful and wanton.
(B) Yes, because the opposing player intended bring about a harmful or offensive contact.
(C) No, because the man impliedly consented to rough play.
(D) No, because the opposing player did not intend to break the man's arm.

73. A medical supply company made transfers of property to a state hospital after the company was insolvent. Subsequently, the company filed for bankruptcy in federal bankruptcy court. The bankruptcy trustee, acting pursuant to the federal Bankruptcy Act, sought to recover those transfers. The state hospital, refusing to comply with the trustee's request, asserted that, as a state entity, it was immune from suit by a private individual, despite a provision in the Bankruptcy Act that abrogated state immunity with respect to such transfers.

Can the trustee force the state to turn over the transferred property?

(A) Yes, because Congress was acting pursuant to the Bankruptcy Clause of Article I, Section 8, Clause 4, in subjecting the state to the Bankruptcy Act.
(B) Yes, because the action was brought in federal court.
(C) No, because the Eleventh Amendment protects a state entity from suit by a private individual for damages in federal court.
(D) No, because Congress lacks the power to abrogate state immunity.

74. An auto collector hired a restorer to refurbish a classic car she had purchased at an auction. The written restoration agreement was signed by the collector and the restorer, and contained only an identification of the vehicle, an enumerated list of the work that was to be done, and the price for the job. The agreement specified, among other things, that the car's engine was to be replaced. When the collector was shown the restored car, she was upset that the engine that was in the car when it was purchased had not been rebuilt, since the complete replacement of the car's engine lowered the value of the car as a classic. The collector refused to pay the agreed-upon price for the restoration, and instead filed suit against the restorer for breach of contract.

At trial, the collector seeks to introduce a note in her handwriting that she had shown to the restorer prior to the execution of the agreement that contained the phrase "rebuild engine." Is this note admissible?

(A) Yes, because the agreement was only partially integrated.
(B) Yes, because the parol evidence rule only applies to oral communications.
(C) No, because of the parol evidence rule.
(D) No, because the Uniform Commercial Code does not apply to this transaction.

75. In order to finance the purchase of a property, the buyer received a loan and in return gave the lender a promissory note secured by a mortgage on the property. Subsequently, the buyer divided the property into two parcels, retaining one of the parcels and selling the other to a friend. The friend took the parcel subject to the mortgage. The buyer and the friend agreed that each would be liable for one-half of the outstanding mortgage. One year later the buyer disappeared. Since the buyer was no longer paying one-half of the mortgage obligation, the lender threatened to foreclose on the property. The friend paid off the outstanding balance of the loan. The applicable jurisdiction recognizes the lien theory of mortgages.

Can the friend bring a foreclosure action against the buyer's parcel?

(A) Yes, because the friend is subrogated to the lender's rights in the parcel.
(B) Yes, because the friend obtained ownership rights in his own parcel by purchase.
(C) No, because the friend does not have an ownership interest in the parcel since the jurisdiction adheres to the lien theory of mortgages.
(D) No, because the friend was not under a legal duty to pay the buyer's portion of the mortgage.

76. A car was parked in front of a man's house for a week without being moved. The man honestly but unreasonably believed that the car had been abandoned. He found a spare key attached to the underside of the car and, using that key, drove the car into his driveway, intending to make it his own. Several days later, the car's owner returned. Seeing his car in the man's driveway, the owner notified the police. The man was charged with larceny. Taking abandoned property is not a crime under the laws of the jurisdiction.

Should the man be convicted of larceny?

(A) No, because taking abandoned property is not a crime.
(B) No, because the man's mistake was honest made.
(C) Yes, because an honest mistake of law does not negate the man's mens rea.
(D) Yes, because the man's mistake was unreasonable.

77.   A mother, upon learning that her son had been assaulted by his middle school teacher, filed a suit on behalf of her son against the school district, claiming that it had negligently hired the teacher. At trial, the mother sought to introduce the testimony of one of the teacher's former students from when the teacher had worked in a different school district. The witness would testify that the teacher had beaten her. The mother had further evidence that this incident had been included in the teacher's personnel file.

Is the former student's testimony likely to be admitted?

(A) No, because character evidence is generally not admissible in civil cases.
(B) No, because character may not be proved I evidence of specific instances of conduct.
(C) Yes, because the teacher's character is an essential element of the mother's claim.
(D) Yes, because character evidence is generally admissible in civil cases.

78.   A defendant was convicted of murder. During the trial, his lawyer made a strategic judgment call to refrain from introducing certain mitigating evidence. The defendant was convicted and sentenced to a long prison term. The lawyer's decision with respect to the mitigating evidence and her overall performance did not fall below an objective standard of competence for attorneys in a similar situation.

After the trial, the defendant's lawyer apologized to the defendant for not introducing the evidence, saying that in hindsight she was wrong not to have done so. The defendant now seeks to reverse his conviction on the grounds that he received ineffective assistance of counsel.

Will the defendant succeed?

(A) No, because decisions regarding trial strategy rest solely with the lawyer.
(B) No, because the defendant's lawyer's performance met the objective standard of care.
(C) Yes, because the lawyer's performance fell below the lawyer's subjective standard, and the defendant was actually prejudiced by the result.
(D) Yes, because the defendant was actually prejudiced by the result of his lawyer's performance.

79. To preserve the environment and enhance the quality of life, a city located on an ocean had restrictive property regulations. The city limited non-residential buildings to its major thoroughfare. In residential areas, single-family dwellings were strongly preferred. People could apply for "special use" permits in residential areas, but they were denied 99% of the time. An organization that operated day-care centers for developmentally disabled children applied for a special-use permit to build and operate, in a residential area, a 7,000 square foot day care center for 15 children. The city denied the application, based primarily upon the increased traffic and noise the center would generate, which would disturb the tranquil quality of life and the environment of the residential neighborhood. The city routinely denied special-use permits to a variety of other groups on similar grounds.

On behalf of the disabled children, the organization brought an action against the city based on a constitutional claim in an appropriate federal court. Will this organization prevail?

(A) Yes, because the city's stated reasons for denying the permit do not constitute a compelling interest sufficient to justify an action that discriminated against the developmentally disabled.
(B) Yes, because the city's reasons for denying the permit do not constitute an important government interest sufficient to justify an action that discriminated against the developmentally disabled.
(C) No, because the city has a compelling interest in preserving the environment and enhancing the quality of life by protecting the tranquility of residential neighborhoods.
(D) No, because the developmentally disabled are not members of a suspect classification, and the city had a rational basis for denying the special-use permit.

80. A telephone company was removing wooden utility poles on a residential street and replacing them with new steel poles. The old poles were approximately 25 feet tall, and weighed several tons each. One morning, telephone company employees were removing an old pole. As a 10-year-old boy walked past the construction site, the old utility pole fell and crushed him to death. When the news was conveyed to the boy's mother, who was at work several miles away, she immediately fainted. For the next 48 hours, the mother was unable to function due to shock over the event. In the following months, the mother had difficulty sleeping due to nightmares as a result of the incident. The mother sued the telephone company for negligent infliction of emotional distress stemming from her son's death. She produced evidence at trial conclusively establishing that the telephone company was negligent in allowing the old utility pole to fall. The applicable jurisdiction has abandoned the zone of danger requirement for this type of action.

Which party is likely to prevail?

(A) The mother, because she was closely related to the boy.
(B) The mother, because she suffered severe emotional distress.
(C) The telephone company, because the mother was not present at the scene of the accident.
(D) The telephone company, because its actions were not extreme and outrageous.

81. In a trademark infringement action, the plaintiff called its financial manager to testify as to the damages suffered by the plaintiff as a consequence of the defendant's alleged infringement. The plaintiff sought to introduce a chart prepared by the manager specifically for the litigation. The chart was based on sales reports, which the plaintiff did not introduce into evidence. The sales reports were properly authenticated as business records, but were so voluminous that they could not be conveniently examined in court. The plaintiff made duplicates available for the defendant's examination and copying. The court overruled the defendant's objection and admitted the chart into evidence.

Did the court err in doing so?

(A) Yes, because the underlying records were not admitted into evidence.
(B) Yes, because the chart was prepared specifically for the litigation.
(C) No, because the chart is a business record.
(D) No, because the documents on which the chart was based were voluminous and could not be conveniently examined in court.

82. A homeowner hired a contractor to finish her basement. They agreed on a price of $20,000 for the job. During the final stages of the remodeling, the contractor discovered that there was mold in the basement, the existence of which had been unknown to either party. The contractor refused to complete the job unless the homeowner paid an additional $2,000 to the contractor for removal of the mold. The homeowner reluctantly agreed, and the contractor finished the basement in accord with the modified contract. The homeowner paid the contractor $20,000.

In a breach of contract action to recover the $2,000, will the contractor prevail?

(A) No, because a contractual modification is not enforceable without consideration.
(B) No, because the unforeseen circumstances did not rise to the level of impracticability.
(C) Yes, because the homeowner agreed to the price increase.
(D) Yes, because the modification was based on a mutual mistake.

83. A driver was speeding through a town's business district. The driver swerved suddenly to avoid hitting a car that was double parked in the middle of a traffic lane, and hit a pedestrian who was crossing the street. The pedestrian filed a complaint in federal district court in the state where the accident occurred against the owner of the car that was double parked. The pedestrian argued that the owner's negligence in leaving his car in the middle of a traffic lane caused the pedestrian to sustain physical injuries, and asserted $100,000 in damages. The plaintiff-pedestrian is a citizen of the state where the accident occurred, and the defendant is a citizen of a neighboring state. The driver of the speeding car is a citizen of the state where the accident occurred and is in the midst of a personal bankruptcy action. The defendant filed a motion to dismiss, arguing that the driver of the speeding car was an indispensable party. Applicable state law provides that tortfeasors may be jointly and severally liable for a plaintiff's injuries.

Is the court likely to grant the defendant's motion to dismiss?

(A) No, because the driver is judgment-proof due to his bankruptcy.
(B) No, because the driver is not subject to compulsory joinder.
(C) Yes, because joining the driver would defeat the court's jurisdiction.
(D) Yes, because the driver's participation is necessary for a just adjudication.

84. In a particular state in the United States, a mortgagee routinely required the mortgagor to convey title to the secured land to the mortgagee via a deed absolute; the mortgagee would reconvey title only upon complete repayment of the loan. The deed absolute transaction also allowed the mortgagee to dispose of the land immediately upon the mortgagor's default, thereby avoiding the cost and delay of foreclosure proceedings. A new election in this state brought into power a majority of pro-consumer legislators. The legislature enacted a statute that immediately outlawed use of the deed absolute and declared that all such deeds would be considered mere liens against the secured property. The statute applied not only to future loans, but also to loans already in existence— even though many of those outstanding loans never would have been made without the extra security provided by the deed absolute.

Mortgagees who had loaned money secured through deeds absolute challenged the constitutionality of the new statute. What is their best argument?

(A) As applied to loans made after the statute was enacted, the law substantially and unreasonably impairs the mortgagees' contract rights in violation of the Contracts Clause.
(B) As applied to loans outstanding at the time the statute was enacted, the law substantia and unreasonably impairs the mortgagees' contract rights in violation of the Contracts Clause.
(C) The statute violates the freedom of contract protected by the Fourteenth Amendment Due Process Clause.
(D) The statute violates the Fourteenth Amendment's Equal Protection Clause by discriminating against mortgagees.

85. A potential renter, a resident of State A, was searching for an apartment. The renter completed an application for a lease at an apartment complex located in State A, which was owned and managed by an apartment management company. The apartment management company's principal place of business was in State A, but it was incorporated in State B. The renter fulfilled all the requirements detailed in the application, yet the management company refused to offer her a lease. Suspecting that the management company refused to rent to her because of her ethnicity, the renter filed a claim under the Federal Fair Housing Act in State A state court seeking damages of $100,000.

If the management company seeks to remove the action to the federal district court located in State A, will it be successful?

(A) Yes, because the federal district court has original federal question jurisdiction.
(B) Yes, because the federal district court has original diversity jurisdiction.
(C) No, because, as a landlord-tenant dispute, the case is properly in state court.
(D) No, because when the state courts and federal courts have concurrent jurisdiction, the plaintiff holds the right to choose where to file the claim.

86. An avid runner was diagnosed with a serious heart condition. The runner's doctor advised her to avoid strenuous physical activity, including running, as such activity would create a substantial risk of cardiac arrest. The runner refrained from such activity for a month, but in that time she gained 15 pounds and felt very unhealthy. Deciding that the health benefits of running outweighed the risk involved, one morning she set out on her normal running path—the shoulder of a flat rural road. Five miles into the run, the runner suffered a heart attack, collapsed, and lapsed into a coma. Two minutes later, the runner's feet and legs—which were partially sticking out into the travel lane—were run over by a car. The driver of the car, who had been traveling at a reasonable speed, was aware of the runner but was unable to avoid her due to a locking up of the car's brakes that the driver had negligently failed to have repaired. The runner survived, but suffered serious injuries to both of her legs. The runner sued the driver for those injuries in a jurisdiction that applies traditional contributory negligence rules.

Is the runner likely to prevail?

(A) No, because the runner was contributorily negligent.
(B) No, because the driver was aware of the runner's predicament before the accident occurred.
(C) Yes, because of the runner's helpless peril at the time of the accident.
(D) Yes, because the driver was negligent in driving the car with brakes in need of repair.

87. A mother made a gift of unimproved real property to her son. The son promptly and properly recorded the deed, but did not inspect the property nor otherwise make use of it by building structures or making other improvements. The son, however, did pay the real estate taxes imposed on the property. Subsequently, the mother, forgetting about her conveyance of the property, sold it at its fair market value. The buyer promptly and properly recorded the deed. The buyer, who was not aware of the son's ownership of the property, began to construct a house on the property. Upon learning about the buyer's construction activities, the son, unaware of his mother's transaction with the buyer, brought an appropriate legal action to halt the buyer's activities and declare title to the property.

Will the buyer be successful in defending against the son's lawsuit?

(A) Yes, because the recording act does not protect a donee of real property.
(B) Yes, because the son did not make productive use of the real property.
(C) No, because the son recorded his deed before his mother made the subsequent conveyance to the buyer.
(D) No, because the son paid the real estate taxes on the property.

88. Following an accident in which a pedestrian was struck and killed by a bus, the pedestrian's children filed a wrongful death action against the bus company. In the complaint, the plaintiffs asserted that the bus company was vicariously liable for the bus driver's negligence, and also liable for its own negligence in hiring the bus driver. In support of both theories of liability, the plaintiffs moved to admit into evidence the bus driver's driving record prior to the driver's employment with the bus company. The driving record included several misdemeanor moving violations and prior suspension of the bus driver's license.

The defendant objected, arguing that the evidence constituted improper character evidence. How should the court rule?

(A) The court may admit the driving record to support both the vicarious liability and negligent hiring theories.
(B) The court may admit the driving record, bu only to support the vicarious liability theory
(C) The court may admit the driving record, but only to support the negligent hiring theory.
(D) The court must exclude the driving record.

89. A state maintained its departments, including its Fish and Game Department, through tax revenues collected primarily from its residents. The department required all recreational deer hunters (i.e., those who hunt purely for sport) to obtain a deer hunting license. The license fee was $25 a year for state residents and $150 a year for out-of-state residents. An out-of-state resident wanted to go deer hunting for sport. He objected to paying a license fee that was six times the fee paid by in-state residents. He sued in an appropriate federal court.

Will the court hold that the licensing fee scheme for recreational deer hunting is unconstitutional?

(A) Yes, because the scheme violates the Equal Protection Clause by discriminating against out-of-state hunters.
(B) Yes, because the scheme violates Article IV Privileges and Immunities Clause by failing accord out-of-state residents the same righ as state residents.
(C) No, because the scheme is constitutionally valid under the Dormant Commerce Clause, as the subject of the fees, deer hunting, is a recreational activity, not a commercial one.
(D) No, because the scheme is constitutionally valid under Article IV's Privileges and Immunities Clause, as recreational deer hunting is not a fundamental right, and a state may charge its residents a lower fee because their taxes support the Fish and Game

90. The owner of a lakefront home in a retirement community that greatly restricts access by nonresidents was aware that her dock needed repair, but was unable to afford the considerable expense to do so. The owner placed a large heavy chair at the entrance to the dock with a sign that read, "Please do not enter. Dock in need of repair."

Two children, a six-year-old boy and a ten-year-old girl, entered the property without permission from, or knowledge of the owner. The children quickly discovered the dock. The girl read the sign aloud to the boy and advised him, "You shouldn't go out on the dock." The boy, responding "But it's not dangerous," climbed over the chair and walked out onto the dock. As the boy ran to the end of the dock, a rotten plank on which the boy stepped gave way, and he fell into the lake and drowned.

As permitted by the applicable jurisdiction, the boy's parents sued the owner in a wrongful death action alleging that her negligence with respect to the dock caused the boy's death. At trial, the boy's parents argued that the dock constituted an attractive nuisance.

Which of the following may protect the owner from liability that otherwise would arise under this doctrine?

(A) The owner lives in a retirement community that greatly restricts access by nonresidents.
(B) The boy was not attracted to the property I the presence of the dock.
(C) The boy was a trespasser.
(D) The boy was aware of the owner's warning.

91. A uniformed police officer learned about a possible burglary of a home and went to investigate.   When the officer arrived, she attempted to get into the home through the front door, but found it locked. Going to the back of the home, the officer found a door slightly open. Drawing her gun, she entered the home and announced that she was a police officer. The homeowner, honestly but unreasonably fearing that the officer was the person who had broken into the home earlier, shot and killed the officer.

The homeowner was charged with murder of the police officer.   The jurisdiction recognizes "imperfect" self-defense. Can the homeowner be convicted of this crime?

(A) Yes, because the homeowner killed the police officer.
(B) Yes, because the homeowner's use of dead force was unreasonable.
(C) No, because the homeowner had no duty to retreat before using deadly force.
(D) No, because the homeowner honestly believed that the police officer threatened him with death or serious bodily injury.

92.   In a civil action properly removed from state court to federal district court based on diversity jurisdiction, a jury of eight persons was empanelled. During the trial, the court excused a juror for good cause. The case was submitted to the jury and the remaining jurors returned a verdict for the plaintiff by a vote of 6-to-1. The law of the state in which the court is located requires a verdict to be rendered by a jury of at least six persons in a civil lawsuit and permits a verdict to be reached by a vote of 5-to-1.

Can the defendant successfully challenge this verdict?

(A) Yes, because the verdict was returned by a jury with seven members.
(B) Yes, because the verdict was not unanimou
(C) No, because at least six members of the jury voted in favor of the verdict.
(D) No, because this is a diversity action and state law permits a verdict by a lesser majority.

93. A retail store that specialized in glass objects entered into a written contract to purchase 100 hand-blown glass ornaments from an artisan. Because of the artisan's popularity, the store paid in full for the ornaments at the time that the contract was executed. The contract specified that the store would pick up the ornaments after notification that they were ready. The contract contained no other terms related to delivery of the ornaments and did not allocate the risk of loss. When the ornaments were ready, the artisan notified the store. The parties arranged for the store to pick up the packaged ornaments no later than 2:00 pm the next day. The employee assigned by the store to make the pickup did not arrive until 6:00 pm. In the late afternoon just before the store employee arrived, a short but intense storm caused a large, healthy tree on the artisan's property to fall over and destroy all the ornaments. Neither party had insured the ornaments against such a loss.

Who bears the risk of the loss with respect to the ornaments?

(A) The store, because the artisan had tendered delivery of the ornaments to the store prior to the loss.
(B) The store, because the artisan's insurance not cover the loss.
(C) The artisan, because the store had not taken possession of the ornaments.
(D) The artisan, because the store was a merchant.

94. A plaintiff properly brought an action based on negligence in federal district court sitting in diversity jurisdiction. At the close of the presentation of the evidence by both parties, both the plaintiff and the defendant filed with the court and served on the opposing party proposed jury instructions. The plaintiff's instructions were silent on the issue of assumption of the risk. Before the parties' closing arguments, the court informed the parties of the jury instructions that it planned to give. With regard to the issue of assumption of the risk, the court rejected the defendant's proposed instruction and substituted its own instruction. The plaintiff objected to the court's proposed assumption-of-the-risk instruction on the record and out of the presence of the jury, but the court overruled the objection. The defendant made no objection. The court then delivered its jury instruction before both parties' closing arguments.

Has the court complied with the Federal Rules of Civil Procedure?

(A) No, because the court must use the defendant's instructions on the issue of assumption of the risk, as the plaintiff did not submit jury instructions on that issue.
(B) No, because the court instructed the jury before the parties' closing arguments.
(C) Yes, because the court is permitted, but not required, to give each party the opportunity to object to the court's jury instructions.
(D) Yes, because the court timely informed both parties of the jury instructions it planned to give and gave them the opportunity to object.

95. A pharmacist was charged with conspiracy to knowingly defraud the government with regard to Medicare payments. The prosecutor called a physician to testify regarding a prescription written by the physician that was filled by the pharmacist. During the defense attorney's cross-examination of the physician, the judge asked the physician, "What did the pharmacist think about this prescription?" The defense attorney immediately objected to the question.

Should the court overrule this objection?

(A) Yes, because a judge may question a witness for the purpose of clarifying a witness's testimony.
(B) Yes, because the answer to the question is relevant and not overly prejudicial.
(C) No, because a judge may not question a witness.
(D) No, because the question calls for an unsupported conclusion.

96. In the Labor Management Relations Act, Congress expressly authorized the president to seize plants to avert a labor shutdown if the president determined that a shutdown would threaten national security. In response to a threatened national strike by America's steel workers, the president ordered the government to seize and operate steel mills to ensure steel production that the president deemed vital to the War on Terrorism and hence to national security. Subsequent to the order, Congress did not explicitly approve or disapprove of the president's action.

One of the companies affected by the president's order filed a suit in an appropriate federal court claiming that the order violated the Constitution. What is the most likely ruling?

(A) Congress unconstitutionally delegated its legislative power to the president because the statutory standard—that a shutdown would "threaten national security"—does not provide a specific, intelligible standard.
(B) The president lacked power as Commander in-Chief to take this action because it involv domestic affairs, not military decisions in th foreign theater of war.
(C) The president had Article II power to take this action.
(D) The president's action would be lawful only if Congress explicitly approved it.

97. The owner of a rural, wooded property devised half of the property to his daughter and the other half to his son. At the time of the devise, the only public road in the area ran along one side of the son's property, but did not adjoin the daughter's property. The daughter, wanting to build a cabin on her property, sought permission from the son to build a road on the son's property to connect with the public road, but the son refused.

In an action by the daughter to compel the son to permit her access across his land to the public road, who will prevail?

(A) The daughter, because access across the son's property is necessary for access to her land.
(B) The daughter, because she sought permission from the son before filing her court action.
(C) The son, because the son never owned the entire wooded property.
(D) The son, because there has been no prior use of his property in the manner that the daughter proposes.

98. A recidivism statute calls for a mandatory life sentence for a defendant who is convicted of three felonies. The defendant was convicted of felony theft three separate times and was sentenced to life in prison after his conviction for the third theft. In each case, the defendant stole the items from stores when nobody was watching. He did not use any weapons, nor was he violent. The defendant challenges the sentence on constitutional grounds.

Will the defendant succeed?

(A) Yes, because the sentence violates the Eighth Amendment prohibition on cruel and unusual punishment because the defendant's crimes were non-violent.
(B) Yes, because the sentence violates the Double Jeopardy Clause.
(C) No, because the Eighth Amendment prohibition on cruel and unusual punishment only applies to degrading or painful sentences involving the use of force.
(D) No, because the recidivism statute is constitutional even when applied to non-violent offenders.

99.   A homeowner hired a contractor to paint the homeowner's residence. The written contract stated that it was the parties' final and complete agreement and that all prior agreements between the parties merged into the written document. Prior to executing the contract, the contractor noted debris in the gutters of the residence. The contractor stated that to prevent such debris from adversely affecting the painting, the gutters should be cleaned. The contractor offered to do this prior to undertaking the painting for $600. The homeowner orally agreed. The homeowner and the contractor then signed the written contract, which did not mention cleaning the gutters. The contractor performed all of the work called for in the written contract as well as cleaning the gutters. The homeowner paid the amount specified in the written contract, but refused to pay an additional $600 for the cleaning of the gutters.

In a breach of contract action by the contractor against the homeowner to recover the $600 payment, which of the following is the strongest argument that the homeowner can make to prevent the contractor from recovering?

(A) The agreement regarding cleaning the gutters only serves to supplement the terms of the written contract.
(B) Since the amount sought for cleaning the gutters was more than $500, it can only be evidenced by a writing.
(C) The contract was a complete integration of the agreement between the contractor and the homeowner.
(D) The parol evidence rule bars evidence about an oral agreement between the parties to a written contract.

100. The fee simple owner of land devised it to a private educational institution "for so long as the land herein conveyed is used for educational purposes; if the land is not so used, then to my daughter and her heirs." At the time of the owner's death, the owner's spouse was deceased and the owner's only two children, a son and a daughter, were alive. The owner devised all of his other real property interests to his son. The daughter died shortly after her father, devising her real property's interests to her only child, who was alive at the time of her death.

Immediately after the owner's death, the institution constructed a classroom building on the land and has held classes in the building each year thereafter.

Thirty years after the owner's death, the educational institution seeks to sell the land to a developer who intends to construct single-family homes on the land. Both the son and daughter's child, who are the owner's only living heirs, are alive.

The applicable jurisdiction has adopted the following statute: "A nonvested property interest is invalid unless when the interest is created, it is certain to vest or terminate no later than 21 years after the death of an individual then alive, or the interest either vests or terminates within 90 years after its creation." The applicable jurisdiction does not impose time limitations on the exercise of interests that follow a defeasible fee property interest.

In order to convey marketable title to the developer, whom must the institution convince to agree to the transfer?

(A) No one, because the institution owns the land in fee simple.
(B) The daughter's child, because she holds an executory interest in the land.
(C) The son, because he holds a possibility of reverter in the land.
(D) The son and the daughter's child, because they are the owner's living heirs.

STOP.

IF YOU FINISH BEFORE TIME IS UP,
CHECK YOUR WORK ON THIS TEST.

PM Session

3 hours

Directions: Each of the questions or incomplete statements below is followed by four suggested answers or completions. You are to choose the best of the stated alternatives. Answer all questions according to the generally accepted view, except where otherwise noted.

For the purposes of this test, you are to assume the application of (1) the Federal Rules of Civil Procedure as currently in effect; and (2) the sections of Title 28 to the U.S. Code pertaining to jurisdiction, venue, and transfer. The terms "Constitution," "constitutional," and "unconstitutional" refer to the federal Constitution unless indicated otherwise. Assume also that Article 2 and Revised Article 1 of the Uniform Commercial Code have been adopted and are applicable when appropriate. All Evidence questions should be answered according to the Federal Rules of Evidence, as currently in effect. Finally, with respect to Torts questions, assume that there is no applicable statute unless otherwise specified; however, survival actions and claims for wrongful death should be assumed to be available where applicable. You should assume that joint and several liability, with pure comparative negligence, is the relevant rule unless otherwise indicated.

101. At trial, in an effort to prove that the defendant suffers from a mental defect, a criminal defense attorney seeks to introduce evidence that his client told several people that he believed he was the President of the United States. The prosecutor contends that the evidence is inadmissible.

Is evidence of the defendant's statement admissible?

(A) No, because the statement constitutes hearsay.
(B) No, because the statement does not meet the requirements of the "state of mind" exception to the hearsay rule.
(C) Yes, because the statement is being offered as circumstantial evidence of the defendant's state of mind.
(D) Yes, because the statement is being introduced by a defense attorney in a criminal trial.

102. A man was arrested and charged with stealing $5 million in an armed bank robbery. The police gave the man his Miranda warnings, and the man indicated that he refused to speak to the police without his lawyer present. The police then placed the man in a holding cell in the police station with an undercover police officer who was posing as a man arrested for drunken driving. The undercover officer asked the man several questions in an attempt to elicit information about the crime and discover where the man's accomplices might be hiding. Believing that he was talking to another prisoner, the man made several self-incriminating statements about the bank robbery, which were secretly taped by a "bug" planted in the holding cell by the police.

Assume that at a subsequent trial for the bank robbery, the defense makes a motion to suppress all evidence regarding the statements the man made in the holding cell to the undercover officer. How should the court rule?

(A) Deny the motion because the man had no expectation of privacy in a police holding cell.
(B) Deny the motion because the man waived any right to counsel by voluntarily speaking to the undercover officer.
(C) Grant the motion because the police violated the man's Sixth Amendment right to counsel.
(D) Grant the motion because the evidence constitutes the fruit of an illegal search violating the man's Fourth Amendment rights.

103. An auto dealership sold a limited-production luxury vehicle as part of its business. It typically sold very few of the vehicles per year, but continued the business because it earned $25,000 in profit on each sale. The vehicles sold at retail for $150,000. A car buyer entered into a contact with the dealership to purchase one of these vehicles with the color scheme and options she desired, which the dealership ordered from the manufacturer. She signed a written order form and put down a $50,000 deposit on the vehicle. The form specified that, in the event that the buyer failed to purchase the vehicle, the deposit was non-refundable, representing liquidated damages that did not constitute a penalty.

Later, the car buyer found a better price on an identical vehicle at another dealership, and purchased that vehicle. She demanded the return of her deposit, but the dealership refused. The dealership had difficulty selling the car, and eventually had to sell it at the discounted price of $100,000.

The car buyer filed a lawsuit seeking to void the non-refundable deposit provision of the order form and seeking the return of her deposit. Is she likely to prevail?

(A) Yes, because the amount of the deposit was not reasonable in relation to the damages that could have been anticipated at the time the order form was signed.
(B) Yes, because the vehicle was not a unique good.
(C) No, because the woman signed the order form, which clearly stipulated that the deposit was not to be interpreted as a penalty.
(D) No, because the deposit was reasonable in relation to the actual damages the dealership suffered.

104. A corporation entered into an agreement with an accountant to audit the corporation's books pending a sale of all of the company's assets. The agreement specified that the accountant would perform "all services relating to the sale of assets of the corporation." The agreement was fully integrated, but did not contain a merger clause. The day after the agreement was executed, the corporation and the accountant amended the agreement to include the evaluation of prospective buyers, for $2,000 per buyer. The accountant evaluated two corporations who were potential buyers. The corporation refused to pay the additional $4,000.

In a breach of contract action, will evidence of the evaluation agreement be excluded?

(A) No, because the agreement regarding the evaluation of prospective buyers was entered into after the execution of the writing.
(B) No, because the amendment was supported by new consideration.
(C) Yes, because the agreement was fully integrated.
(D) Yes, because the second agreement dealt with the same subject matter as the first agreement.

105. The president of the United States received reliable information from federal law enforcement authorities that (1) a known terrorist group was planning a terrorist attack on America which would occur within the next two weeks, (2) the terrorists, all of whom were fluent in a particular dialect, were already in America, and (3) the terrorist group's leaders would provide to these terrorists certain details regarding the attack through coded messages contained in a U.S. newspaper published in the particular dialect. There were four such newspapers—in New York, Washington, Los Angeles, and Detroit. The president immediately ordered all four newspapers to shut down for two weeks and notified the newspapers that they were to be fully compensated for any losses they incurred because of the closure order. The newspapers immediately challenged the order as unconstitutional.

Which of the following is the president's best argument that the order should be upheld?

(A) It is not a prior restraint on speech or the press.
(B) The federal government can always suppress subversive speech as long as it pays just compensation to the person whose expression has been suppressed.
(C) The words that would be published constitute a clear and present danger to national security.
(D) Because national security is at issue, the burden is on the newspapers to establish the right to publish the information.

106. A chef decided to start a food truck business. He borrowed $60,000 from a bank to buy a food truck, and secured the loan by mortgaging his home. The bank recorded the mortgage the day after this loan was made. The following week, the chef borrowed an additional $50,000 from his mother to buy cooking appliances for the truck. He also secured the loan by a mortgage on his home, and his mother recorded this mortgage in a timely manner. The food truck business proved to be a bad investment for the chef, and he was unable to make any payments on his bank loan. He approached his father for help paying off the bank loan and his father agreed to loan him $40,000, secured by a mortgage on the chef's home. The father recorded his mortgage in a timely manner. The father believed that the bank loan would be paid off in its entirety by the father's $40,000 loan. He was unaware of the loan by the chef's mother, who was his ex-wife. The chef used the $40,000 from his father's loan to partially pay off the bank loan. When the chef failed to make monthly payments to his mother, she brought a foreclosure action against the chef.

In the foreclosure action, whose mortgage will be deemed to have priority?

(A) The mother's mortgage, as a purchase-money mortgage.
(B) The mother's mortgage, because the father recorded his mortgage after the mother did.
(C) The father's mortgage, because his loan was used to pay off the bank's mortgage.
(D) The father's mortgage, because otherwise the chef would be unjustly enriched.

107. A man shopping in a department store found a suit that he liked but could not afford. He noticed that the store had a system for identifying sale merchandise: all merchandise with a sticky red label on the tag was 50% off the original price. The man then went to an office supply store and purchased a set of identical labels. He returned to the department store with one of the labels, and placed the label on the suit's price tag. The man then took the suit to the register, paid the reduced price for the suit, and took the suit home.

Of which one of the following crimes should the man be convicted?

(A) Forgery
(B) Embezzlement
(C) Larceny by trick
(D) False pretenses

108. In December, a contractor was hired by a power utility company to perform repair work on a large transformer. The contractor performed the work negligently and as a result severely damaged one of the conducting coils in the transformer. The damage resulted in a two-day power outage in a town with a large industrial park. An electronics manufacturer was a tenant in the industrial park, and the power outage crippled its ability to meet the strong demand for its products during the critical holiday buying season. While none of the electronic manufacturer's machines were damaged, it can prove with certainty that the power outage directly caused it to lose $750,000 in business. The electronics manufacturer sued the power utility company and the contractor for negligently causing its sales losses.

If, at the end of the plaintiff's case, both defendants move for summary judgment, and all the foregoing facts are undisputed, how should the court rule on the motions?

(A) Deny both motions, because both parties were substantial factors in the electronics manufacturer's loss.
(B) Deny both motions, because the burden of proof has shifted to both defendants to exonerate themselves.
(C) Grant the motion as to the contractor, but deny the motion as to the power utility company, because liability is assigned to the principal under the respondeat superior doctrine.
(D) Grant both motions, because the electronics manufacturer suffered no tangible injury to its equipment or employees.

109. A federal statute provides that "all persons within the United States shall have the same right in every state to make and enforce contracts as is enjoyed by white persons." The Supreme Court interpreted this statute as applying to all contracts, including private contracts.

A black citizen of a state in the United States claims that an appliance store in her state violated this statute by refusing to enter into a sales contract with her because of her race. The appliance store defended on the ground that the statute is unconstitutional.

A federal court would be most likely to uphold this statute by relying upon which provision of the Constitution?

(A) The Thirteenth Amendment
(B) The Contracts Clause
(C) The General Welfare Clause
(D) The Equal Protection Clause of the Fourteenth Amendment

110. An employee brought an action in federal district court based on sexual harassment claims under Title VII. The employer, in his answer, alleged that the employee voluntarily terminated her employment after the termination of a consensual sexual relationship with her supervisor. In the alternative, the employer alleged that the employee's poor job performance justified her termination. The court, finding that these allegations were mutually exclusive, ruled that the employer could not plead both and ordered the employer to strike one.

Are the court's ruling and order correct?

(A) Yes, because, while alternative allegations are permissible, inconsistent ones are not.
(B) Yes, because the employer's allegations were made in an answer rather than a complaint.
(C) No, because a court on its own may not strike a defense from a pleading.
(D) No, because alternative and inconsistent allegations are permitted.

111.   The owner of an undeveloped lot agrees to sell the lot to a buyer. The written agreement identifies the parties, describes the property in sufficient detail, specifies the price to be paid, and spells out the payment terms. The agreement is signed by the owner. In accord with the agreement, the buyer pays the required down payment to the owner. Subsequently, the buyer constructs a garage on the lot as the first step towards building a three-story residence, but, due to a financial reversal, abandons his construction efforts.

May the seller bring an action to compel the buyer to complete the purchase?

(A) No, because of the Statute of Frauds.
(B) No, because the owner's remedy at law is adequate.
(C) Yes, because of the doctrine of part performance.
(D) Yes, because of the doctrine of detrimental reliance.

112.   A fisherman who lived next to a lake owned a large sport-utility vehicle equipped with a trailer hitch. He used the vehicle primarily to tow his large fishing boat. One afternoon, a neighbor asked if she could borrow the fisherman's vehicle for a short time in order to tow her boat back from the dock, as her car was at the repair shop. The fisherman agreed to let the neighbor use the vehicle to tow her boat, but asked her to return the vehicle immediately afterward. The neighbor drove the vehicle to the dock and towed her boat back without incident. Before returning the vehicle, the neighbor decided to buy a gift for the fisherman as a token of appreciation. While the neighbor was driving the vehicle to the store to buy the gift, she was involved in a serious accident. The neighbor was not seriously hurt, but the vehicle was a total loss.

If the fisherman sues his neighbor for conversion, will he prevail?

(A) Yes, because the neighbor exceeded the scope of consent.
(B) Yes, because the neighbor's use of the vehicle constituted a frolic rather than a mere detour.
(C) No, because the neighbor was acting for the fisherman's benefit.
(D) No, because the fisherman had consented to the activity and the damage was accidental.

113.　A man carried a handgun for protection, but failed to register it.　In the applicable jurisdiction, possession of an unregistered handgun is a felony.　The man had little experience with firearms, and negligently carried the gun in a holster designed to fit a different handgun model. While the man was shopping for groceries one day, the gun slipped out of the holster, fell to the floor, and accidentally discharged.　The bullet struck a fellow shopper, who died as a result of the incident.

The crimes below are listed in descending order of seriousness.　Which is the most serious homicide crime for which the man can be convicted?

(A)　Felony murder
(B)　Voluntary manslaughter
(C)　Involuntary manslaughter
(D)　No crime

114.　Congress enacted the Health Care Act (HCA) "to ensure all Americans access to health care at a reasonable cost." Congress delegated to an executive agency, the Department of Health & Human Services (HHS), responsibility for promulgating regulations to implement the HCA. The HCA further provided that a joint House/Senate committee can repeal or revise the HHS regulations if the committee determines that they inadequately fulfill the HCA's purpose.

Would a court be likely to hold that the HCA is unconstitutional?

(A)　Yes, because it delegates legislative power to an executive agency.
(B)　Yes, because it contains a legislative veto provision.
(C)　No, because Congress is reasonably trying to vindicate its Article I legislative power by ensuring the accountability of executive agencies that make law.
(D)　No, because the joint committee action to repeal or revise an HHS regulation would not constitute the exercise of executive power.

115. A man became intoxicated after drinking at a neighborhood bar for several hours. He left the bar and went to a party at a friend's house, where he struck up a conversation with a woman at the party. After a few minutes, the man grabbed the woman's arm, pulled her into an empty room, and attempted to have sexual intercourse with her. The woman struggled with the man, and, before intercourse occurred, was able to break free and exit the room. The man was arrested and charged with attempted rape. At trial, the man testified that at the time of the incident he believed that the woman had consented to sexual intercourse with him.

If the jury believes the man's testimony, should he be convicted?

(A) No, because the man's intoxication prevented him from understanding the wrongfulness of his act.

(B) No, because the man believed that the woman had consented to intercourse.

(C) Yes, because the man's intoxication was voluntary.

(D) Yes, because rape is a crime of malice and intoxication is not a defense to malice crimes.

116. A famous jazz pianist and a nightclub owner executed a contract that called for the pianist to perform at the nightclub five times per week for six months. The contract prohibited the pianist from giving public performances during the contract period at any other venue located within a specified distance of the nightclub.

Three months into the contract term, the pianist received a more lucrative offer to play a series of shows at a restaurant located within the contractually prohibited area. The pianist accepted the offer. Upon learning about this arrangement, the nightclub owner filed a suit seeking an injunction to prevent the pianist from performing at the restaurant. The nightclub owner has made no attempt to hire another performer to replace the pianist. The judge determines that the contract restriction on the pianist is reasonable.

Is the judge likely to grant the injunction?

(A) No, because the pianist's contractual duties are in the nature of a personal service, and hence enforcement would constitute unconstitutional involuntary servitude.

(B) No, because the nightclub owner has failed seek a replacement entertainer.

(C) Yes, because the restriction is a valid non-compete clause.

(D) Yes, because an injunction generally may be sought as an alternative to damages in a breach of contract action.

117.   A defendant on trial for forging checks took the stand in his own defense. On direct examination, the defendant denied having forged any checks; he stated that before he graduated from college the year before, he worked in his university's academic records office, indicating that he was "a trustworthy person." On cross-examination, the prosecutor asked the defendant if he had falsified records while working in the academic records office. The defendant denied that he had done so. The prosecutor then wanted to call to the stand his former supervisor from the university to testify that she had to investigate the defendant after allegations of misconduct, and that when questioned, he had admitted to her that he had falsified records. The defendant was removed from his position, but no formal charges had been brought against him.

Should the prosecutor be allowed to call the defendant's former supervisor to the stand to testify as to the falsified records?

(A) Yes, in order to impeach the defendant and to present propensity evidence.
(B) Yes, but only to impeach the defendant.
(C) No, because the testimony would contain hearsay.
(D) No, because the testimony would be extrinsic.

118.   An automotive enthusiast owned a sports car that was the fastest production car available in the United States. The enthusiast was friendly with a neighbor, who was 25 years old and had a clean driving record. The neighbor wanted to borrow the sports car to drive to a social event and impress some clients. The enthusiast allowed the neighbor to borrow the sports car, but told him very clearly and sternly that he was to drive very carefully, that he was not to exceed the speed limit, and that he was to bring the sports car back as soon as the event concluded. After the event concluded, the neighbor drove the car around for an additional two hours, often at very high speeds. Eventually, he slammed into another car while driving over 100 miles per hour. The driver of the other car survived, but sustained serious injuries in the accident. The driver of the other car sued the enthusiast in a jurisdiction without an owner liability statute, claiming that the enthusiast negligently entrusted his neighbor with the vehicle. The foregoing facts are undisputed.

If the enthusiast files a motion for a directed verdict, which party is likely to prevail?

(A) The enthusiast, because his specific instructions regarding use of the car were ignored.
(B) The enthusiast, because the neighbor had no history of negligent behavior.
(C) The other driver, because the jurisdiction does not have an owner liability statute.
(D) The other driver, because the neighbor's negligent behavior is imputed to the enthusiast.

119. In order to purchase her residence, a homeowner gave a lender a promissory note in exchange for a loan. The note was secured by a mortgage on the residence. Five years later, the homeowner gave a second lender a promissory note in exchange for a loan, in order to add another room to the residence. This note was also secured by a mortgage on the residence. Three years later, the homeowner gave a third lender a promissory note in exchange for a loan in order to construct a deck on the residence. This note was also secured by a mortgage on the residence. Each mortgage was properly recorded promptly after execution.

Recently, the homeowner has failed to make timely payments with regard to the first mortgage. The first lender has declared the homeowner in default and, in accord with the terms of the mortgage, accelerated the obligation. After properly notifying the junior mortgagees, the first lender forecloses on the mortgage. At the properly noticed foreclosure sale, the third lender purchases the residence.

To which of the following mortgages is the residence now subject?

(A) Only the first mortgage.
(B) Only the second mortgage.
(C) Both the first and the second mortgages.
(D) Neither the first nor the second mortgages.

120. A city fire department required all firefighter applicants to pass a demanding physical fitness test. The test was designed to ensure that firefighters could handle the physical rigors of the job, such as lifting heavy equipment, carrying injured people, and withstanding intense heat. Applicants of a specific ethnic background failed this physical fitness test at twice the rate of applicants at large. Moreover, in this particular city, people of this ethnic background were historically the victims of many forms of discrimination.

A man of this ethnic background applied to be a firefighter but was rejected because he failed the physical fitness test. He sued the fire department based on a constitutional claim of discrimination.

Will he prevail?

(A) Yes, because the fire department's physical fitness test had a negative disparate effect on applicants of a specific ethnic group.
(B) Yes, because the unusually high current failure rate of applicants from this ethnic group on this test most likely has resulted from past intentional governmental discrimination.
(C) No, because the plaintiff failed to establish that he had any property interest in potential employment with the fire department that has been denied because of the test.
(D) No, because there is no evidence that the fire department used the test to intentionally discriminate against people of this ethnic group.

121.   A patron at a resort ranch took part in a supervised horseback trail ride. Prior to the ride, the patron executed a valid release that enumerated the inherent risks of horseback riding and, by its terms, relieved the resort from liability from any loss, damage, or injury to the guest's person or property suffered during the ride attributable to the negligence of the ranch or its employees. The patron was injured by a fall from the horse. The horse reared in response to negligent behavior of another rider who was also a patron at the ranch. The patron filed suit against the ranch and the other rider for damages resulting from his injuries that totaled $400,000. At trial, it was determined that the ranch was 75% at fault for the patron's injuries due to its selection and training of the horse, and that the other rider was 25% at fault. The applicable jurisdiction recognizes the validity of such releases and has enacted both a modified comparative negligence statute and a pure several liability statute.

How much can the patron recover from the ranch?

(A) Nothing
(B) $100,000
(C) $300,000
(D) $400,000

122.   A class action was filed in federal court against an insurance company by its policyholders. The complaint, alleging that the company had violated state law, asserted that the court had subject-matter jurisdiction pursuant to the Class Action Fairness Act of 2005.   The complaint sought total damages of $4 million. The individual damages for the 900 class members ranged from $100 to $10,000. Of the five named plaintiffs, one is a citizen of the same state as the company; the other four are citizens of other states. The company filed a motion to dismiss this action for lack of subject-matter jurisdiction.

Which of the following reasons supports this motion?

(A) There is not complete diversity of citizenship between the parties.
(B) The aggregate amount in controversy does not meet the statutory requirement.
(C) No member of the class has a claim that exceeds $75,000.
(D) The number of class members does not meet the statutory requirement.

123. A homeowner who sought to sell his home entered into an agreement with a real estate agent to market the home. The agreement specified that the agent was entitled to a commission if the agent procured a buyer who was "ready, willing, and able" to purchase the home in accord with the contract terms. The agent found a buyer who agreed to pay the seller's asking price for the home and who pre-qualified for a loan to finance the purchase. The buyer and seller entered into a contract of sale. Among the provisions in the contract was a home inspection clause, which permitted the buyer to enter the property and conduct an inspection of the home. After conducting the inspection, during which the buyer learned of the antiquated nature of the electrical system that did not satisfy the electrical code for newly constructed homes, the buyer, in accord with the inspection clause, presented the seller with a request to upgrade the electrical wiring. Because of the cost of such an upgrade, the seller refused. Under the terms of the inspection clause, the inability of the buyer and seller to agree resulted in the voiding of the contract.

Is the agent entitled to a commission to be paid by the homeowner?

(A) No, because the contract was subject to a condition precedent that was not satisfied.
(B) No, because the buyer who demanded the seller upgrade the electrical wiring was responsible for the termination of the contract.
(C) Yes, because the buyer entered into a contract to purchase the home.
(D) Yes, because the seller, by refusing to upgrade the wiring for economic reasons, was responsible for the termination of the contract.

124. A concert violinist received an offer by mail to play a concerto with a local symphony orchestra. She checked her schedule, and thinking that she had the date free, mailed a letter to the symphony orchestra accepting the offer. Later that day, as she was checking her calendar about another matter, she realized that she had a rehearsal for another performance on that date. The violinist called the orchestra manager and declined the offer to play the concerto.

In a breach of contract action by the orchestra against the violinist, will the orchestra prevail?

(A) Yes, because the acceptance was sent before the rejection phone call was made.
(B) Yes, because the phone call was not a proper means of rejecting a written offer under the "mirror image" rule.
(C) No, because the agreement constitutes an unenforceable personal service contract.
(D) No, because the "mailbox rule" does not apply to a rejection.

125. A defendant was convicted of bank robbery in federal court. Subsequently, the defendant was indicted in the state where the bank was located for the crimes of robbery and conspiracy to commit robbery. The defendant moved to dismiss the state prosecution of these offenses on double jeopardy grounds.

Should the defendant's motion be granted?

(A) Yes, as to both offenses.
(B) Yes, as to the robbery offense only.
(C) Yes, as to the conspiracy offense only.
(D) No, as to either offense.

126. A company believed that its former employee was providing confidential information to a competitor and that the competitor was taking actions that affected the company's patents. The company filed a motion for a temporary restraining order (TRO) in federal court, arguing that its competitor was violating both state and federal law. The company signed a written oath establishing that immediate and irreparable injury would result unless the TRO was granted. The company did not provide notice of the motion to its competitor. At the TRO hearing, the CEO of the company testified that the company had not attempted to provide notice to its competitor, but that it intended to provide notice prior to any action on a preliminary injunction. The judge granted a TRO enjoining the competitor from taking certain actions, and ordered that it be in effect for 10 days until a hearing on a preliminary injunction could be held. The TRO stated the date and time issued, the irreparable harm suffered by the company, and the reasoning behind the ex parte issuance.

What is the competitor's best argument that the TRO was improper?

(A) A federal court may not issue an ex parte injunction.
(B) A federal court does not have jurisdiction to grant a TRO based on state law claims.
(C) A plaintiff did not file a written certification explaining why notice was not provided to the competitor.
(D) A TRO may not be in effect longer than seven days.

127. Article I, § 4 of the Constitution provides: "The times, places and manner of holding elections for Senators and Representatives shall be prescribed by each state legislature, but Congress may . . . make or alter such regulations." Congress enacted a statute requiring every state to allow voters to register to vote in federal elections either by mail or at a state motor vehicle department.

If a state refuses to comply with the statute and is sued by the federal government, will the state likely prevail?

(A) Yes, because Congress cannot "commandeer" state legislatures to enact statutes.
(B) Yes, because Congress cannot "commandeer" state executive officials to carry out federal programs.
(C) No, because Article I, § 4 permits Congress to require states to change their laws regarding federal elections.
(D) No, because the statute, which applies to federal elections only, does not interfere with a traditional government function.

128. During a trial for attempted murder, the prosecutor seeks to introduce into evidence the victim's properly-authenticated emergency room report. The report describes the victim's stab wounds and treatment. The report also includes a statement that the victim made to his doctor during a check-up the following day, naming the defendant as his assailant. The prosecutor wants to introduce the record to prove the extent of the victim's injuries, and as evidence that the defendant was responsible for the victim's harm.

Is the victim's emergency room report admissible?

(A) The report is admissible under the business records exception, but the victim's statement within it is not.
(B) The report is admissible as a whole, because it falls under the business records exception.
(C) The report is admissible under the business records exception, and the statement within it is admissible as a statement made for the purpose of medical treatment.
(D) Neither the report nor the statement is admissible, because the victim is alive and available to testify.

129.   A plaintiff sued a defendant for state law negligence in a federal district court sitting in diversity jurisdiction. The plaintiff was injured after tripping and falling at the defendant's place of business and is seeking damages for injuries resulting from the fall. The defendant has liability insurance that would cover any judgment that the plaintiff might win in the case. There have been no agreements between the parties or orders by the court regarding discovery in the case.

What is the defendant's obligation with regard to the disclosure of the defendant's liability insurance?

(A) The defendant's liability insurance agreement is not subject to discovery.
(B) The defendant need only provide a copy of the liability insurance agreement to the plaintiff if the plaintiff makes a request for production of documents concerning such agreements.
(C) The defendant need only provide information to the plaintiff concerning any insurance agreement if the insurer is joined as a party to the litigation.
(D) The defendant must make the insurance agreement available to the plaintiff even if the plaintiff does not ask for it.

130.   A buyer purchased a motor home from a private seller. After taking possession of the motor home, the buyer discovered that the bedroom of the motor home was infested with bed bugs, and pest control treatments were unsuccessful in eradicating the problem. The buyer honestly claims that he would not have purchased the motor home had he known of the infestation.

At the time of the sale, the seller knew of the infestation but did not disclose the condition to the buyer. When the buyer commented to the seller at the time of the sale that the buyer assumed that the motor home did not have bed bugs, the seller simply did not respond. The buyer was justified in relying on the seller's silence as an assertion that the mobile home did not contain bed bugs. The seller's actions violated her duty of good faith and fair dealing.

What is the best description of the status of the contract between the buyer and the seller?

(A) The contract is voidable by only the buyer.
(B) The contract is voidable by either the buyer or the seller.
(C) The contract is voidable by neither the buyer nor the seller.
(D) The contract is void.

131. The owner of a residence devised it to his wife for her life and remainder to his son. The son, after his father's death, regularly stopped by the residence to look after his mother and the residence. On some of the visits, the son would perform routine maintenance on the property, such as changing the air filter for the heating and air conditioning unit. When the mother permitted a companion to occupy the residence with her, the son became estranged from his mother and stopped visiting her. Recently, a neighbor who had visited the mother called the son. The neighbor indicated that mother was in good health, but that the condition of the premises was deplorable. The son contacted his mother. She asked him to come over, which he did, but denied him access to the premises when he arrived.

Can the son gain entry to the residence to inspect the premises?

(A) No, because the right to possess the premises belongs to the mother.
(B) No, because the mother has denied him entry to the residence.
(C) Yes, because he has a license coupled with an interest.
(D) Yes, because the mother, by permitting someone else on the premises, is estopped from denying her son permission to enter the premises.

132. A woman took her car to an unscrupulous auto mechanic's garage for a tune-up. The woman's car had a new and expensive set of tires that the mechanic coveted. The woman left her car at the garage overnight. Later that night, after the woman had left the premises, the mechanic took the tires off the woman's car, put them into a back room of his garage, and replaced the tires with a cheap, old set. That same evening, the woman's friend told her about the mechanic's unscrupulous nature, and that he had a habit of stealing tires. The woman went back to the garage the next morning. Noticing that the tires on her vehicle were different, she demanded that the new, expensive tires be put back on the vehicle. The mechanic complied, and the woman left the premises.

The woman reported the mechanic to the police, and the mechanic is charged with larceny. Based on the foregoing facts, should he be convicted of the crime?

(A) Yes, because the mechanic moved the tires from the car to the back room.
(B) Yes, because the mechanic had a present intent to permanently deprive the woman of the tires.
(C) No, because the car was left with the mechanic by consent.
(D) No, because the tires were returned to the woman before she was permanently deprived of them.

133. A man and his friend attended their 10-year high school reunion party. There, the two struck up a conversation with another former classmate. Neither the man nor his friend had seen the classmate since high school. At the end of the reunion party, the three decided to walk to a nearby bar. As they were walking to the bar, the friend suggested a shortcut through an alley. In the alley, the friend grabbed the classmate, took out a gun, and threatened to rob him. The man, despite the classmate's pleas to help him, continued walking on towards the bar. Once there, the man ordered a beer and watched a sporting event on television, while his friend robbed the classmate in the alley.

The man was charged as an accomplice to robbery. Should he be convicted of the crime?

(A) No, because the man did not commit an actus reus for which he could be criminally liable.
(B) No, because there was no agreement between the man and his friend to rob the classmate.
(C) Yes, because the man's actions aided and abetted the friend in committing the robbery.
(D) Yes, because the man was aware that the friend was robbing the classmate.

134. Based on an advertisement in a local newspaper, a state resident bought a cross-country roundtrip ticket on a national airline for $450. The ad did not mention that the airline charged $75 for any changes to a ticket. Because of illness, the state resident had to change her return flight, and the airline charged her $75. The state resident refused to pay, citing a state law that required any ad for the sale of tickets for any event or trip to clearly disclose any monetary penalties for changing tickets.

The airline sued the state resident in federal court for the unpaid fee, arguing that the state law is invalid, citing a federal statute prohibiting states from enforcing any law "relating to the rates, routes, or services" of any airline. Will the airline prevail?

(A) Yes, because, under the Freedom of Press Clause of the First Amendment, the content of commercial speech may not be regulated.
(B) Yes, because Congress has occupied the field of airline rates, routes, and services and hence has preempted the state law.
(C) No, because the court will apply the presumption against preemption.
(D) No, because the state law does not conflict with the federal statute.

135. In a case properly brought in federal district court, the plaintiff alleges that the state police, acting under a longstanding custom of using excessive force against people of a certain ethnicity in traffic stops, beat him up during a routine traffic stop. The plaintiff requests $100,000 in damages to remedy this injury and, fearing that the state police are targeting him, also requests preliminary and permanent injunctions prohibiting the police from using excessive force against him. The court issues an order refusing to grant the plaintiff a preliminary injunction and setting the case for trial.

Three weeks later, the plaintiff appeals this order to the appropriate U.S. Court of Appeals. Can the appellate court hear this appeal?

(A) Yes, if the appellate court, in the exercise of its discretion, concludes that an appeal is warranted.
(B) Yes, as a matter of right.
(C) No, because the district court's order is not a final judgment.
(D) No, because the appeal was not filed in a timely manner.

136. A defendant on trial for battery arising from a barroom brawl sought to introduce the testimony of his grandmother, who would testify that the defendant had a reputation in her church community for being a "helpful and trustworthy person." Further, the grandmother would offer her testimony regarding an incident that took place when the defendant was 13 years old wherein he refused to engage in a schoolyard fight with one of his classmates. The prosecution objects to the grandmother's testimony in its entirety.

Should the court allow the grandmother to testify?

(A) Yes, the grandmother's testimony should be admissible in its entirety, because the defendant is allowed to present evidence of his own good character.
(B) The grandmother should be allowed to testify as to the schoolyard incident, but not as to the defendant's reputation.
(C) The grandmother should be allowed to testify as to the defendant's reputation, but not as to the schoolyard incident.
(D) No, the grandmother should not be allowed to testify as to either of these issues, because the testimony is not relevant.

137. A biotech start up firm secured a loan from a private investor to purchase land and to build a laboratory facility on that land with a mortgage on the land and the facility. Subsequently, the firm sold the developed property to a partnership. The deed stated that the partnership took the property subject to the mortgage. Later, the partnership sold the developed property to a corporation. Each deed was properly recorded promptly after its applicable closing. Immediately after closing, the president of the corporation, in exchange for adequate consideration, promised the partnership that the corporation would assume the mortgage.

For four months, neither the corporation nor the previous owners of the facility made the required monthly payments on the mortgage obligation to the lender. The lender has filed an action against the corporation for the past due amounts.

Is the corporation liable for these amounts?

(A) No, because, since the partnership was not personally liable for the obligation, the corporation is protected by the shelter principle from personal liability.
(B) No, because the corporation's assumption agreement was not in writing.
(C) Yes, because the corporation assumed the mortgage.
(D) Yes, because the loan was tied to a purchase money mortgage.

138. A defendant is on trial for cocaine possession. The cocaine was found during a warrantless search of the defendant's car by a police officer. The search occurred immediately after the defendant was arrested for driving a car with an inoperative taillight, a misdemeanor punishable only by a fine. The defendant had been placed in a police car prior to the search. The cocaine was found inside a closed bag on the back seat of the passenger compartment of the defendant's car. The defendant now moves to suppress the cocaine.

Will the defendant's motion be granted?

(A) Yes, because the defendant was in the police car at the time of the search.
(B) Yes, because the arrest was unreasonable and the cocaine seized was a fruit of the poisonous tree.
(C) No, because the police may search a car without a warrant under the automobile exception.
(D) No, because the search was a lawful search incident to arrest.

139. At a defendant's burglary trial, the defendant testified that the crime was committed not by him, but by an acquaintance whose whereabouts are unknown. The defense seeks to introduce properly authenticated evidence of the acquaintance's final judgment of conviction by a jury for another burglary, in order to prove that the acquaintance was the type of person who could have committed the burglary for which the defendant is on trial. The prosecution has objected to the introduction of this evidence.

Should the court admit the evidence?

(A) No, because the evidence is inadmissible as character evidence.
(B) No, because the acquaintance is not available to testify.
(C) Yes, because there is a hearsay exception for a final judgment of conviction.
(D) Yes, because the defendant may present character evidence.

140. An adult woman was vacationing at a friend's house on a lake. One afternoon, the woman watched her friend maneuver his motorized personal watercraft around the lake; the friend took a particularly violent spill that temporarily knocked the wind out of him but left him otherwise unharmed. The next morning, without the friend's knowledge, she decided to take the personal watercraft out on the lake herself. Due to her inability to control the vehicle, it flipped over. As a consequence, the woman suffered serious physical injuries.

The woman brought a lawsuit against the friend to recover damages for her injuries. The applicable jurisdiction has adopted comparative negligence rules.

Prior to the submission of the case to the jury, the friend requested that the court specifically instruct the jury on the assumption of the risk defense. Should the court grant this request?

(A) Yes, because the woman voluntarily assumed the risk of being injured.
(B) Yes, because assumption of the risk is an absolute bar to recovery.
(C) No, because the defendant did not have the requisite knowledge for this defense.
(D) No, because assumption of the risk is not recognized as a separate defense.

141.   Concerned about problems caused by overpopulation, a state legislature enacted a statute imposing criminal penalties on any person who is the biological parent of more than two children. The stated purpose of the statute was to preserve the state's natural resources and improve the quality of life for the state's residents.

After the statute took effect, a married couple who already had two children conceived a third. After the wife gave birth to this child, the couple was arrested and convicted under the statute.

Which of the following is the strongest argument for voiding their convictions?

(A) The statute is an invalid exercise of the state's police power because there is no rational basis for concluding that the statute would further the government's stated interests.
(B) The statute places an unconstitutional burden on the fundamental privacy and procreative rights of married persons.
(C) The statute grants too much discretion to a prosecutor to determine who will be permitted to bear children.
(D) The statute denies the couple their Equal Protection rights.

142.   A man recently inherited an extensive collection of beetles from his father, a famous entomologist. The man called a local natural history museum to offer the collection in exchange for the museum's promise to use the beetles in an exhibit named after the man's father. The museum told the man that they did not currently have the time or space to create a new exhibit, but that they may be interested at a later time. The man told the museum that his offer would remain open for at least one month. A week later, a university called the man and offered him $5,000 in exchange for the collection. The man's father had been one of their most successful graduates, and the university wanted to display his collection in their library. The man agreed and delivered the beetle collection in exchange for the money. One week later, the museum learned that the father's entire collection was already on display in the library of the father's university. The museum immediately called the man to accept his offer, but the man could no longer deliver the collection.

If the museum sues the man to enforce his offer to give them the beetle collection, which of the following is the man's strongest defense?

(A) The man did not make assurances in writing to keep the offer to the museum open.
(B) The man's offer was revoked before the museum attempted to accept it.
(C) The man's promise to not revoke the offer for at least one month was not supported by consideration.
(D) The museum cannot enforce the man's promise to make a gift without showing detrimental reliance.

143. A homebuyer was discussing the purchase of a house with the seller. Of particular concern to the buyer was whether the house had a termite problem. The seller, aware of the buyer's concern, ordered an inspection from a licensed inspection company. The company issued a report stating that the house was free of termites. In fact, the company's inspector was negligent, and the house's foundation had a modest termite problem. Relying on the report, the seller told the buyer that the house was free of termites.

The buyer is seeking to avoid the contract. Will he prevail?

(A) Yes, because the buyer reasonably relied on the misrepresentation.
(B) Yes, because enforcing the contract would be unconscionable.
(C) No, because the misrepresentation did not rise to the level of a mutual mistake.
(D) No, because the inspector, not the seller, was negligent.

144. Eleven years ago, the owner of a condominium unit located in another state, upon his death, bequeathed the condominium unit to his wife for her life and then to their son. A year after the owner's death, the wife had a stroke that left her incapacitated. The son sought and was granted both personal and financial guardianship over his mother. Six months later the son suddenly died. By will, the son devised his real property to his daughter, who was unaware of the condominium unit and took no action with regard to it. The daughter assumed guardianship over her grandmother who remains alive but unable to care for herself.

Shortly after the owner's death, the wife granted an acquaintance the right to occupy the condominium unit for the following month. At the end of that month, the acquaintance tried unsuccessfully to obtain the wife's permission to remain longer. Deciding to remain despite the lack of permission, the acquaintance, since that time, has resided in the unit, maintaining it as well as paying the annual condominium fees and real estate taxes on it.

The applicable statutory period to acquire title by adverse possession is 10 years.

The acquaintance brings an appropriate action to determine title to the condominium unit.

What type of ownership interest in the condominium unit will the acquaintance be found to possess?

(A) Fee simple absolute
(B) A life estate measured by the wife's life
(C) A remainder interest
(D) None

145. The plaintiff, a State A citizen, sues the defendant, a State B citizen, in State B federal court and credibly claims breach of contract resulting in damages of $106,000. The contract was executed in State C and contains a clause providing that "in a litigated dispute, the laws of State D shall govern." The State B federal court properly asserts jurisdiction. The key issue is the parol evidence rule. States A, B, C, and D take four different approaches to this rule, which typifies the division among the other 46 states. State B law also provides that, in contract cases, its courts should apply the law of the state specified by the parties in their contract. State C has the identical choice-of-law rule. State B's rules are valid under the U.S. Constitution's Full Faith & Credit and Due Process Clauses.

The court should apply the parol evidence rule of which state?

(A) State A
(B) State B
(C) State C
(D) State D

146. After consuming too much alcohol, an actor tripped over his own feet and smashed face first into a sidewalk. The actor delayed seeking medical attention for his facial injuries for several days, which aggravated those injuries. When the actor finally sought treatment from a plastic surgeon, the plastic surgeon negligently performed the operation on the actor's face. After surgery, the actor failed to follow the surgeon's post-operative instructions. All of the actor's actions coupled with the surgeon's negligence contributed to the actor's permanent facial scarring.

The actor received reimbursement for some of his medical expenses from an insurer under a health insurance policy.

The actor sued the plastic surgeon for damages attributable to the surgeon's medical treatment of the actor's facial injuries. The applicable jurisdiction has not modified the common law collateral-source rule.

Assuming that the monetary effect of each of the following can be established with reasonable certainty, which can be taken into account to reduce the damages to which the actor would otherwise be entitled due to the surgeon's negligence?

(A) The plaintiff's negligent behavior that initially led to his facial injuries.
(B) The plaintiff's failure to promptly seek medical care.
(C) The plaintiff's failure to follow the surgeon's post-operative instructions.
(D) The reimbursement for medical expenses received by the plaintiff.

147.   A brother and sister were suspects in a bank robbery, but the police were having difficulty finding any evidence in their investigation. The police told the brother that if he testified against his sister, he would be granted use immunity for his testimony. The brother agreed. At the sister's trial, the brother testified that he and his sister had each used a gun in the robbery, and that he had helped her threaten the bank teller with his gun. He also testified that after the robbery, he had hidden his gun in a safe in an abandoned shed in the woods behind his apartment. The sister was convicted based on the brother's testimony. After the trial, the police found the safe in the abandoned shed and located the brother's gun. The brother was then charged with felony assault with a firearm for threatening the bank teller with the gun during the robbery. The brother has refused to take the stand at his trial.

Can the gun be offered as evidence at the brother's trial for felony assault with a firearm?

(A) No, because the police cannot lay a proper foundation to admit the gun unless the brother takes the stand.

(B) No, because the police used the brother's testimony from the sister's trial to locate the gun.

(C) Yes, because the brother is not entitled to transactional immunity for his testimony.

(D) Yes, because the brother was not granted immunity from the felony assault charge.

148.   A real estate broker pitched an idea for a reality-based television show to network executives. After the show was created and ran for a season, the broker sued the network in federal court, alleging that the network had orally agreed to compensate him for his idea. The jury rendered a special verdict in favor of the broker, finding that an oral agreement existed. Before the court entered judgment on the jury's verdict, the network moved for a judgment as a matter of law. In support of its motion, the network maintained that the jury's finding that an oral agreement existed was against the clear weight of the evidence.

How should the court rule on the network's motion?

(A) Deny the motion, because the sufficiency of the evidence is a matter entrusted solely to the jury.

(B) Deny the motion, because the motion was untimely.

(C) Grant the motion, because the motion was made before court pronounced judgment.

(D) Grant the motion, because the jury's verdict was against the clear weight of the evidence.

149.   A pest control company fumigated one of two buildings in an apartment complex with a toxic gas in order to eliminate unwanted insects. Even though the company exercised reasonable care, the gas escaped into the other building, which adjoined the fumigated building, where the gas caused serious illness to a tenant in that building. The tenant had received a written advance notice about the fumigation that advised the tenant of the need to vacate his apartment during the hours the fumigation was conducted. The tenant chose instead to remain there in order to watch a favorite television program. The applicable jurisdiction treats fumigation as an ultrahazardous activity.

The injured tenant filed an action against the pest control company. Who will prevail?

(A) The tenant, because the pest control company is strictly liable for the harm that resulted from the fumigation.
(B) The tenant, because the pest control company was negligent in conducting the fumigation.
(C) The pest control company, because the tenant was not a resident of the fumigated building.
(D) The pest control company, because the tenant assumed the risk.

150.   A physician entered into a written agreement to purchase land from his aunt. The agreement, which was secured by not only the land itself but also all future improvements, required the physician to make annual installment payments to the aunt. The deed from the aunt to the physician was recorded, but it made no mention of this agreement. The agreement itself was not recorded. The following year, the physician obtained a loan from the local bank to build a house on the land in exchange for a mortgage on the property and any structures built on it. The physician informed the bank about the agreement with his aunt. The bank required the aunt to sign an agreement subordinating her loan to the bank's loan. The mortgage agreement was recorded, but the agreement between the bank and the aunt was not recorded. After the house was built, a patient successfully sued the physician for malpractice. The judgment was promptly and properly recorded so that it became a lien against the residence of the physician. The patient was unaware of the physician's financial dealings with his aunt or the bank. The physician failed to make timely payments on the mortgage. In accord with the terms of the mortgage, the bank declared the full mortgage obligation due and properly foreclosed on the property. At the time of the foreclosure sale, which was properly conducted, the physician's outstanding balance with regard to the agreement with his aunt was $100,000, and with regard to the mortgage was $500,000. The total amount owed with respect to the judgment was $400,000. After expenses, the sale of the mortgaged property netted only $550,000. The applicable jurisdiction has the following two statutes: "Every conveyance not recorded is void as against any subsequent purchaser or mortgagee in good faith and for valuable consideration from the same vendor whose conveyance is first duly recorded." "Any judgment properly filed shall, for twelve years from filing, be a lien on the real property then owned or subsequently acquired by any person against whom the judgment is rendered."

What is the amount due to the aunt from the sale?

(A) $100,000, because the aunt's interest predated the other interests.
(B) $100,000, because the aunt's interest was a seller-financed purchase money security interest.
(C) $50,000, because the aunt's interest has priority over the patient's judgment lien, but not the bank's mortgage.
(D) Nothing, because both the patient's judgment lien and the bank's mortgage have priority over the aunt's interest.

151.   In a state known for its game fish, there are many guide-led fishing expeditions marketed to tourists. The state enacted a statute that required all fishing guides who charge a fee to have a license. The purpose of the statute is to protect the state's game fish from overfishing. The license costs $100 for in-state residents and $300 for out-of-state residents.

If an out-of-state resident challenges the constitutionality of this statute, what is the most likely result?

(A) The statute will be struck down under the Privileges and Immunities Clause of Article IV, Section 2.
(B) The statute will be struck down under the Equal Protection Clause.
(C) The statute will be upheld because engaging in fishing is not a fundamental right.
(D) The statute will be upheld because regulation of fishing is traditionally a state, rather than national, function.

152.   A defendant is on trial for robbery. A witness picked the defendant's picture out of a photo array that was conducted by a police officer at the police station after the defendant's arrest. The photo array was impermissibly suggestive. No counsel was present for the defendant at the photo array. Later, at trial, the witness identified the defendant.   Because of the witness's extended opportunity to view the defendant at the time of the crime, this identification was reliable.

The defendant moves to suppress the identification.   Should the court grant this motion?

(A) Yes, because the defendant's right to counsel was violated.
(B) Yes, because the identification procedure was impermissibly suggestive.
(C) No, because the identification was reliable.
(D) No, because the photo array was conducted by a police officer at a police station.

153. In a trial for murder in which the defendant asserted the affirmative defense of self-defense, the defendant's attorney introduced evidence that the victim had a reputation as a violent person. In turn, the prosecutor wanted to introduce the testimony of a witness, the victim's wife, who would testify that in her opinion, the victim was a peaceful person who would not have provoked a fight. Additionally, the prosecutor wanted to introduce evidence that the defendant has a reputation for being violent.

Should the court allow the prosecutor's evidence to be admitted?

(A) Yes, as to both.
(B) No as to the testimony regarding the victim, because the victim's character is not relevant to the defendant's actions, but yes as to the testimony regarding the defendant's reputation.
(C) No, as to the testimony regarding the defendant's reputation, because the defendant did not "open the door" by putting his own character at issue, but yes as to the testimony regarding the victim.
(D) No, as to both.

154. The driver of a truck was involved in an accident with a car driven by a citizen of a foreign country. The truck driver filed suit in a federal district court in the state in which the accident occurred, where the truck driver was domiciled. The driver of the car was a permanent legal resident of the United States and was domiciled in this state as well. The truck driver alleged damages of $35,000 in good faith due to personal injuries and damages of an additional $50,000 due to property losses. As permitted by state law under a direct action statute, the suit named only the insurer of the car as a defendant. The insurer was incorporated in a neighboring state and had its headquarters in a distant state. The insurer timely moved to dismiss the action due to lack of subject-matter jurisdiction.

How should the court rule on this motion?

(A) Grant the motion, because alienage jurisdiction does not exist.
(B) Grant the motion, because diversity of citizenship does not exist.
(C) Deny the motion, because the amount in controversy exceeds $75,000.
(D) Deny the motion, because the insurer is not a citizen of the forum state.

155.   The owner of an office building leased space to a physician in general practice for a term of five years. The physician's written lease with the owner restricted use of the space to a doctor's office, but permitted the assignment of the office with the written permission of the owner, which, according to the terms of the lease, could be withheld for any reason. At the end of second year of the lease, the physician decided to move to another building and rented the space to a lawyer for one year. The lawyer's monthly payments were the same as those called for in the lease between the owner and the physician. The owner's permission was not sought, but the owner accepted rental payments directly from the lawyer. At the end of the third year of the lease, the physician found a psychiatrist to rent the space for a year. As with the lawyer, the psychiatrist's monthly payments were to be the same as those called for in the lease between the owner and the physician. When contacted by the physician, the owner at first orally agreed, and then, upon learning the identity of the psychiatrist, refused due to personal animosity towards the psychiatrist.

Can the owner be compelled to accept the psychiatrist as a tenant?

(A) Yes, because the lease does not restrict the physician from subletting the office space.
(B) Yes, because the owner has waived the right to object by accepting the physician's previous sublet of the office space.
(C) No, because the physician did not obtain the owner's written permission.
(D) No, because the owner properly exercised his right to reject the psychiatrist as a tenant.

156.   A toy company specialized in producing high-end toy racecars. Three months prior to the holiday shopping season, the toy company received an order of 50,000 racecars from a major retailer. The toy company immediately contracted with two of its major suppliers, a metalworking company and a paint company, to provide essential parts and paint for the racecars. The metalworking company and the paint company both were extremely busy with orders from other manufacturers, but agreed to supply needed parts and paint for the racecars.

One month later, the metalworking company, without justification, informed the toy company that it would not be able to perform the contract. The toy company found a replacement metal parts supplier, but the new supplier was only able to provide 25,000 parts. Consequently, the toy company reduced its order with the paint company by 25,000 units.

The paint company then sued the metalworking company, seeking the profits it lost because of the reduced order. The contract between the toy company and the metalworking company was silent on the issue of third-party liability. Is the paint company entitled to such relief?

(A) Yes, because the paint company is a volume seller of paint.
(B) Yes, because the paint company has a vested right to enforce the contract between the toy company and the metalworking company.
(C) No, because the paint company is not an intended beneficiary of the contract between the toy company and the metalworking company.
(D) No, because the contract between the toy company and the metalworking company did not explicitly grant third-party rights in the paint company.

157. An American helicopter manufacturer contracted with a foreign hospital located in a severely war-torn region to sell five helicopters specially outfitted for medical use. The helicopter manufacturer, in turn, contracted with a subcontractor to provide five flight systems for use in the helicopters. The subcontractor was not informed about the contract between the helicopter manufacturer and the foreign hospital, nor the location where the helicopters would be used.

After the two contracts were formed, the country in which the hospital was located descended deeply into civil war. The United Nations imposed an embargo against all shipments to that country. The helicopter manufacturer directed the subcontractor to stop all work on the contract, and to place any completed systems into storage. At that point, the subcontractor had finished three of the five flight systems called for by the subcontract. The systems were custom-built, and could not be used for any other purpose.

The subcontractor sued the helicopter manufacturer for breach of contract. Is the subcontractor likely to prevail?

(A) Yes, because the subcontractor was a vested third-party beneficiary of the contract between the helicopter manufacturer and the foreign hospital.
(B) Yes, because the helicopter manufacturer assumed the risk of the failure of the contract.
(C) No, because the contract was rendered impracticable by the United Nations embargo.
(D) No, because the failure of the contract between the helicopter manufacturer and the foreign hospital frustrated the purpose of the subcontract.

158. A man was having an affair with a woman. The man and the woman had been seen together many times in public enjoying romantic dinners. One evening, when the man claimed to be going out with friends, his wife followed him. Instead of going to meet his friends, the man met the woman at a secluded restaurant. The two sat in a dark booth, and the wife snuck in and sat unseen in the booth next to them. During their conversation, which the wife recorded using her cell phone, the woman admitted that she was pregnant with the man's child. The wife was so upset about the news that she ran out of the restaurant and forgot her cell phone. A waiter found the phone and gave it to his son, who sold used cell phones for a living. While clearing out the contents of the phone, the son discovered the recorded conversation between the man and the woman regarding her pregnancy. The son anonymously posted the recording on a popular video-sharing website. The woman's attorney eventually figured out who posted the video. Now the woman wants to sue the son for invasion of privacy.

If all of the following torts are recognized in the relevant jurisdiction, which of the following causes of action would provide the woman with her best chance of recovery against the son?

(A) Intrusion upon seclusion
(B) Misappropriation of the right to publicity
(C) Public disclosure of private facts
(D) False light

159. A secretary was charged with and convicted of felony theft for depositing cash payments made by her employer's customers into her personal account and destroying the company's records (e.g., invoices, shipping records) related to those payments. Her employer then brought a civil action for conversion based on the same conduct. The employer has requested, over the secretary's objection, that she be precluded from contesting whether she has engaged in conversion since the elements for tortious conversion and felony theft were the same under the applicable state law.

How should the court rule?

(A) For the secretary, because the employer was not a litigant in the criminal case.
(B) For the secretary, because this case is a civil, not a criminal, action.
(C) For the employer, because offensive issue preclusion is permitted.
(D) For the employer, because theft crimes are an exception to the general rule preventing offensive preclusion.

160. A state statute makes the possession of all venomous snakes unlawful. The state legislature's purpose in enacting the statute was to address the problem of a rising number of fatal snakebites occurring within the state.

A religious entity based in the state teaches that God will protect its members against all harm, and that therefore its members must handle venomous snakes during the entity's religious services to witness their true faith. An ordained minister of the entity, who sincerely believes all of the religious entity's teachings, sued in an appropriate federal court to have the statute declared unconstitutional because it prevents him from exercising his religious beliefs.

Is the court likely to uphold the statute?

(A) Yes, because it is a neutral law of general applicability.
(B) Yes, because it does not have the primary effect of advancing religion and does not excessively entangle the government in religion.
(C) No, because it is not the least restrictive means of achieving the state's compelling interest in public health and safety.
(D) No, because it interferes with an integral part of the religious entity's worship services.

161.   In reporting on the death of a city official whose bullet-ridden body was found in a barren apartment, a newspaper attributed the death to a "drug deal that went sour." The newspaper reporter who filed the report had serious doubts about the official's involvement with drugs. Later, the newspaper determined that the official neither used nor sold illegal drugs, but instead was killed because he had been involved in a fraud scheme that went awry.

The executor of the official's estate brought an action for defamation against the newspaper. The executor is unable to establish special damages. Who will prevail?

(A) The executor, because presumed damages are permitted for a libel action.
(B) The executor, because the newspaper acted with malice.
(C) The newspaper, because the city official was dead.
(D) The newspaper, because the statement regarding the city official's involvement in criminal activity was substantially true.

162.   A city located in the southern part of State A experienced very high temperatures throughout the year. As a result, the city's residents paid high energy bills due to the necessity of using air conditioners. State B was located just north of State A. Much of State B's energy industry consisted of manufacturers providing consumers with renewable-energy sources, including residential solar panels. In past years, many residents of the southern city in State A had purchased residential solar panels from State B manufacturers in order to reduce their electric bills. Recently, many of these State B manufacturers moved their headquarters to a northern city in State A because it reduced their shipping costs to the southern part of State A. To support this emerging renewable-energy industry in its state, State A enacted a statute requiring that all residential solar panels be purchased from in-state manufacturers only. As a result, a renewable-energy manufacturer located in State B lost all of its prospective business in State A. The manufacturer wants to challenge the constitutionality of the statute.

Is the manufacturer likely to succeed?

(A) Yes, because the statute impairs the manufacturer's business relationships.
(B) Yes, because the statute discriminates against out-of-state manufacturers.
(C) No, because the traditional government function exception allows State A to regulate in favor of its own energy industry.
(D) No, because the statute treats all out-of-state manufacturers the same.

163. A borrower owed a substantial sum of money to an unsavory lender. One afternoon, the lender knocked on the borrower's door. When the borrower opened the door, the lender was holding a baseball bat and said, "If you don't get me the money you owe within the next two hours, I'll break your legs." The borrower was extremely frightened, and immediately gave the lender the cash needed to satisfy the debt.

If the borrower later sues the lender for assault, will the borrower prevail?

(A) Yes, because the lender threatened the borrower with harmful or offensive bodily contact.

(B) Yes, because the lender intended to place the borrower in apprehension of harmful or offensive bodily contact.

(C) No, because the lender's words alone cannot give rise to an assault claim.

(D) No, because the lender gave the borrower two hours to deliver the money.

164. In a pre-trial hearing, a judge determined that a defendant's confession was given voluntarily to a police detective after the detective had given Miranda warnings to the defendant. At this hearing, the defendant testified. At trial, the defense did not contest the defendant's receipt of Miranda warnings, but sought to question the police detective about the manner in which the defendant was interrogated after receiving the warnings in order to call into question whether the confession was voluntary. The defense does not plan to call the defendant to the witness stand.

Should the court permit this line of questioning?

(A) No, because there had been a judicial determination that the confession was voluntary.

(B) No, because the defense did not challenge the defendant's receipt of Miranda warnings.

(C) Yes, because a party may introduce evidence that is relevant to the weight and credibility of other evidence.

(D) Yes, because a defendant may testify at a hearing regarding a preliminary question without being required to testify at trial.

165. A man asked a friend to burn down the man's residence so the man could collect the fire insurance proceeds. The friend stated that she would be willing to set fire to the residence for $20,000. The man offered $10,000, but the friend refused. Later, the man set fire to an office building that he owned in order to collect the fire insurance proceeds. The man honestly, but unreasonably and incorrectly, believed that there was no one in the building when he set the fire. There was a person in the office building at the time of the fire who escaped unharmed. The man is charged with solicitation and arson. The relevant statute defines arson as "the malicious burning of any dwelling or occupied structure."

Can the man be convicted of these crimes?

(A) No, as to both solicitation and arson.
(B) Yes, as to both solicitation and arson.
(C) Yes, as to arson only.
(D) Yes, as to solicitation only.

166. The holder of a trademark sued an entrepreneur in federal court for damages resulting from the breach of an agreement that granted the entrepreneur exclusive use of a trademark in a specified geographic area. Although the weight of the evidence regarding the breach was clearly against the entrepreneur, there was substantial evidence to support the entrepreneur's position. The jury rendered a verdict in favor of the entrepreneur and the trial court entered a judgment accordingly. On appeal, the trademark holder sought to have the judgment set aside because the verdict was against the weight of the evidence.

How should the appellate court rule?

(A) Set aside the judgment, because the verdict was against the weight of the evidence.
(B) Set aside the judgment, because the issue was one that should have been decided by the court.
(C) Affirm the judgment, because there was substantial evidence to support the verdict.
(D) Affirm the judgment, because the appellate court is precluded from setting aside a jury verdict by the Seventh Amendment.

167. A plaintiff and a defendant are in settlement negotiations to resolve the plaintiff's lawsuit to recover for injuries she suffered when she fell off a horse at the defendant's stable. In exchange for the plaintiff's agreeing to drop the case, the defendant offered to pay the plaintiff $5,000, which would cover her medical expenses and leave a little extra for pain and suffering. The plaintiff counter-offered $7,000, which the defendant refused. The case went to trial. The plaintiff prayed for $20,000 in damages, and reiterated during her testimony that that amount was the least amount she could accept to make her whole. The defendant testified that the plaintiff's injuries were not severe enough to warrant a $20,000 judgment, and added, "The plaintiff was willing to settle for $7,000; it's ludicrous that she is now asking for $20,000." The plaintiff's attorney objected to the defendant's statement.

How should the court rule on the plaintiff's objection?

(A) Sustain it, because the testimony contains hearsay not within any exception.
(B) Sustain it, because the testimony discloses communications regarding a settlement offer.
(C) Overrule it, because the testimony contains a prior inconsistent statement.
(D) Overrule it, because the testimony impeaches the plaintiff's credibility.

168. The owner of a parcel of land validly devises the parcel "to my wife for life, but if she remarries, then to my son for his life; then to my son's children who attain the age of 21." At the time of the conveyance, the son has one child, a daughter.

Subsequently, the son is killed in an automobile crash. At the time of the crash, the son also has a second daughter. A year after the son's funeral, the owner's wife remarries.

The oldest daughter, who is now 21, contacts a lawyer about ownership of the parcel of land. Her sister is currently 18 years old.

The jurisdiction follows the common law Rule Against Perpetuities, has abolished the common law rule regarding the destructibility of contingent remainders, and follows the rule of convenience with regard to class gifts.

Which of the following prevents the oldest daughter from owning the entire parcel in fee simple absolute?

(A) The Rule Against Perpetuities.
(B) Her sister's interest in the parcel.
(C) Her father's death and grandmother's remarriage before she turned 21 years old.
(D) Her grandmother is still alive.

169. A widow and widower were engaged to be married. After some discussion as to how to pay for the wedding, the son of the widow and the daughter of the widower each orally agreed to give $50,000 to the other's parent as a gesture of approval of the upcoming union. The son and daughter shook hands in agreement as to the arrangement, but before either gift had been made, the two became embroiled in a serious disagreement, and both agreed to forego making the gifts. In spite of this, the son of the widow did make a gift of $50,000 to the widower at the time of the wedding.

Soon after the marriage of the widow and widower, the widower died. Subsequently, the widow learned of the arrangement and sued the daughter of widower to compel her to pay $50,000. Is the widow likely to prevail?

(A) Yes, because the widow was an intended beneficiary of the agreement between the children.
(B) Yes, because the agreement between the children was not required to be in writing.
(C) No, because the agreement between the children was unenforceable as promises to make gifts.
(D) No, because the agreement between the children was rescinded before the widow's rights vested.

170. Congress has enacted many laws regulating navigation generally, but not regarding the specific subject of water pollution by ships sailing on navigable bodies of water. A state enacted a law prohibiting any ship from discharging specified pollutants, including oil, into the navigable waterways of the state. Violation of the law was punishable by fines based on the amount of the discharge. The law is necessary to the important state interest of preventing pollution; there are no reasonable alternatives available. In addition, the benefits of the law to the state outweigh the burdens it imposes on interstate commerce.

A ship owner from another state is fined pursuant to this law for discharging oil into a waterway in the state. Will the ship owner's challenge to the state law as unconstitutional be successful?

(A) Yes, because the law regulates interstate commerce, which may be regulated only by Congress.
(B) Yes, because the fine constitutes an impermissible ad valorem tax.
(C) No, because the law is necessary to the important state interest of preventing pollution and there are no reasonable alternatives available.
(D) No, because the law does not discriminate against interstate commerce and does not impose an undue burden on interstate commerce.

171.   In a well-trafficked downtown location, a voyeur concealed a video camera near a sidewalk grate. As the voyeur was aware, a natural spurt of air coming up from the grate would occasionally lift a woman's skirt and reveal her underwear. In reviewing the video taken one day, the voyeur discovered a short sequence involving a prominent female politician who at the time was not wearing underwear. The voyeur contacted the politician and demanded a substantial payment in exchange for not posting the video on the Internet.

The politician sued the voyeur in an invasion of privacy action based on intrusion upon her seclusion. The voyeur moved to dismiss the action for failure to state a cause of action. Should the court grant this motion?

(A) No, because the politician did not consent to the video.
(B) No, because the video intruded into her privacy in a manner highly offensive to a reasonable person.
(C) Yes, because the video was made in a public place.
(D) Yes, because the video was not revealed to a third party.

172.   A 16-year-old entered into a written agreement to buy a car from a dealership. He made a small down payment and took out a loan from the dealership for the remainder of the purchase price. The deal was fair in every respect, and the same as the car dealership would give any other customer. After the sale was finalized, the salesman's supervisor reviewed the contract, and upon researching the matter further, discovered that the boy was only 16. He told the salesperson to call the boy and cancel the contract, which he did.

In a breach of contract action brought on behalf of the boy, the court held for the boy. What was the reason?

(A) The contract is one for necessities.
(B) The contract cannot be disaffirmed because of the boy's part performance.
(C) The contract is not voidable because the terms were fair.
(D) The dealer did not have the right to void the contract.

173. Two vehicles were involved in an automobile accident. The driver of one car ran to the other car and said, "Ma'am, are you ok? Oh my goodness, I didn't even see that stop sign. I'm calling an ambulance right now." The injured woman sued the other driver. At trial, the other driver testified that the woman was the one who ran the stop sign. The woman's attorney then seeks to introduce the other driver's statement as evidence that he ran a stop sign and caused the accident.

Upon proper objection, should the court admit the statement into evidence?

(A) Yes, both as substantive evidence and for impeachment purposes.
(B) No, because as a prior inconsistent statement, it can only be used to impeach the other driver.
(C) No, because the declarant is available to testify and subject to cross-examination.
(D) No, because the statement is hearsay not within any exception.

174. A city airport is one of the busiest in the nation and caters to travelers of all kinds, particularly sports stars. The airport had struggled for many years to maintain order at security checkpoints when these sports stars were recognized by fans. For security reasons, the board of the city's airport commission used government funds to build a special terminal with a separate, faster security checkpoint where sports stars could go without having to interact with the general public. A recent study that was given to the board showed that female sports stars earn an average of $150,000 per year, whereas male sports stars earn an average of $400,000 per year. The same study suggested that although there is a correlation between an athlete's income and his or her popularity among fans, the two factors are not directly proportional. To prevent the need for a costly and time-consuming application process for athletes wanting to use the special terminal, the board required that a sports star must earn a yearly salary of at least $300,000 to use the private terminal. A female sports star who earns $175,000 per year would like to use the special terminal, but is not permitted to do so. The female sports star sued the board, claiming that the minimum salary requirement violates her constitutional rights.

Which of the following argument's best supports the female sports star's challenge to the minimum salary requirement?

(A) The requirement is not rationally related to the likelihood of a sports star's presence causing a security disruption.
(B) The requirement is discriminatorily applied to female sports stars.
(C) The requirement has a disparate effect on female sports stars.
(D) The board's prior knowledge of the study evidences a discriminatory intent in setting the minimum salary requirement.

175. The plaintiff sues a large out-of-state corporation in federal court. The plaintiff claims that the corporation's widget had a defect that caused him a serious injury and requests $300,000 in damages. The corporation has a great legal department and a large group of professionals with a thorough understanding of each of its products. The plaintiff's attorney hires a widget expert, and pays her $30,000 to consult with him and to provide a report on the corporation's widgets. The report concludes that the widgets were properly designed and manufactured, although it is possible that the widget used by the plaintiff had a defect. The plaintiff's attorney decided not to have the expert testify at trial. During discovery, the corporation requested all of the plaintiff's expert reports related to the litigation.

Must the plaintiff's attorney disclose the expert's report?

(A) Yes, because the expert's report is relevant to the parties' claims or defenses and is not privileged.
(B) Yes, because the benefit of the expert's report to the corporation outweighs the burden of the discovery request.
(C) No, because the corporation's request was likely calculated to harass and unduly burden the plaintiff.
(D) No, because the plaintiff's attorney hired the expert as a consultant to prepare for the trial, not to testify at the trial.

176. A hospital placed an order to purchase scalpel blades from a medical supply company. The hospital specified that the blades were to be shipped immediately. Upon receipt of the order, the supply company discovered that it did not have the type of blade ordered by the hospital, and shipped instead a different type of blade, along with a note that these blades were not the type ordered by the hospital but were sent as an accommodation.

The hospital rejected and returned the shipped blades, then sued the supply company for breach of contract. Will the hospital be successful in its suit?

(A) Yes, because of the perfect tender rule.
(B) Yes, because acceptance of the hospital's order could be made by shipment as well as by a promise.
(C) No, because the hospital order could only be accepted by shipment of the type of scalpel blades ordered.
(D) No, because the medical supply company did not accept the hospital's offer.

177. A man owned a fleet of small airplanes available for charter within the region. He was flying with customers one day when he was forced to make an emergency landing in a field. A farmer on the land tried to prevent the man from landing on his field and destroying his crops by standing in the landing path of the plane and waving the plane into an adjacent barren field. While the farmer was gesturing to the airplane, a piece of metal from the plane came loose and struck his shoulder, injuring him. The farmer sued the man, who in his answer contended that the farmer's actions barred recovery. The farmer's attorney provided evidence that the man had not completed an inspection on the plane for nearly two years and that an inspection would have quickly notified him of the loose piece of metal on the plane.

Is the owner of the airplane likely liable to the farmer for the injury?

(A) Yes, because he owned the plane that injured the farmer.
(B) Yes, because he had not had the plane inspected for two years.
(C) No, because he acted as a reasonable person would have acted in an emergency landing.
(D) No, because the farmer stood in the landing path.

178. At about 5:00 a.m., firefighters responded to a house fire. The fire was brought under control in about an hour and completely extinguished approximately two hours later. In the early afternoon, a city fire inspector came to the house with an administrative warrant. The warrant authorized the inspector to search for the cause of the fire and seize items related to it. The inspector first searched the basement of the house, finding a barely recognizable electric curling iron plugged into a partially melted timer, which was set to turn on at about 4:00 a.m. In addition, the inspector found the iron in a large soot blackened tub. Nearby were several empty gallon containers labeled "turpentine." The inspector seized the iron, timer, tub and empty turpentine containers, believing that they constituted evidence necessary to establish the cause of the fire. While the ground level of the house was almost completely destroyed by the fire, the second level was in much better condition. On the second floor, the inspector noticed that there were several empty frames, their pictures apparently having been removed, hanging on the walls. Also the inspector noted that none of the three upstairs bedrooms contained electronic equipment, such as televisions or computers, despite the presence of empty power strips plugged into outlets in these rooms. The inspector seized the empty frames and power strips, believing that they constituted evidence the homeowner had deliberately set the fire. The family who lived in the house was away on vacation at the time of the fire and did not return until the following day. The homeowner was charged with arson.

Can the homeowner successfully object to the introduction into evidence of the items seized by the inspector from the second floor of the house?

(A) No, because the items were seized by a fire inspector rather than a police officer.
(B) No, because the search was conducted under exigent circumstances.
(C) No, because the search was conducted pursuant to an administrative warrant.
(D) Yes, because the seizure of these items exceed the scope of the warrant.

179.	A plaintiff initiated a libel action against her former boyfriend after he posted a written statement on his web site accusing the plaintiff of being able to afford a new car only because she worked as a prostitute. At trial, the defendant called a neighbor of the plaintiff to testify that he paid the plaintiff to have sex with him. The plaintiff objected to the testimony.

Should the court admit this testimony for the purpose of proving that the plaintiff is a prostitute?

(A) No, because the introduction of evidence of sexual conduct in a civil action is prohibited.
(B) No, because the testimony is inadmissible character evidence.
(C) Yes, because the evidence is relevant to the defendant's defense.
(D) Yes, because character evidence must be in the form of specific acts rather than reputation or opinion testimony.

180.	A state amended its constitution to provide that "English is the state's official language and applies to all state employees during the performance of government business." A state employee sued the state's governor to enjoin application of this provision to her. She alleged that she worked in the state's Department of Motor Vehicles and often communicated with customers in Spanish, thereby facing possible adverse employment action in violation of her First and Fourteenth Amendment rights. The governor defends against this action by invoking the political question doctrine.

Will the governor likely be successful?

(A) Yes, because the case presents a hotly contested question involving sensitive political issues.
(B) Yes, because a judicial decision would unnecessarily embarrass the governor.
(C) No, because the law does not require the judge to make any discretionary policy determinations.
(D) No, because the state constitutional provision has been properly challenged as violating individual constitutional rights.

181. Two friends, a chef and an electrician, together purchased a beachfront residence. They took title to the residence as joint owners, with the chef owning a 75% interest and the electrician a 25% interest.

The chef, during the time he used the residence, prepared elaborate meals. He advertised those meals, attracted a paying clientele, and made a net profit from them.

The electrician pointed out to the chef that the electrical system in the house was in dangerous condition. The chef, agreeing with the electrician that repair of the system was necessary, stated that he had neither the time nor the expertise to fix it himself and couldn't afford the cost of doing so. The electrician repaired it and demanded that the chef contribute to the cost of the repair. The chef refused.

The electrician brought an action for partition. The court ordered the sale of the residence. It was purchased by a third party for its appraised value.

In allocating the sale proceeds, should the court take into account either the chef's net profit from the meals or the electrician's repair of the electrical system?

(A) Only the electrician's repair of the electrical system.
(B) Only the chef's net profit from the meals.
(C) Both must be taken into account.
(D) Neither should be taken into account.

182. After a man suffered a major epileptic seizure, he reported the seizure to his state's Motor Vehicle Administration, in compliance with the following statute:

Driver's license holders diagnosed with epilepsy shall be required to report their epilepsy and seizures to the State Motor Vehicle Administration (SMVA). The SMVA shall refer their license applications to the Medical Advisory Board for review. The Board may, in its discretion, suspend or revoke a person's driver's license or refuse to renew a license for longer than 90 days if the person's driving may be adversely affected by a seizure.

Pursuant to its authority, the Medical Advisory Board revoked the man's driver's license. Nonetheless, the man kept driving his car to work, and one morning, he hit a pedestrian with his car. The pedestrian was crossing the street in a crosswalk.

There is no evidence that the man was suffering an epileptic seizure at the time of the incident. The pedestrian sued the man, and during trial, argued that the man's actions constituted negligence per se. Will the pedestrian's argument be successful?

(A) No, because the man was not suffering a seizure at the time of the accident.
(B) No, because the harm suffered by the pedestrian was not of the type contemplated by the statute.
(C) Yes, because the man was driving in violation of the Medical Advisory Board's order.
(D) Yes, because the pedestrian is in the class of persons intended to be protected by the statute.

183. The defendant was convicted in state court of armed robbery by a unanimous vote of a six-person jury. The applicable statute provides for a sentence of not more than 20 years' imprisonment. However, if the defendant was previously convicted of specified crimes, including felony theft, the sentence could be increased to not more than 30 years' imprisonment. Upon the introduction of evidence by the prosecution, the judge determined that the defendant had been previously convicted of a felony theft and sentenced the defendant to 25 years in prison. On appeal, the defendant has challenged both his conviction and his sentence.

Should the appellate court uphold the conviction and the sentence?

(A) Yes as to the conviction, because a six-person jury is permissible in a criminal trial, and yes as to the sentence, because it was validly imposed by the judge.
(B) Yes as to the conviction, because a six-person jury is permissible in a criminal trial, but no as to the sentence, because it was not imposed by a jury.
(C) No as to the conviction, because a six-person jury is not permissible in a criminal trial, but yes as to the sentence, because it was validly imposed by the judge.
(D) No as to the conviction, because a six-person jury is not permissible in a criminal trial, and no as to the sentence, because it was not imposed by a jury.

184. A homeowner entered into an oral agreement with a landscaper to landscape the grounds surrounding her home for $75,000 while she was away for the summer. While the homeowner had described the overall effect that she wanted the landscaper to create as "stately," she left the choice of plants and other materials and their placement up to the landscaper. In order to secure the homeowner's assent, the landscaper promised her that she would be satisfied with the job or she would not have to pay him. Upon the homeowner's return in the fall, the landscaper sought payment from the homeowner. The homeowner refused to pay because, in her honest opinion, the landscaper had failed to create the effect she desired.

The landscaper filed a breach of contract action to recover $75,000 from the homeowner. At trial, the landscaper offers evidence that the landscaping was done in conformity with standards set forth by a national organization of landscapers and testimony from several witnesses that the homeowner was being unreasonable because the grounds were stately. Will the landscaper likely prevail?

(A) No, because the homeowner was not satisfied with the landscaping.
(B) No, because the contract was not in writing.
(C) Yes, because the landscaper performed in accordance with recognized standards.
(D) Yes, because the homeowner was being unreasonable in refusing to acknowledge that the landscaping had made the grounds stately.

185. A plaintiff brought an action in civil court against the defendant for battery. The defendant contended that he had acted in self-defense, which depended on the defendant's knowledge that the plaintiff carried a knife. Prior to calling the defendant to testify, the defendant's attorney sought to call as his first witness a former companion of the plaintiff who lived with the plaintiff at the time of the incident. The defendant's attorney proffered that the companion would testify that, although the companion could not be sure that the plaintiff carried a knife on the day in question, the plaintiff, as he dressed each morning, always snapped a sheath around the lower part of his right leg and inserted a knife into the sheath. The plaintiff's attorney objected to the introduction of this testimony as irrelevant, since the defendant had not yet introduced evidence that the defendant himself was aware that the plaintiff carried a knife.

May the court admit the companion's testimony subject to the defendant's subsequent introduction of such evidence?

(A) Yes, because the court may admit otherwise irrelevant evidence when its probative value substantially outweighs the danger of unfair prejudice.

(B) Yes, because the fact that the plaintiff carried a knife may be conditionally admitted even though its relevance depends on the existence of the defendant's knowledge of that fact.

(C) No, because the relevance of the fact that the plaintiff carried a knife depended on the defendant's knowledge of that fact, which had not been introduced into evidence.

(D) No, because the companion was not sure that the plaintiff carried a knife on the day in question.

186. A city passed an ordinance prohibiting all "adult entertainment establishments," defined as "enterprises that sell, trade, or depict materials that are obscene or pornographic." The city justified its law on the basis of reputable studies showing that (i) obscene and pornographic material degrades females and increases the tendency towards anti-social behavior of people who view it; and (ii) adult entertainment establishments are linked with criminal activity such as prostitution and drug dealing. The city also emphasized that the three cities bordering it all allow adult entertainment establishments.

An entrepreneur who wishes to open an adult bookstore in the city sues the city in an appropriate federal court and claims that the ordinance is unconstitutional. Will she likely prevail?

(A) Yes, because the city's ordinance deprives her of her right to earn a living in violation of the Due Process Clause of the Fourteenth Amendment.

(B) Yes, because the First Amendment prohibits the city from banning all adult entertainment establishments.

(C) No, because the plaintiff has not been deprived of her constitutional right to earn a living, as she can open her adult bookstore in one of the three nearby cities.

(D) No, because the city has legitimate reasons for banning adult entertainment establishments that are not based on the content of the material they are selling, trading, or depicting.

187. A tenant rented an apartment in a multi-family dwelling on a month-to-month basis. Under the terms of the lease, the tenant had an absolute duty to repair the premises. At the time that the tenant rented the apartment, the landlord made the tenant aware of several housing code violations that constituted a substantial threat to the tenant's health and safety. After waiting a reasonable time for the landlord to correct the violations, the tenant, in accord with a statutory provision, placed the monthly rent payment in an escrow account, rather than submitting it to the landlord.

After failing to receive the rent for two months, the landlord filed an action seeking eviction of the tenant.

If the tenant raised the landlord's failure to correct the housing code violations as a defense, will the tenant be successful?

(A) No, because the tenant had a contractual duty to repair the premises.
(B) No, because the tenant was aware of the violations when the tenant assumed control of the premises.
(C) Yes, because of the implied warranty of habitability.
(D) Yes, because the landlord's actions constituted a constructive eviction.

188. Arriving home from work, a husband found his wife engaged in sex with his best friend. The husband flew into a rage and verbally threatened to shoot both of them, although he did not own a gun. The best friend quickly left and the husband eventually calmed down and regained his self-control after his wife promised not to see the best friend again. Nevertheless, the husband left the house to purchase a handgun. After making his purchase, he stopped by a local bar and became inebriated.

In the meantime, the best friend returned to drop off the husband's favorite hat, which the husband had left at the best friend's house the day before. Only the wife was home, but as the wife was giving the best friend a goodbye hug, the husband returned home, still inebriated. As both the wife and the best friend attempted to explain the innocent nature of their being together, the husband, his shock over their relationship returning, pulled the trigger. His shot missed the best friend and instead killed the wife.

The husband was charged with common-law murder of his wife. Which of the following would be his best argument against the charge?

(A) He didn't intend to kill his wife.
(B) His intoxicated state prevented him from forming the intent necessary to commit the crime.
(C) The sight of his best friend and his wife together again reignited his feelings regarding his wife's adultery.
(D) A reasonable person would not have cooled off from the initial discovery of the adultery.

189. A federal statute provides that, in a federal action challenging the constitutionality of a state statute where the state itself is not a defendant, the court must permit the state to defend the statute; if the state declines to do so, a predetermined private law firm in each state has the right to make this defense.

A plaintiff was arrested by city police officers for violation of a state criminal statute that prohibited the obstruction of governmental administration because the plaintiff had filmed a public encounter between the officers and a group of protesters. The plaintiff, seeking money damages, sued the city and the police officers in federal court for violation of her civil rights under the First and Fourth Amendments. Among the plaintiff's contentions was the state statute was unconstitutional. The state declined to defend the statute.

If the predetermined law firm in the state seeks to defend the statute, the firm should file a motion based on which of the following rules?

(A) Intervention as of right.
(B) Compulsory joinder.
(C) Permissive joinder.
(D) Interpleader.

190. The Occupational Safety and Health Act of 1970 (OSHA) required all private employers in America to meet certain minimum federal standards to ensure safe and healthful work environments. Recently, Congress amended OSHA, extending its coverage requirements to state and local government employers.

A state sued in an appropriate federal court, challenging the constitutionality of this amendment. Will the court likely uphold the amendment as constitutional?

(A) No, because the amendment violates the Tenth Amendment.
(B) No, because the amendment violates fundamental principles of federalism, because Congress has directly impaired the states' ability to carry out their integral governmental functions.
(C) Yes, because the amendment merely affects the activities of states acting in their proprietary capacity.
(D) Yes, because the amendment is a valid exercise of Congress's Commerce Clause power.

191. When a mortgagor defaulted on her loan obligation, the bank forced a foreclosure sale. Among the claims on the sale proceeds were attorney's fees associated with the foreclosure sale, the unpaid portion of the bank loan associated with the mortgage five years ago, and a debt owed by the mortgagor to a contractor who had recently performed work on the property. The original purchase-money mortgage had previously been paid off. All creditors filed claims in the appropriate court to receive the funds of the foreclosure in satisfaction of the debt. Within the state, none of the interested parties were afforded additional rights or liens on the property other than those regulating regular foreclosure actions.

What is the appropriate order of the application of the money from the foreclosure sale to these debtors?

(A) Contractor, Bank, Attorney
(B) Attorney, Bank, Contractor
(C) Bank, Attorney, Contractor
(D) Bank, Contractor, Attorney

192. A pedestrian was walking next to a building under construction. Suddenly, he was hit in the head by a falling brick. As a consequence, the pedestrian suffered a skull fracture and a severe brain injury. The pedestrian sued the construction company. At trial, the pedestrian did not introduce any direct evidence of the construction company's negligence, but proved that the construction company's employees were in control of its bricks at all relevant times, and that a brick does not ordinarily fall from a building under construction without negligence. The construction company offered uncontroverted proof that the pedestrian was negligent by walking so close to an active construction site. The jurisdiction in which the lawsuit is proceeding applies pure comparative negligence rules.

At the close of all evidence, the construction company moved for a directed verdict. Should the court deny this motion?

(A) Yes, because the pedestrian's negligence does not reduce the likelihood of the construction company being negligent.
(B) Yes, because res ipsa loquitur requires a finding of negligence.
(C) No, because a party who is negligent may not prevail under a res ipsa loquitur theory.
(D) No, because the pedestrian has not produced any direct evidence of the company's culpability.

193. A plaintiff sued a defendant for injuries she sustained when she slipped on a wet floor in the defendant's restaurant. The plaintiff saw a physician and underwent physical therapy sessions to treat her injuries. During one session, the plaintiff said to her physical therapist, "You know, I saw the 'Caution, Floor is Wet' sign before I fell, but I was in such a hurry to get back to my table that I ignored it." Another patient undergoing physical therapy with another therapist overheard the statement, and informed the defendant, who happened to be his friend. The defendant wants to introduce the testimony of his friend, as whether the plaintiff had notice of the wet floor is at issue in the case. The plaintiff objects to the testimony.

Should the court allow the friend to testify as to the plaintiff's statement?

(A) No, because the statement is inadmissible hearsay.
(B) No, because the statement is privileged.
(C) Yes, because the statement is not hearsay.
(D) Yes, because the statement was made for the purposes of medical diagnosis or treatment.

194. A gas station entered into a contract with an oil distributor to purchase a specified quantity of gasoline for resale. The contract specified, per the gas station's insistence, that the gasoline was to be a minimum of 99.5% free of impurities, as determined by industry-standard measurements. Another contract provision specified that the gasoline was to be delivered by July 31 at the latest.

The oil distributor delivered the gasoline to the gas station on July 30. Before accepting the delivery, the gas station manager checked the purity of the gasoline. The gasoline was only 99.3% free of impurities, and the manager rejected it. The oil distributor immediately informed the gas station manager that it intended to cure the defect by delivering a new shipment as soon as possible. The oil distributor delivered a new shipment of gasoline to the gas station on August 1, but the gas station manager rejected the new shipment. Both parties agree that the gasoline in the second shipment was 99.7% free of impurities.

Later, the oil distributor sued the gas station for breach of contract. Is it likely to prevail?

(A) No, because the oil distributor had no right to cure its defective tender.
(B) No, because an acceptable shipment needed to be delivered by July 31.
(C) Yes, because the second shipment was a conforming tender, and the gas station was required to accept it.
(D) Yes, because the oil distributor properly cured its defective tender within a reasonable time.

195. A chef and her friend were cooking dinner. As the friend handed a knife to the chef, the knife slipped and fell, slicing into the chef's foot. While the chef's foot was being treated at the hospital, the chef contracted a severe infection, which eventually necessitated the amputation of her foot. The chef sued the hospital and her friend in a jurisdiction that applies traditional joint and several liability rules, allows contribution, and uses a pure comparative negligence system. The jury determined that the chef suffered $1 million in damages, and apportioned the fault as follows: 30% to the chef, 55% to the friend, and 15% to the hospital.

How much, if anything, may the chef collect from the hospital, and how much, if anything, may the hospital seek in contribution from the friend?

(A) The chef may collect $150,000 from the hospital, and the hospital may not seek contribution from the friend.
(B) The chef may collect $150,000 from the hospital, and the hospital may seek $150,000 in contribution from the friend.
(C) The chef may collect $700,000 from the hospital, and the hospital may seek $550,000 in contribution from the friend.
(D) The chef may collect $700,000 from the hospital, and the hospital may not seek contribution from the friend.

196. A homeowner held title to her residence in fee simple absolute. During her ownership, the homeowner converted a first floor room into a library. She designed floor-to-ceiling bookcases with elaborate decorative items. She contracted with a carpenter to build and install the bookcases in the room. The bookcases were affixed to the walls of the rooms with screws rather than nails so that they could be more easily removed. She intended to take the bookcases with her if she ever moved.

In the sales brochure that was prepared by the homeowner's real-estate broker and approved of by the homeowner, the room was described as a library, but no specific mention was made of the bookcases.

The contract of sale did not contain a reference to the bookcases. After the contract of sale was entered into, the homeowner had the bookcases removed from the house and repaired the damage to the walls caused by their removal.

On a walk-through of the premises prior to closing, the buyer discovered that the bookcases had been removed. The buyer, after balking at the transfer of the property without the bookcases, agreed to accept the deed but reserved the right to pursue an action regarding the removal of the bookcases.

In the action based on the removal of the bookcases brought by the buyer for money damages, which of the following would not be a strong argument that the specified party could make in support of its position?

(A) The seller argues that the damage done to the room from the removal of the bookcases was repaired.
(B) The seller argues that the seller's subjective intent, at the time of installation, was to remove the bookcases if the house was ever sold.
(C) The buyer argues that the bookcases were specially designed for use in the library.
(D) The buyer argues that the bookcases were important to the function of the room as a library.

197.   A woman met a man at a party at the home of a third person. The woman noticed that the man was wearing an expensive gold watch. As the party was winding down and the woman and man were alone, the woman slipped a sedative into the man's drink. Waiting until the man passed out, the woman then removed the watch from the man's wrist and left the party. Later, the party's host discovered the man asleep, and revived him. When the man discovered that his watch was missing, the man called the police. The man, who lived at home with his parents, had taken the watch from his father's dresser for the evening, without his father's permission.

The woman was arrested and charged with robbery. Can she be convicted of the crime?

(A) Yes, because the woman used force to permanently deprive the man of the watch he was wearing.
(B) Yes, because the taking took place at a dwelling.
(C) No, because the watch belonged to the man's father and the man did not have permission to use it.
(D) No, because the man was unconscious when his watch was taken.

198.   Over the course of one night, an attorney went to three different bars: Bar A, Bar B, and Bar C. The attorney stayed at each bar for roughly equal amounts of time, and each bar served him enough liquor to make him legally intoxicated. At the end of the night, the attorney left Bar C and was driving home erratically. A block away from his home, the attorney lost control of his car, careened into oncoming traffic, and collided with his neighbor's car. The attorney died in the collision, and his neighbor was permanently disfigured. The neighbor sued Bar A in a jurisdiction that has adopted standard dram shop laws. Bar A filed a motion to dismiss the suit for failing to state a claim upon which relief can be granted.

How should the court rule on the motion?

(A) Deny the motion, and order Bar B, Bar C, and the attorney's estate joined as defendants.
(B) Deny the motion, because a reasonable fact finder could determine that the neighbor's injuries were a continuing consequence of Bar A's actions.
(C) Grant the motion, because the attorney's criminal act of driving drunk was a superseding cause that cut off Bar A's liability.
(D) Grant the motion, because Bar A's negligence was not the "but-for" cause of the neighbor's injuries.

199. In a valid contract, the plaintiff promised to pay the defendant $87,000 to fumigate the plaintiff's commercial office building within seven days to stop a major insect infestation. The defendant performed the fumigation, and plaintiff paid the $87,000. Two months later, the plaintiff filed a complaint in the State A federal district court, making three main allegations. First, "Plaintiff is a State Z citizen, Defendant is a State A citizen, the amount in controversy is $87,000, and the court has diversity jurisdiction." Second, "Defendant breached its contract with Plaintiff (copy attached) by failing to render adequate performance, and Plaintiff has been unable to sell his commercial office building." Third, "Plaintiff demands judgment of $87,000, the amount Plaintiff lost as a result of Defendant's breach."

What would be the defendant's best response?

(A) Filing a Rule 12(b) motion to dismiss for lack of subject matter jurisdiction.

(B) Filing a Rule 12(b)(6) motion to dismiss for failure to state a claim upon which relief can be granted.

(C) Filing an answer denying the plaintiff's allegation that the defendant breached the contract.

(D) Filing a motion for summary judgment on the grounds that there is no genuine issue of material fact and that the defendant is entitled to judgment as a matter of law.

200. In a criminal trial for attempted murder, the prosecutor seeks to introduce a statement made by the victim immediately after he was attacked by the defendant. The victim, very seriously injured, shouted the defendant's name and said, "I can't believe you shot me! I'm dying!" At the time of the trial, the victim has mostly recovered from his injuries, but suffered permanent memory loss, has no recollection of the incident at all, and has no recollection of making the statement. The prosecutor seeks to introduce the statement as a dying declaration, but the defendant objects.

Should this statement be admissible under the "dying declaration" exception to the hearsay rules?

(A) No, the statement is not admissible as a dying declaration.

(B) No, because the victim did not die.

(C) Yes, because the victim is unavailable due to his inability to remember.

(D) Yes, because the proceeding in which the statement will be introduced is a criminal trial.

STOP.
IF YOU FINISH BEFORE TIME IS UP, CHECK YOUR WORK ON THIS TEST.

ANSWER KEY

Log in to your course to submit your answers and view detailed answer explanations.

Question	Answer	Subject	Chapter	Section	ID
1	A	Contracts & Sales	Formation Of Contracts	Mutual Assent	2366
2	B	Evidence	Relevance	General Considerations	4321
3	A	Torts	Harms To Personal Property And Land	Nuisance	1425
4	C	Civil Procedure	Choice Of Law: The Erie Doctrine	Determining Applicable State Law	4924
5	D	Real Property	Titles	Conveyance By Will, Trust, And Operation Of Law	1894
6	B	Evidence	Presentation Of Evidence	Mode And Order Of Presentation Of Evidence	618
7	C	Criminal Law	Inchoate Crimes	Conspiracy	167
8	A	Constitutional Law	Procedural Due Process	Procedural Due Process Applied	1390
9	B	Contracts & Sales	Formation Of Contracts	Mutual Assent	2367
10	C	Real Property	Disputes About The Use Of Land	Covenants Running With The Land	2019
11	C	Contracts & Sales	Formation Of Contracts	Defenses To Formation	2370
12	B	Constitutional Law	Intergovernmental Immunities	State Immunity	1393
13	D	Evidence	Presentation Of Evidence	Introduction Of Evidence	3004
14	D	Criminal Procedure	Fifth Amendment Rights And Privileges	Fifth Amendment In The Trial Context	376
15	C	Criminal Law	General Principles	Mens Rea- State Of Mind	168
16	A	Civil Procedure	Subject Matter Jurisdiction	Federal Question Jurisdiction	5010
17	C	Torts	Products Liability	Strict Products Liability	1441
18	C	Civil Procedure	Personal Jurisdiction	In General	4905
19	D	Real Property	Mortgages And Security Interests	Pre-Foreclosure Rights And Duties	2025
20	D	Contracts & Sales	Discharge	Frustration Of Purpose	2383
21	B	Torts	Defenses To Intentional Torts Involving Personal Injury	Self Defense	1437
22	C	Constitutional Law	Freedom Of Expression And Association	Regulation Of Time, Place, And Manner Of Expression	1445
23	D	Civil Procedure	Trial Procedure	Motion For A New Trial	5011
24	B	Evidence	Presentation Of Evidence	Introduction Of Evidence	3050
25	D	Real Property	Titles	Delivery And Recording Of Deed	2004
26	C	Evidence	Presentation Of Evidence	Mode And Order Of Presentation Of Evidence	3039
27	B	Torts	Intentional Torts Involving Personal Injury	Intentional Infliction Of Emotional Distress	1461

Question	Answer	Subject	Chapter	Section	ID
28	A	Contracts & Sales	Formation Of Contracts	Warranties In Sale-Of-Goods Contracts	2369
29	D	Criminal Procedure	Trial	Jury Trial	370
30	C	Constitutional Law	The Powers Of Congress	Other Article I Powers	1396
31	B	Real Property	Titles	Delivery And Recording Of Deed	2001
32	B	Torts	Negligence	Defenses To Negligence	1435
33	A	Real Property	Mortgages And Security Interests	Foreclosure	2024
34	B	Civil Procedure	Subject Matter Jurisdiction	Federal Question Jurisdiction	4897
35	D	Criminal Law	Homicide	Types Of Homicide	170
36	C	Torts	Intentional Torts Involving Personal Injury	Intentional Infliction Of Emotional Distress	1443
37	B	Evidence	Hearsay Exceptions	Declarant's Availability Immaterial	629
38	D	Torts	Strict Liability	Animals	1483
39	D	Civil Procedure	Post-Trial Procedure	Claim Preclusion (Res Judicata)	5012
40	D	Contracts & Sales	Conditions And Performance	Types Of Conditions	2371
41	C	Evidence	Privileges And Other Policy Exclusions	Privileges	622
42	D	Real Property	The Land Sale Contract	Performance	2013
43	B	Constitutional Law	Equal Protection	Quasi-Suspect Classifications	5858
44	B	Contracts & Sales	Formation Of Contracts	Implied-In-Fact Contracts And Quasi-Contracts	2372
45	A	Evidence	Relevance	General Considerations	624
46	B	Constitutional Law	The Powers Of Congress	Power To Enforce The Thirteenth, Fourteenth, And Fifteenth Amendments	1402
47	A	Criminal Procedure	Fourth Amendment: Application To Arrest, Search And Seizure	Arrest: Unreasonable Seizure Of Persons	371
48	A	Real Property	Disputes About The Use Of Land	Covenants Running With The Land	2016
49	C	Contracts & Sales	Statute Of Frauds	Writing Required	2373
50	D	Contracts & Sales	Assignment Of Rights And Delegation Of Duties	Delegation Of Duties	2374
51	C	Torts	Negligence	Vicarious Liability	1481
52	B	Civil Procedure	Personal Jurisdiction	In Personam Jurisdiction	4909
53	C	Constitutional Law	Takings Clause	Types Of Taking	1404
54	D	Civil Procedure	Personal Jurisdiction	In General	4980
55	C	Real Property	Titles	Delivery And Recording Of Deed	1651
56	C	Constitutional Law	Equal Protection	Quasi-Suspect Classifications	1405

Question	Answer	Subject	Chapter	Section	ID
57	D	Evidence	Witnesses	Impeachment	626
58	A	Constitutional Law	State Regulation And Taxation Of Commerce	The Dormant Commerce Clause	1407
59	B	Criminal Law	Other Crimes	Crimes Against Property	171
60	B	Civil Procedure	Personal Jurisdiction	Jurisdiction Over Things	4982
61	B	Criminal Procedure	Fifth Amendment Rights And Privileges	The Privilege Against Compulsory Self-Incrimination	373
62	A	Evidence	Hearsay	What Is Not Hearsay	628
63	C	Contracts & Sales	Breach Of Contract And Remedies	Remedies Under The Ucc	2376
64	D	Evidence	Relevance	Character Evidence	4186
65	B	Real Property	Disputes About The Use Of Land	Easements	2377
66	D	Torts	Products Liability	Strict Products Liability	1439
67	B	Criminal Procedure	Fourth Amendment: Application To Arrest, Search And Seizure	Search And Seizure	375
68	A	Contracts & Sales	Breach Of Contract And Remedies	Anticipatory Repudiation	2378
69	B	Real Property	The Land Sale Contract	Equitable Conversion	2010
70	A	Criminal Law	Other Crimes	Rape And Other Sex Crimes	172
71	B	Civil Procedure	Personal Jurisdiction	In Personam Jurisdiction	5013
72	B	Torts	Defenses To Intentional Torts Involving Personal Injury	Consent	1431
73	A	Constitutional Law	Judicial Power	Source And Scope	1379
74	C	Contracts & Sales	Parol Evidence Rule	Integration	2384
75	A	Real Property	Mortgages And Security Interests	Foreclosure	2043
76	B	Criminal Law	General Principles	Mens Rea- State Of Mind	173
77	C	Evidence	Relevance	Character Evidence	4320
78	B	Criminal Procedure	Sixth Amendment	Ineffective Assistance Of Counsel	372
79	D	Constitutional Law	Equal Protection	General Considerations	1413
80	C	Torts	Negligence	Special Rules Of Liability	1414
81	A	Evidence	Witnesses	Impeachment	632
82	C	Contracts & Sales	Formation Of Contracts	Consideration	2379
83	B	Civil Procedure	Subject Matter Jurisdiction	Diversity Jurisdiction	4895
84	B	Constitutional Law	Prohibited Legislation	Obligation Of Contracts	1395
85	A	Civil Procedure	Subject Matter Jurisdiction	Removal Jurisdiction	5023
86	A	Torts	Negligence	Defenses To Negligence	2385
87	C	Real Property	Titles	Delivery And Recording Of Deed	1608
88	C	Evidence	Relevance	Specific (Bad) Acts	4201

Question	Answer	Subject	Chapter	Section	ID
89	D	Constitutional Law	Privileges And Immunities Clauses	Article Iv	1418
90	A	Torts	Negligence	The Standard Of Care	1457
91	D	Criminal Law	Defenses	Specific Defenses	174
92	D	Civil Procedure	Subject Matter Jurisdiction	Removal Jurisdiction	4921
93	B	Contracts & Sales	Breach Of Contract And Remedies	Remedies Under The Ucc	2381
94	A	Civil Procedure	Subject Matter Jurisdiction	Supplemental Jurisdiction	4916
95	D	Evidence	Presentation Of Evidence	Mode And Order Of Presentation Of Evidence	3037
96	C	Constitutional Law	The Powers Of The President	Domestic Power	1422
97	A	Real Property	Disputes About The Use Of Land	Easements	2015
98	D	Criminal Procedure	Trial	Cruel And Unusual Punishment	384
99	C	Contracts & Sales	Parol Evidence Rule	Integration	2382
100	B	Real Property	Ownership	Present Estates	2026
101	C	Evidence	Hearsay	What Is Hearsay	623
102	C	Criminal Procedure	Sixth Amendment	Applicability: Right To Counsel	380
103	D	Contracts & Sales	Breach Of Contract And Remedies	Remedies: Damages For Breach Of Contract	2386
104	A	Contracts & Sales	Parol Evidence Rule	When The Parol Evidence Rule Is Inapplicable	2387
105	C	Constitutional Law	Freedom Of Expression And Association	Regulation Of Content	1421
106	B	Real Property	Mortgages And Security Interests	Pre-Foreclosure Rights And Duties	2020
107	D	Criminal Law	Other Crimes	Crimes Against Property	177
108	D	Torts	Negligence	Damages	1466
109	A	Constitutional Law	The Powers Of Congress	Power To Enforce The Thirteenth, Fourteenth, And Fifteenth Amendments	1424
110	A	Civil Procedure	Subject Matter Jurisdiction	Supplemental Jurisdiction	4920
111	C	Real Property	The Land Sale Contract	Formation	2007
112	A	Torts	Defenses To Intentional Torts Involving Personal Injury	Consent	1471
113	C	Criminal Law	Homicide	Types Of Homicide	178
114	B	Constitutional Law	Federal Interbranch Relationships	Congressional Limits On The Executive	1426
115	B	Criminal Law	General Principles	Mens Rea- State Of Mind	179
116	C	Contracts & Sales	Breach Of Contract And Remedies	Specific Performance	2388
117	D	Evidence	Witnesses	Impeachment	638
118	B	Torts	Negligence	Vicarious Liability	1475

Question	Answer	Subject	Chapter	Section	ID
119	D	Real Property	Mortgages And Security Interests	Foreclosure	2021
120	D	Constitutional Law	Equal Protection	General Considerations	1429
121	A	Torts	Negligence	Defenses To Negligence	2405
122	B	Civil Procedure	Multiple Parties And Claims	Class Actions	4922
123	A	Real Property	The Land Sale Contract	Formation	2006
124	A	Contracts & Sales	Formation Of Contracts	Mutual Assent	2389
125	D	Criminal Procedure	Post-Trial Considerations	Double Jeopardy	377
126	A	Civil Procedure	Subject Matter Jurisdiction	Federal Question Jurisdiction	4892
127	C	Constitutional Law	The Powers Of Congress	Other Article I Powers	1432
128	A	Evidence	Hearsay	What Is Hearsay	625
129	D	Civil Procedure	Pretrial Procedure And Discovery	Mandatory Disclosures	4936
130	A	Contracts & Sales	Formation Of Contracts	Defenses To Formation	2391
131	C	Real Property	Disputes About The Use Of Land	Easements	2051
132	C	Criminal Law	Other Crimes	Crimes Against Property	180
133	A	Criminal Law	General Principles	Parties To A Crime	181
134	B	Constitutional Law	Federal Preemption Of State Law	Express Preemption	1434
135	B	Civil Procedure	Post-Trial Procedure	Appeals	5014
136	D	Evidence	Relevance	Character Evidence	640
137	C	Real Property	Mortgages And Security Interests	Transfer	2052
138	A	Criminal Procedure	Fourth Amendment: Application To Arrest, Search And Seizure	Search And Seizure	379
139	A	Evidence	Relevance	Character Evidence	4185
140	D	Torts	Negligence	Sharing Liability Among Multiple Defendants	1487
141	B	Constitutional Law	Substantive Due Process	Fundamental Rights	1436
142	A	Contracts & Sales	Formation Of Contracts	Mutual Assent	2392
143	A	Contracts & Sales	Formation Of Contracts	Defenses To Formation	2393
144	B	Real Property	Titles	Adverse Possession	1885
145	D	Civil Procedure	Choice Of Law: The Erie Doctrine	Determining Applicable State Law	5015
146	C	Torts	Negligence	Damages	1394
147	D	Evidence	Presentation Of Evidence	Mode And Order Of Presentation Of Evidence	5910
148	A	Civil Procedure	Personal Jurisdiction	In Personam Jurisdiction	4983
149	D	Torts	Strict Liability	Defenses To Strict Liability	1491
150	C	Real Property	Titles	Delivery And Recording Of Deed	2054

Question	Answer	Subject	Chapter	Section	ID
151	A	Constitutional Law	Privileges And Immunities Clauses	Article Iv	1440
152	C	Criminal Procedure	Pretrial Procedures	Eyewitness Identification Procedures	381
153	A	Evidence	Relevance	Character Evidence	642
154	B	Civil Procedure	Subject Matter Jurisdiction	Diversity Jurisdiction	4908
155	A	Real Property	Landlord And Tenant	Assignment And Subletting	2030
156	C	Contracts & Sales	Third-Party Beneficiary Contracts	Intended And Incidental Beneficiaries	2395
157	B	Contracts & Sales	Discharge	Impracticability	2396
158	D	Torts	Negligence	The Standard Of Care	1497
159	A	Civil Procedure	Personal Jurisdiction	Jurisdiction Over Things	4988
160	A	Constitutional Law	Freedom Of Religion	Free Exercise	1442
161	C	Torts	Defamation, Invasion Of Privacy, And Business Torts	Defamation	1493
162	D	Constitutional Law	Prohibited Legislation	Obligation Of Contracts	1444
163	D	Torts	Intentional Torts Involving Personal Injury	Assault	1463
164	C	Evidence	Presentation Of Evidence	Introduction Of Evidence	3003
165	B	Criminal Law	Inchoate Crimes	Solicitation	166
166	B	Civil Procedure	Personal Jurisdiction	In General	5044
167	B	Evidence	Privileges And Other Policy Exclusions	Public Policy Exclusions	646
168	B	Real Property	Ownership	Future Interests	1889
169	D	Contracts & Sales	Third-Party Beneficiary Contracts	Vesting Of Beneficiary's Rights	2397
170	D	Constitutional Law	State Regulation And Taxation Of Commerce	The Dormant Commerce Clause	1447
171	B	Torts	Defamation, Invasion Of Privacy, And Business Torts	Invasion Of Privacy	1494
172	D	Contracts & Sales	Formation Of Contracts	Defenses To Enforcement	2398
173	A	Evidence	Hearsay	What Is Not Hearsay	2399
174	A	Constitutional Law	Equal Protection	General Considerations	1449
175	D	Civil Procedure	Pretrial Procedure And Discovery	Discovery Scope And Limits	5016
176	D	Contracts & Sales	Formation Of Contracts	Mutual Assent	2400
177	D	Torts	Negligence	Vicarious Liability	1495
178	C	Criminal Procedure	Fourth Amendment: Application To Arrest, Search And Seizure	Search And Seizure	383
179	C	Evidence	Relevance	Specific (Bad) Acts	3021
180	D	Constitutional Law	Judicial Power	Judicial Review In Operation	1452
181	A	Real Property	Ownership	Concurrent Estates	2028
182	A	Torts	Negligence	The Standard Of Care	1459
183	A	Criminal Procedure	Post-Trial Considerations	Sentencing	2401

Question	Answer	Subject	Chapter	Section	ID
184	A	Contracts & Sales	Conditions And Performance	Satisfaction Of Conditions	2402
185	B	Evidence	Relevance	General Considerations	3008
186	B	Constitutional Law	Freedom Of Expression And Association	Regulation Of Content	1454
187	C	Real Property	Landlord And Tenant	Duties Of Landlord	2029
188	C	Criminal Law	Homicide	Types Of Homicide	182
189	A	Civil Procedure	Multiple Parties And Claims	Intervention	5017
190	D	Constitutional Law	The Powers Of Congress	Commerce	1456
191	B	Real Property	Mortgages And Security Interests	Foreclosure	4265
192	A	Torts	Negligence	Breach Of Duty	1498
193	C	Evidence	Hearsay	What Is Not Hearsay	649
194	B	Contracts & Sales	Breach Of Contract And Remedies	Remedies Under The Ucc	2404
195	C	Torts	Negligence	Sharing Liability Among Multiple Defendants	1499
196	B	Real Property	Disputes About The Use Of Land	Fixtures	1588
197	A	Criminal Law	Other Crimes	Crimes Against Property	175
198	B	Torts	Negligence	Causation	1500
199	B	Civil Procedure	Pleadings	Motions Against The Complaint	5018
200	A	Evidence	Hearsay Exceptions	Declarant Unavailable As A Witness	650

Themis
Bar Review

Practice Exam Four

Practice Exam Four

Start Time:_____

End Time:_____

1. Ⓐ Ⓑ Ⓒ Ⓓ
2. Ⓐ Ⓑ Ⓒ Ⓓ
3. Ⓐ Ⓑ Ⓒ Ⓓ
4. Ⓐ Ⓑ Ⓒ Ⓓ
5. Ⓐ Ⓑ Ⓒ Ⓓ
6. Ⓐ Ⓑ Ⓒ Ⓓ
7. Ⓐ Ⓑ Ⓒ Ⓓ
8. Ⓐ Ⓑ Ⓒ Ⓓ
9. Ⓐ Ⓑ Ⓒ Ⓓ
10. Ⓐ Ⓑ Ⓒ Ⓓ
11. Ⓐ Ⓑ Ⓒ Ⓓ
12. Ⓐ Ⓑ Ⓒ Ⓓ
13. Ⓐ Ⓑ Ⓒ Ⓓ
14. Ⓐ Ⓑ Ⓒ Ⓓ
15. Ⓐ Ⓑ Ⓒ Ⓓ
16. Ⓐ Ⓑ Ⓒ Ⓓ
17. Ⓐ Ⓑ Ⓒ Ⓓ
18. Ⓐ Ⓑ Ⓒ Ⓓ
19. Ⓐ Ⓑ Ⓒ Ⓓ
20. Ⓐ Ⓑ Ⓒ Ⓓ
21. Ⓐ Ⓑ Ⓒ Ⓓ
22. Ⓐ Ⓑ Ⓒ Ⓓ
23. Ⓐ Ⓑ Ⓒ Ⓓ
24. Ⓐ Ⓑ Ⓒ Ⓓ
25. Ⓐ Ⓑ Ⓒ Ⓓ

26. Ⓐ Ⓑ Ⓒ Ⓓ
27. Ⓐ Ⓑ Ⓒ Ⓓ
28. Ⓐ Ⓑ Ⓒ Ⓓ
29. Ⓐ Ⓑ Ⓒ Ⓓ
30. Ⓐ Ⓑ Ⓒ Ⓓ
31. Ⓐ Ⓑ Ⓒ Ⓓ
32. Ⓐ Ⓑ Ⓒ Ⓓ
33. Ⓐ Ⓑ Ⓒ Ⓓ
34. Ⓐ Ⓑ Ⓒ Ⓓ
35. Ⓐ Ⓑ Ⓒ Ⓓ
36. Ⓐ Ⓑ Ⓒ Ⓓ
37. Ⓐ Ⓑ Ⓒ Ⓓ
38. Ⓐ Ⓑ Ⓒ Ⓓ
39. Ⓐ Ⓑ Ⓒ Ⓓ
40. Ⓐ Ⓑ Ⓒ Ⓓ
41. Ⓐ Ⓑ Ⓒ Ⓓ
42. Ⓐ Ⓑ Ⓒ Ⓓ
43. Ⓐ Ⓑ Ⓒ Ⓓ
44. Ⓐ Ⓑ Ⓒ Ⓓ
45. Ⓐ Ⓑ Ⓒ Ⓓ
46. Ⓐ Ⓑ Ⓒ Ⓓ
47. Ⓐ Ⓑ Ⓒ Ⓓ
48. Ⓐ Ⓑ Ⓒ Ⓓ
49. Ⓐ Ⓑ Ⓒ Ⓓ
50. Ⓐ Ⓑ Ⓒ Ⓓ

51. Ⓐ Ⓑ Ⓒ Ⓓ
52. Ⓐ Ⓑ Ⓒ Ⓓ
53. Ⓐ Ⓑ Ⓒ Ⓓ
54. Ⓐ Ⓑ Ⓒ Ⓓ
55. Ⓐ Ⓑ Ⓒ Ⓓ
56. Ⓐ Ⓑ Ⓒ Ⓓ
57. Ⓐ Ⓑ Ⓒ Ⓓ
58. Ⓐ Ⓑ Ⓒ Ⓓ
59. Ⓐ Ⓑ Ⓒ Ⓓ
60. Ⓐ Ⓑ Ⓒ Ⓓ
61. Ⓐ Ⓑ Ⓒ Ⓓ
62. Ⓐ Ⓑ Ⓒ Ⓓ
63. Ⓐ Ⓑ Ⓒ Ⓓ
64. Ⓐ Ⓑ Ⓒ Ⓓ
65. Ⓐ Ⓑ Ⓒ Ⓓ
66. Ⓐ Ⓑ Ⓒ Ⓓ
67. Ⓐ Ⓑ Ⓒ Ⓓ
68. Ⓐ Ⓑ Ⓒ Ⓓ
69. Ⓐ Ⓑ Ⓒ Ⓓ
70. Ⓐ Ⓑ Ⓒ Ⓓ
71. Ⓐ Ⓑ Ⓒ Ⓓ
72. Ⓐ Ⓑ Ⓒ Ⓓ
73. Ⓐ Ⓑ Ⓒ Ⓓ
74. Ⓐ Ⓑ Ⓒ Ⓓ
75. Ⓐ Ⓑ Ⓒ Ⓓ

76. Ⓐ Ⓑ Ⓒ Ⓓ
77. Ⓐ Ⓑ Ⓒ Ⓓ
78. Ⓐ Ⓑ Ⓒ Ⓓ
79. Ⓐ Ⓑ Ⓒ Ⓓ
80. Ⓐ Ⓑ Ⓒ Ⓓ
81. Ⓐ Ⓑ Ⓒ Ⓓ
82. Ⓐ Ⓑ Ⓒ Ⓓ
83. Ⓐ Ⓑ Ⓒ Ⓓ
84. Ⓐ Ⓑ Ⓒ Ⓓ
85. Ⓐ Ⓑ Ⓒ Ⓓ
86. Ⓐ Ⓑ Ⓒ Ⓓ
87. Ⓐ Ⓑ Ⓒ Ⓓ
88. Ⓐ Ⓑ Ⓒ Ⓓ
89. Ⓐ Ⓑ Ⓒ Ⓓ
90. Ⓐ Ⓑ Ⓒ Ⓓ
91. Ⓐ Ⓑ Ⓒ Ⓓ
92. Ⓐ Ⓑ Ⓒ Ⓓ
93. Ⓐ Ⓑ Ⓒ Ⓓ
94. Ⓐ Ⓑ Ⓒ Ⓓ
95. Ⓐ Ⓑ Ⓒ Ⓓ
96. Ⓐ Ⓑ Ⓒ Ⓓ
97. Ⓐ Ⓑ Ⓒ Ⓓ
98. Ⓐ Ⓑ Ⓒ Ⓓ
99. Ⓐ Ⓑ Ⓒ Ⓓ
100. Ⓐ Ⓑ Ⓒ Ⓓ

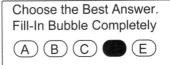
Themis
BarReview

PRACTICE EXAM FOUR

TIME: THREE HOURS

Welcome to Practice Exam Four. This exam consists of 100 questions covering all subject areas tested on the MBE. This exam will take approximately three hours (an average of 1.8 minutes per question). After you have completed this exam, log in to your course to submit your answers, view detailed answer explanations, and compare your performance to other Themis students.

1. The prosecutor called a witness to the stand at a trial for armed robbery. The prosecutor sought to question the witness about the defendant's statements during the armed robbery. The witness was present at the scene of the crime and had video recorded the entire incident on his cellular phone, although the video and audio quality was poor. The prosecutor did not introduce the witness's video recording into evidence.

Is the witness's testimony admissible?

(A) No, because the defendant's statements constitute hearsay not within any exception.

(B) No, because the best evidence rule requires the admission of the video recording.

(C) Yes, because the witness had personal knowledge of the defendant's statements.

(D) Yes, because the witness may testify as to the contents of the video recording.

2. An accountant made a gift of rental property to her son. Subsequently, the accountant, desperate for money, sold the rental property to a buyer. Prior to the sale, the accountant, who kept the books for the property, supplied the buyer with the records that indicated the rent received and the expense associated with the property. The accountant also fraudulently stated that her son was managing the property for her. The buyer did not directly question the son, who was unaware of the accountant's actions with regard to the property. The day after the sale, the buyer and son met by chance. The son learned of his mother's sale of the property and the buyer learned of the gift of the property to the son. The next day the buyer properly recorded her deed, but not before the son had properly recorded his donative deed. The accountant vanished with the sale proceeds. The recording act of the jurisdiction reads: "No conveyance or mortgage of real property shall be good against subsequent purchasers for value and without notice unless the same be recorded according to law."

In an action to determine ownership of the rental property between the buyer and the son, will the buyer be successful?

(A) Yes, because the son received the property as a donee.

(B) Yes, because the buyer purchased the property without notice of the prior transfer.

(C) No, because the son recorded his deed first.

(D) No, because the buyer learned of the prior transfer before recording his deed.

3.   A manufacturer of plywood ordered an adhesive from a commercial seller. The seller shipped the adhesive with an invoice. Printed on the invoice was a notice that limited the manufacturer's right to bring any action arising from the sale to one year after the accrual of the cause of action. The manufacturer paid the invoice without objection. The statutory period for bringing a cause of action based on sale of goods contracts is four years. The manufacturer filed a suit that arose from the contract two years after the cause of action accrued.

Can the seller successfully challenge the suit as time barred?

(A)   Yes, because the manufacturer failed to object to the invoice notice.
(B)   Yes, because merchants are free to set whatever limitations period for bringing an action that arises from a sale of goods.
(C)   No, because the one-year limitation term is not part of the contract.
(D)   No, because the statutory limitations period cannot be shortened.

4.   A state law provided that before an abortion may be performed a woman must (a) have a consultation with a physician, who should try to persuade the woman to have her baby, and (b) wait another 24 hours before seeking an abortion. A woman in the middle of her first trimester of pregnancy challenges the constitutionality of the law.

Would a court be likely to strike down this law?

(A)   No, because the state has a rational basis for requiring the consultation and 24-hour waiting period.
(B)   No, because the state's purpose is not to hinder women's right to choose abortion, but merely to persuade women to choose birth and to ensure that their decisions are deliberate.
(C)   Yes, because the law violates the woman's liberty interest in abortion protected by the Fourteenth Amendment.
(D)   Yes, because a state's power to regulate abortions does not include the power to impose waiting periods.

5. A wealthy businessman contracted with an animal trainer to perform a show with live animals, including a lion, at the businessman's New Year's Eve party for $100,000. On the day of the party, the trainer called the businessman and informed him that she could not perform a show with a lion that evening, but could do a show with a white tiger instead. However, she refused to perform unless the businessman agreed to pay her $125,000. The businessman agreed. The show was a spectacular success with the guests. After the show, the businessman paid the trainer $100,000. The trainer filed a breach of contract action against the businessman for $25,000.

Is the trainer likely to prevail?

(A) Yes, because there was consideration for the contract modification.

(B) Yes, because, since the show was a success, the trainer substantially performed the contract.

(C) No, because the trainer had a pre-existing duty to perform the contract for $100,000.

(D) No, because a threat to breach a contract unless an additional amount is paid constitutes duress.

6. A man went to visit his grandfather, who was very ill. The grandfather and grandson reminisced about hunting trips they had taken on property owned by the grandfather. The grandfather told his grandson that he wanted him to have the property after the grandfather died. The grandson was unaware that his grandfather had sold the property earlier that month to a rancher who lived on an adjacent piece of property. Shortly after the grandfather died, the grandson planned a short trip to look over the property. The rancher, spotting the grandson, told the grandson that he now owned the land, and ordered the grandson to leave immediately. The grandson called the rancher a liar and refused to leave. The rancher went back to his house to think over his options. By the time he decided to report the grandson, however, the grandson had left to catch his flight home. The rancher has sued the grandson for trespass.

Is the rancher likely to succeed in his claim against the grandson?

(A) No, because the grandson honestly believed he owned the property.

(B) No, because the rancher cannot prove he suffered damages.

(C) Yes, because the grandson refused to leave after being told he did not own the land.

(D) Yes, because mistake of fact is not a defense to a trespass to land claim.

7.   A defendant entered a guilty plea in state court for conduct stemming from a single incident in which the defendant broke into the victim's apartment with the intent of committing a rape and did so.   The judge entered a judgment against the defendant on both the burglary and rape charges.   Pursuant to state law, sentences for two or more crimes must run concurrently unless the judge finds that the crime was an indication of the defendant's willingness to commit more than one crime. The judge, making such a finding with respect to burglary, ordered that the sentences for burglary and rape run consecutively. The defendant filed an appeal, challenging the consecutive sentences as unconstitutional.

Should the court rule in the defendant's favor?

   (A)   No, because a judge may determine whether a defendant's sentences run consecutively.
   (B)   No, because, where a defendant enters a guilty plea, the defendant has waived his right to a trial by jury, and the judge may find a fact that results in the enhancement of the defendant's sentence.
   (C)   Yes, because the Double Jeopardy Clause of the Fifth Amendment as applied to the states through the Fourteenth Amendment prohibits punishment for both a crime and its lesser included offense.
   (D)   Yes, because a jury, not a judge, must find any fact essential to a defendant's punishment.

8.   A professional assassin was hired to kill a man.   The assassin used locksmith tools to silently break open the back door of the man's house in the middle of the night.   He then went upstairs to the man's bedroom and saw the man seemingly asleep on his stomach.   The assassin took out a gun fitted with a silencer, shot the man twice in the head, and turned to leave the room. As the assassin was leaving the room, he noticed a large diamond ring on the man's dresser; he took the ring and left the house.   Unbeknownst to the assassin, the man had suffered a heart attack several hours before the break-in, and was already dead before the shooting.

The crimes below are listed in descending order of seriousness.   What is the most serious crime for which the assassin can be convicted?

   (A)   Murder
   (B)   Attempted murder
   (C)   Burglary
   (D)   Larceny

9.   A defendant was charged with attempted murder. The defendant had previously served a ten-year prison sentence after being convicted of embezzlement in a trial in which the attempted murder victim was the primary witness. The prosecution alleged that, shortly after the defendant was released from prison, the defendant shot at the victim in revenge for the victim's testimony at the prior trial. Before trial, the prosecution notified the defendant that it intended to introduce evidence that the defendant had been convicted of embezzlement. The defendant, who will not testify at his current trial, objected to the introduction of this evidence regarding his previous conviction. At a pre-trial evidentiary hearing, the judge found that the probative value of the conviction outweighed, but not substantially so, its prejudicial effect.

Is the evidence of the prior conviction likely to be admitted?

(A)   No, because the probative value of the embezzlement conviction did not substantially outweigh its prejudicial effect.

(B)   No, because the prior crime was committed more than 10 years ago.

(C)   Yes, because the evidence of the defendant's prior conviction is relevant to show that the defendant acted in conformity with his criminal nature in attempting to murder the witness from his prior trial.

(D)   Yes, because the evidence of the prior conviction demonstrates motive.

10.   A police officer saw an automobile parked on the right side of a major highway with its hazard lights blinking. Upon approaching the vehicle, the officer found a man sitting behind the steering wheel holding the vehicle's keys. The man told the officer that the vehicle had run out of gas, that he had just returned from obtaining gas, and that he was now ready to leave. The officer believed that the man's appearance and behavior were consistent with the use of the stimulant methamphetamine and therefore asked the man for his driver's license and registration. The man was able to produce a valid license, but no registration, claiming that the vehicle had been borrowed from a friend. The officer then asked the man if he would consent to a search of the vehicle and the man agreed to the search. The officer ordered the man to step out of the vehicle and stand with his hands on the hood of the officer's police cruiser while he conducted the search of the vehicle. The search revealed a small plastic bag under the driver's seat that the officer believed to contain methamphetamine. On questioning by the officer, the man admitted that the bag belonged to him and was immediately arrested. At no point during this exchange did the officer provide the man with Miranda warnings. The bag was subsequently found to contain methamphetamine and the man was charged with criminal possession of a controlled substance.

On the man's pre-trial motion to suppress his admission about the bag belonging to him, the court should find that the statement:

(A)   Should not be suppressed because the man consented to the search of the vehicle.

(B)   Should not be suppressed if the police officer had probable cause to search the vehicle.

(C)   Should be suppressed if it is found that the plastic bag was not in "plain view" of the police officer.

(D)   Should be suppressed if the man is found to have been in custody for purposes of the Fifth Amendment at the time he was questioned by the officer about the bag.

11. A widower who owned his residence in fee simple absolute contracted to sell it to a couple. The contract did not require either party to acquire or maintain casualty insurance on the premises, but the widower had a casualty insurance policy in force. About a month before the closing date, the widower, who had remained in the residence, died. About a week after his death, the residence was seriously damaged by a large tree falling on the residence due to a windstorm. As a result of the casualty, the widower's estate has received a payment from the insurer. The jurisdiction has adopted the doctrine of equitable conversion.

In an action brought by the widower's estate to enforce the contract, what is the likely outcome?

(A) The couple cannot be compelled to purchase the residence, because the doctrine of equitable conversion does not apply to residential transactions.

(B) The couple can be compelled to purchase the residence, but they are entitled to an offset in the amount of the insurance proceeds against the purchase price.

(C) The widower's estate is entitled to retain the proceeds and recover the full purchase price from the couple, because the widower did not have duty to insure the residence.

(D) The widower's estate is entitled to retain the proceeds but cannot compel the couple to purchase the residence, because the death of the widower terminated the contract.

12. A plaintiff initiated a negligence suit in federal district court against a defendant based on an automobile accident. The accident occurred as the defendant, tired from a long trip, was driving through a state to reach his home in a neighboring state. The forum court, in a state with two federal districts, was located in the eastern district. The accident occurred in the western district of this state. The defendant, who is a citizen of a foreign country but is also a lawful, permanent resident of the United States, filed a timely motion to dismiss the action for lack of subject-matter jurisdiction. The court properly rejected the motion. In his answer, the defendant raised the defense of improper venue.

The plaintiff contemplates making the following replies; which correctly reflects the law?

(A) Venue is proper because an alien may be sued in any judicial district.

(B) Venue is proper because the accident occurred in the forum state.

(C) Because the court has ruled that it has subject-matter jurisdiction over the suit, venue is also proper.

(D) The defendant waived this defense by failing to assert it in his motion to dismiss.

13. A defendant was charged with the statutory rape of an underage victim. In the jurisdiction, statutory rape is a strict liability crime defined as sexual intercourse with an individual under the age of 18. The defendant filed a timely motion of intent to offer evidence that the alleged victim had engaged in consensual sexual activity with a third party in order to show that the alleged victim consented to sex with the defendant. The prosecutor objected to the introduction of this evidence.

Should the court permit the defendant to introduce this evidence at trial?

(A) Yes, because the evidence is probative of the alleged victim's willingness to engage in sexual intercourse with the defendant.

(B) Yes, because evidence of a victim's consent to sexual intercourse is admissible as an exception to the "rape shield" rule.

(C) No, because the evidence is not relevant.

(D) No, because evidence of a victim's past sexual conduct is never admissible in rape cases.

14. The State Department issued a travel warning advising Americans to abstain from travel to a specific foreign country because the country was coping with a deadly outbreak of a newly discovered influenza strain. Despite the warnings, more Americans traveled to the foreign country because the travel warning led to a drastic decrease in airline fees and other travel expenses. In response, Congress passed the "Outbreak Prevention Act," which expressly limits travel to specific destinations in the foreign country for six months, which corresponds with the end of the influenza season. The Act does not explicitly ban travel to the entire foreign country for the six-month period but does ban travel to specific cities hit hardest by the outbreak.

Does this act violate the right to travel?

(A) Yes, because the right to travel is a fundamental right.

(B) Yes, because the language in the Act is not narrowly tailored.

(C) No, because there is no fundamental right to travel internationally.

(D) No, because the prevention of illness represents the required compelling interest.

15. A plaintiff has an extreme aversion to any physical contact, especially with strangers. As a result, he tries very hard to avoid circumstances under which he might be touched. Recently, when the plaintiff was walking down the street, the defendant, a friendly old man, approached the plaintiff to ask directions. The plaintiff leaped back, concerned that the man might touch him. Laughing at what he perceived to be the plaintiff's jumpiness, the man reached out his hand and patted the plaintiff on the shoulder, saying, "Calm down there, Sonny. I don't bite!" Shuddering at the unwanted contact, the plaintiff wrenched away, causing what turned out to be a severe back injury. The plaintiff brought a suit for battery against the man in a jurisdiction that applies the "single intent" rule.

If the plaintiff's claim is unsuccessful, what would be the most likely reason?

(A) The man did not intend to do him any physical injury.
(B) The harm was much worse than could have been anticipated.
(C) Being patted on the shoulder is not offensive to a reasonable person.
(D) The plaintiff explicitly consented to being patted on the shoulder.

16. A plaintiff brought an action against a defendant in federal district court sitting in diversity jurisdiction for civil damages resulting from an alleged battery by the defendant. By agreement of the parties, the case was tried by the court without a jury. The plaintiff presented a witness who testified that the defendant had hit the plaintiff with no provocation. The defendant presented two other witnesses, who each testified that the plaintiff had threatened the defendant prior to the defendant striking the plaintiff. The trial judge found in favor of the plaintiff, specifically finding that the testimony of the plaintiff's witness was more persuasive to her than the testimony of the two defense witnesses. On appeal, a three-judge panel of the court of appeals reviewed the trial transcript. The appellate judges all, in good faith, agreed that the testimony of the two defense witnesses was more persuasive than the testimony of the plaintiff's witness and that it is likely that the trial judge erred in her findings. There are no other issues of fact or law in the case.

Should the court of appeals overturn the trial court's decision?

(A) Yes, because they reviewed the transcript de novo for factual errors and believed that the trial judge was incorrect in her ruling.
(B) Yes, because they would be overturning a finding of law, not fact.
(C) No, because the appellate court cannot consider factual findings by the trial court judge on appeal.
(D) No, because they would be overturning a finding of fact, not law.

17. A retailer from State A entered into a contract with a wholesaler from State B for the purchase and delivery of various sporting goods. The contract was executed in State A. Immediately before the delivery date, the wholesaler informed the retailer that he would no longer be able to deliver the sporting goods at the agreed-upon price. The retailer subsequently brought an action against the wholesaler in federal district court in State C for breach of contract, alleging $75,000 in damages. The retailer hired a process server who left the summons and complaint under the front door of the wholesaler's home. In his answer to the complaint, the wholesaler specifically denied each of the retailer's allegations. At the conclusion of discovery, the wholesaler filed a motion to dismiss.

Which ground may the wholesaler properly raise in his motion to dismiss?

(A) Lack of subject matter jurisdiction.
(B) Insufficient service of process.
(C) Improper venue.
(D) Lack of personal jurisdiction.

18. While working on an addition to a residence, a carpenter took an expensive necklace from the owner's bedroom. The owner walked into the bedroom from an adjoining bathroom as the carpenter was slipping the necklace into his pocket. The carpenter exited the bedroom and fled the premises in his truck. As the carpenter drove away, the owner called the police. Notified of the theft by a police dispatcher, a nearby patrolman spotted the carpenter and gave chase. After several miles, the carpenter abandoned his truck and headed into a wooded area. The patrolman called for backup. Sometime later, a police helicopter flew over the area in an attempt to locate the carpenter who, by that time, was several miles away, having coffee at a convenience store. The helicopter developed mechanical problems and crashed, killing the helicopter pilot. Later, the carpenter was apprehended and charged with felony murder of the helicopter pilot.

Which of the following, if established, would not be a defense to the charge?

(A) The helicopter pilot's death was not causally connected to the carpenter's felony.
(B) The helicopter pilot's death did not occur during the commission of the felony.
(C) The carpenter did not commit an inherently dangerous felony.
(D) The carpenter did not act maliciously with regard to the death of the helicopter pilot.

19. A homeowner hired a contractor to build a retaining wall on the west side of the homeowner's property. The contractor built the wall to the homeowner's specifications. However, the wall soon began to show signs of cracking and bulging. The homeowner noticed the cracking and bulging but did nothing about it. Several weeks later, the wall collapsed, destroying a portion of the homeowner's house. The homeowner sued the contractor. A jury determined that the contractor was partially at fault because the construction was shoddy, and that the homeowner was partially at fault because he should have taken action to repair the wall. The jury concluded that the contractor and homeowner were each 50 percent at fault.

Will the homeowner be able to collect any damages from the contractor?

(A) No, because the homeowner failed to mitigate damages after noticing that the wall was showing signs of strain.

(B) No, because the homeowner was equally at fault for the resulting damages.

(C) Yes, because the contractor was strictly liable for the wall collapse.

(D) Yes, because the contractor was at least partially liable for the collapse.

20. A farmer owned a large tract of land that he subdivided into two adjacent parcels. The farmer's house was situated on the north parcel, which had direct access to a state highway. The south parcel was undeveloped and did not have access to the highway, although it was accessible by a local road. To make the south parcel marketable, the farmer executed and recorded an easement across the western edge of the north parcel so that the south parcel would have direct access to the state highway. The farmer later sold the south parcel to a writer, who subsequently built a house and an access road to the state highway across the western edge of the north parcel. The farmer and writer lived as neighbors for twenty years and became close friends. When the farmer died, he devised the north parcel in his will "to the writer, for life, and then to my nephew." The writer moved into the farmer's former residence and did not use the access road again. When the writer died fifteen years later, his sister inherited the south parcel. She did not live on the south parcel and did not use the access road to the highway when she visited the property, but instead accessed it via the local road. The farmer's nephew did not visit the north parcel for several years until he moved into the farmer's prior residence. When he moved in, the nephew blocked the access road from the south parcel to the state highway. Upon discovering this, the sister filed suit against the nephew and requested an injunction that would allow her to use the access road to the state highway.

Will the sister prevail in her suit against the nephew?

(A) Yes, because the access road constituted an express easement.

(B) Yes, because the access road constituted an easement by necessity.

(C) No, because the easement merged into the underlying estate when the writer was bequeathed the north parcel in the farmer's will.

(D) No, because the easement had been abandoned.

21. An inmate in state prison filed a complaint against a state prosecutor, alleging that the prosecutor had violated the inmate's constitutional rights in obtaining a conviction against him. Ten days after being served with the complaint, the defendant filed a motion to dismiss under Rule 12(b)(6), arguing that he was immune from suit. Five days later, the plaintiff filed an amended pleading, adding certain factual allegations to his original pleading. The judge reviewed the complaint as amended, and determined that the complaint failed to state a claim upon which relief could be granted and that the additional allegations in the proposed amendment did not save the complaint from dismissal.

Was the plaintiff entitled to amend his complaint?

(A) No, because the plaintiff lost his right to amend his pleading after the defendant filed a motion to dismiss.

(B) No, because the plaintiff's amendment to his complaint would have been futile.

(C) Yes, because the plaintiff had the right to amend his complaint once as of right any time before the complaint was dismissed.

(D) Yes, because the plaintiff had the right to amend his complaint as of right once within 21 days of being served with the motion.

22. A farmer was tried for the death of a farmhand whom the farmer ran over with a combine. The jury unanimously found that the farmer acted with reckless indifference to the safety of the farmhand in operating the combine, though they did not determine that the farmer had intentionally run over the farmhand with the combine.

The crimes below are listed in ascending order of seriousness. What is the most serious crime for which the farmer is likely to be convicted?

(A) Involuntary manslaughter.
(B) Voluntary manslaughter.
(C) Depraved heart murder.
(D) Premeditated murder.

23. In a civil action brought in federal district court, the judge conducted voir dire of the prospective jurors. The judge refused to permit either attorney to directly question the prospective jurors. The judge did permit the attorney for each party to submit questions for her to ask the prospective jurors, but refused to ask particular questions that she found to be improper.

Has the judge conducted voir dire in accordance with the federal rules?

(A) Yes, because the judge gave each party's attorney the opportunity to submit questions to be asked of the prospective jurors.

(B) Yes, because only the judge may examine prospective jurors.

(C) No, because the judge did not permit each party's attorney to directly question the prospective jurors.

(D) No, because the judge refused to ask particular questions submitted by the attorneys.

24. A supermarket owned and operated a box baler, a device that compresses large cardboard boxes for compact disposal. The box baler was located outdoors, in back of the supermarket. An applicable state law requires that all operational box balers be equipped with an automatic shut-off feature in order to prevent serious injury to the operator or other user of the baler. The supermarket's box baler was not equipped with the feature. A man was walking his dog on the supermarket's property when he suddenly lost control of the dog. The dog ran to the back of the supermarket and jumped into the box baler, which was in the middle of its compression cycle. The dog's leg was crushed by the box baler before the store employee who was operating the machine could turn it off. The dog's owner sued the supermarket for the costs of veterinary care, and produced expert testimony that the dog's leg would not have been crushed had the box baler been equipped with an automatic shut-off feature.

If the dog's owner files a motion for summary judgment, how should the court rule on the motion?

(A) Grant the motion, because the box baler statute conclusively establishes liability.

(B) Grant the motion, because the supermarket is strictly liable for the dog's injury.

(C) Deny the motion, because a reasonable fact finder could conclude that the store was not negligent.

(D) Deny the motion, because the owner did not establish that he suffered a physical harm.

25.   A guest at a party becomes enraged over the host's advances towards the guest's wife. Threatening to burn down the host's home, the guest sets a chair on fire.   In addition to consuming the chair, the fire causes extensive smoke damage to the room before it is put out.

The guest is charged with common-law arson. Should he be convicted?

(A)   No, because the fire did not damage the home.

(B)   No, because the guest did not enter the home with the intent to set it on fire.

(C)   Yes, because the structure was the host's home.

(D)   Yes, because the guest had ill will towards the host.

26.   A number of immigrants from a South American country had settled in a U.S. city. Most of the immigrants were legal U.S. residents. After the economy declined and the unemployment rate in the region increased, tensions between ethnic groups in the area arose. The city council passed an ordinance that prohibited a non-citizen from serving on the city's police force. A legal U.S. resident, who was not a U.S. citizen, applied for a position on the police force and was denied based on the ordinance. He sued the city on Equal Protection grounds.

What statement most accurately describes the burden of proof?

(A)   The applicant must show that the ordinance is not rationally related to a legitimate state interest.

(B)   The applicant must show that the ordinance is not the least restrictive means to achieve a compelling government interest.

(C)   The city must show that the law is substantially related to a legitimate government interest.

(D)   The city must show that the ordinance is the least restrictive means to achieve a compelling government interest.

27. A plaintiff filed a complaint against his former employer in federal court, alleging that the plaintiff had been terminated based on his race in violation of federal law. The complaint included a short and plain statement of the plaintiff's claim and the facts upon which it was based, but not detailed factual allegations. Ten days after the complaint was filed, the defendant filed an answer. The following day, the defendant filed a motion to dismiss the complaint, asserting that the plaintiff had failed to state a claim upon which relief could be granted. The defendant attached to the motion an affidavit from the plaintiff's former supervisor stating that the plaintiff was terminated based upon his performance and described an incident in which the plaintiff made a mistake that caused the employer to lose an important customer. The court granted the motion to dismiss, noting that the facts described in the affidavit undermined the plaintiff's claims.

Was the court's ruling granting the motion to dismiss proper?

(A) No, because the defendant waived any objection based on the pleadings by filing an answer.

(B) No, because the court considered matters outside the pleadings.

(C) Yes, because the plaintiff did not state with particularity the circumstances constituting discrimination.

(D) Yes, because the motion included a credible affidavit with facts that undermined the plaintiff's claims.

28. A diamond wholesaler had a long-standing relationship with a retail jeweler in the community. The wholesaler had recently received a shipment of exquisite diamonds that he wished to show the jeweler. The wholesaler offered to sell the jeweler any one of five exquisite diamonds for $4,000. The jeweler agreed and the jeweler and the wholesaler entered into a signed, written agreement containing the agreed-upon terms. The jeweler informed the wholesaler that he would need to take some time in making the selection and would provide his decision in a couple of days. Eager to have the sale promptly completed and to foster a continuing relationship with the jeweler, the wholesaler sent the jeweler a signed letter the next day stating that the jeweler could choose any two of the five exquisite diamonds. When the jeweler arrived at the wholesaler's business to select two of the diamonds, the wholesaler only permitted the jeweler to choose one.

Can the jeweler introduce evidence of the signed letter in an action against the wholesaler?

(A) Yes, because the written agreement was a partial integration.

(B) Yes, because the wholesaler's letter was sent after the original contract was executed.

(C) No, because the parties' agreement was fully integrated.

(D) No, because the letter contradicts the terms of the written agreement.

29. A lamp retailer contacted an electronics manufacturer about purchasing some wiring. The electronics manufacturer replied that the wiring would cost $20/yard. The retailer replied that it was willing to pay $10/yard as long as the wiring was copper. After several emails back and forth, they executed a contract in writing by email. The contract specified that the manufacturer would provide 2000 yards of wiring to the retailer for $13/yard. No mention was made of the wiring material.

The manufacturer shipped the retailer 2000 yards of aluminum wiring. When the retailer objected, saying he was paying for copper wiring, the manufacturer replied that the copper wiring would cost $30/yard.

The retailer sued, claiming that the manufacturer had breached the agreement to sell copper wiring for $13/yard.

Will the court likely allow the retailer to introduce into evidence the emails specifying copper wiring?

(A) Yes, because the emails are evidence of how a term within the contract should be interpreted.
(B) Yes, because the parties did not intend for the contract to be a total integration.
(C) No, because the emails were written before the final contract was executed.
(D) No, because the contract does not make any mention of specific wiring material.

30. The electronic security devices at many national landmarks, parks, and historical federal buildings across the country were outdated and ineffective. Due to the resulting increase in national security risks at these tourist locations, Congress enacted a federal statute creating an excise tax of 10 cents on all electronic devices purchased in the country. The purchase of electronic devices among the various states is not directly proportional to the population of each state. The tax was imposed solely to raise money to replace the outdated electronic security devices.

Is the tax constitutional?

(A) Yes, because it has a reasonable relation to revenue production.
(B) Yes, because it is necessary to a compelling governmental interest.
(C) No, because it violates the uniformity requirement of the Constitution.
(D) No, because it is an impermissible direct tax.

31. An indigent defendant was convicted of violating a state statute prohibiting vagrancy. The defendant unsuccessfully challenged his conviction in a state appellate court on the grounds that the law is unconstitutionally vague on its face. Seeking discretionary review of the appellate court's decision in the state's highest court, the indigent has sought to retain the counsel provided by the state for his trial and initial appeal to prepare this appeal.

Is the state constitutionally required to provide the indigent with counsel for this appeal?

(A) Yes, because the criminal statute is allegedly unconstitutional on its face.

(B) Yes, because denial of appointed counsel to an indigent defendant violates the Equal Protection Clause.

(C) No, because the appeal is discretionary.

(D) No, because an indigent defendant is not entitled to appointed counsel to pursue any appeal.

32. Seeking damages, a plaintiff pursued a breach of contract claim in federal district court with subject matter jurisdiction based on diversity. The plaintiff, as part of its complaint, made a demand for a jury trial. The state in which the federal district court sits requires the use of a special verdict in civil actions unless a party requests otherwise. The plaintiff requested that the court use a special verdict. The district court directed the jury to return a general verdict.

Is it likely that the plaintiff can successfully challenge the use of a general verdict?

(A) No, because the federal rules mandate the use of a general verdict in a civil action.

(B) No, because selection of the form of the verdict is subject to the discretion of the federal district court.

(C) Yes, because the rules of the state in which the federal court sits mandate the use of a special verdict in a civil action.

(D) Yes, because the federal rules require the use of a special verdict in a civil action.

33. In response to a devastating oil spill, Congress enacts the Federal Hazardous Materials Act, which provides for specific methods for the deconstruction and remediation of sites previously used to acquire natural resources. The Act included information on specific oil rigs, mines, and other miscellaneous land across the United States and requires that a federally approved organization oversee the deconstruction and remediation. The Act forbids state laws that regulate the sites specifically mentioned in the Act in a manner inconsistent with the methods described in the Act. The governor of a state known for extensive drilling approves a statute providing for the monitoring of all drilling sites in the state, including those referenced in the Act, from the time drilling begins until remediation is complete. The statute contains very detailed instructions on how to monitor the sites. The state requirements mostly conform to the Federal Hazardous Materials Act, except that a state-approved engineer may inspect the sites and issue an "oversight waiver," which makes overseeing the deconstruction and remediation unnecessary.

Is the state law valid?

(A) Yes, because it applies detailed instructions on how to monitor the sites and mostly conforms to the federal statute.

(B) Yes, because it is does not discriminate against out-of-state commerce.

(C) No, because the Act specifically forbids inconsistent state regulation.

(D) No, because the statute unfairly discriminates against oil companies not located within the state.

34. A father was throwing a baseball with his young son in their backyard, very close to the low fence that divided their yard from their next-door neighbor's. The son threw the ball too high, as he often did, and the baseball sailed over the fence and onto their neighbor's property. Although the neighbor had told the father never to enter her property without permission, the father knew that the neighbor was not home, and entered the neighbor's property to retrieve the baseball. While there, the father stepped into a hole created by a mole, breaking his ankle. The neighbor had been aware of the moles but had taken no action with regard to them. The father subsequently sued the neighbor for negligence.

Will the father prevail?

(A) Yes, because the neighbor was aware of the mole problem on his property.

(B) Yes, because the neighbor had a duty to inspect the property for dangerous conditions.

(C) No, because the father was injured by a natural condition on the neighbor's land.

(D) No, because the father was an undiscovered trespasser on the neighbor's property.

35. A defendant is convicted of murder and properly sentenced to life imprisonment. Subsequently, the family members of the victim bring a wrongful death action against the defendant. They seek to introduce a properly authenticated, certified copy of the final judgment to show that the defendant wrongfully killed the victim. The defendant objects to the introduction of the judgment.

May the plaintiffs introduce the copy of the final judgment from the defendant's criminal case?

  (A) No, because a copy of the judgment does not satisfy the original document rule.
  (B) No, because the judgment is inadmissible hearsay.
  (C) Yes, because the defendant was found guilty of a crime punishable by death or imprisonment of more than one year.
  (D) Yes, because any criminal judgment is admissible in a subsequent civil action.

36. A defendant is on trial for criminal battery of a patron at a bar. The defendant admitted that he hit the patron, but claims that he acted in self-defense when the patron mistook him for the boyfriend of the patron's ex-wife and attacked him.   The defendant's attorney called the defendant's mother as a witness and offered her testimony that the defendant has a reputation in the community as a peaceful and nonviolent person.

Is the testimony of the defendant's mother admissible?

  (A) Yes, because the defendant's reputation for nonviolence is inconsistent with criminal battery.
  (B) Yes, because a criminal defendant is always permitted to offer reputation evidence of the defendant's good character.
  (C) No, because the prosecution has not presented evidence of the defendant's bad character.
  (D) No, because the defendant's mother is an unreliable character witness.

37. In a phone conversation with a longtime friend, the owner of a ranch granted the friend a 90-day option to purchase the ranch for $10 million. As per the terms of their option agreement, the friend gave the owner $1,000 cash the following day. Later that same day, the owner was stricken with an illness that has left the owner unable to manage her own affairs. As a consequence, a guardian for the owner's property has been appointed. The friend proposed to the guardian that he would purchase the ranch immediately for $9.5 million. The guardian rejected this offer. Subsequently, but prior to the expiration of the 90-day period, the friend presented the guardian with a valid check for $10 million, which the guardian refused to accept.

In an action brought by the friend to compel the guardian to sell the ranch, if the court rules for the guardian, what is the reason?

(A) The option was not in writing.
(B) The option terminated at the time that the owner became incapacitated.
(C) The option was revoked by the friend's counteroffer.
(D) The option constituted a restraint on alienation of the ranch.

38. An elderly man was having financial difficulties. He wanted to hire someone to take care of his property and maintain his home, as he could no longer handle repairs or maintenance tasks. After learning of the man's needs, a long-time neighbor entered into a contract with a local landscaping company that would also perform repairs around the house. The written contract provided that the landscaping company would perform all landscaping and any necessary repairs for the man each month for one year, and the neighbor would pay $200 every month to the company. Following the execution of the contract, the neighbor told the man about the contract with the landscaping company. After two months of performance under the contract, the landscaping company sent written notice to the neighbor stating clearly that the company will no longer do any work under the contract. The man immediately brought suit for breach of contract against the landscaping company.

Will the man prevail in his suit for breach of contract against the landscaping company?

(A) No, because the man gave no consideration to make the agreement enforceable.
(B) No, because the man must bring suit against the neighbor.
(C) Yes, because the man was an intended beneficiary of the contract.
(D) Yes, because promissory estoppel applies.

39. A collector owned an Elizabethan-era tapestry in need of professional restoration and cleaning. The collector set up an appointment for a restorer to view the tapestry. After examining the tapestry, the restorer quoted the collector a price for the restoration and cleaning. The restorer told the collector that her offer would remain open for a week. Two days later, the restorer posted a note to the collector to tell him that she could not in fact perform the restoration due to a scheduling conflict. The next day the collector, before receiving this note, phoned the restorer and told her that he accepted her offer. The collector is suing the restorer for breach of contract.

Will the collector prevail?

(A) No, because the offer was not supported by consideration.
(B) No, because under the "mailbox rule," the restorer's revocation was effective before the collector accepted the offer.
(C) Yes, because the collector had until the end of the week to accept the offer.
(D) Yes, because the offer was not properly revoked before acceptance.

40. A woman purchased a new bicycle from a bicycle shop, which was the exclusive local retail store for Speed Bikes, a well-known bicycle manufacturer. After purchasing the bicycle, the woman went on a short ride. While riding, the front wheel unexpectedly turned sharply to the left, causing the woman to fall off of the bicycle and sustain minor injuries. The woman inspected the wheel closely and noticed that the wheel frame was bent. She immediately called the bicycle shop to inquire as to the bicycle shop's policy for fixing wheel frames. Because the bicycle shop had recently received a number of complaints regarding bent wheel frames on Speed Bikes, the employee on the telephone responded, "We apologize and will provide you with a new wheel, as well as a $25 gift card for your trouble." The woman later brought an action for strict products liability against the bicycle shop. At trial, the woman sought to introduce the employee's statement into evidence after the employee denied ever making it.

Is the employee's statement admissible?

(A) Yes, but only to impeach the employee.
(B) Yes, because it is an opposing party's statement.
(C) No, because it is an offer to compromise.
(D) No, because it is inadmissible hearsay.

41. A plaintiff properly brought a civil action in federal district court, sitting in diversity jurisdiction, seeking damages for negligence against a corporate defendant. The trial concluded on March 13 with a verdict for the defendant. The court entered judgment for the defendant on March 14. The plaintiff filed a motion for new trial on March 15. The motion was denied by a signed written order entered on March 24.

Which of the following must the plaintiff do to commence an appeal?

(A) File a notice of appeal within 30 days after March 14th.
(B) File a notice of appeal within 60 days after March 14th.
(C) File a notice of appeal within 30 days after March 24th.
(D) File a notice of appeal within 60 days after March 24th.

42. Two brothers owned a tract of land, located in a race-notice jurisdiction, as tenants in common. The younger brother lived in a house he built on the land, while the older brother lived out of state. Twelve years ago, the younger brother granted one of his neighbors the right to use a path across the land to access a fishing pond and go fishing; this easement, which was in writing, was never recorded. The neighbor uses the path regularly every summer. One summer, the brothers agree to enter a contract to sell the land. The neighbor happened to be using the path to access the fishing pond while the two brothers gave the buyer a tour of the property. The younger brother said to the buyer, "That's your new neighbor; he has permission to use this path to go fishing. Don't worry; he only uses the path for two or three months out of the year." The next day, the neighbor informed the brothers that he expects to have continued access to the path and fishing pond.

In the event that the brothers sell the land to that buyer, what right does the neighbor most likely have with respect to the land?

(A) The neighbor has a right to continued access to the land, because he has acquired an easement by prescription.
(B) The neighbor has a right to continued access to the land, because the buyer had notice of the easement.
(C) The neighbor has no rights in the land, because he did not use the easement continuously.
(D) The neighbor has no rights in the land, because only the younger brother and not the older brother granted the easement.

43. Congress has enacted, and the President has signed legislation (Act), that requires health care facilities receiving federal funds to adopt special procedures that deal with highly infectious diseases. Concerned with the possibility that inconsistent lower court decisions regarding the interpretation and application of the Act could delay its enforcement, the Act provides that legal challenges to it can be initiated only by filing an action in the United States Supreme Court.

Is the provision that authorizes direct review of the interpretation and application of the Act by the U.S. Supreme Court constitutional?

(A) No, because Congress lacks the authority to adjust the original jurisdiction of the U.S. Supreme Court.

(B) No, because Congress, unlike state legislatures, does not have a police power to legislate for the general welfare.

(C) Yes, pursuant to Congress's Spending Power under Article I, section 8 of the U.S. Constitution.

(D) Yes, pursuant to Congress's authority to set the Supreme Court's jurisdiction under Article III, section 2 of the U.S. Constitution.

44. A tenant and a landlord entered into a two-year lease for a residential apartment. Four months into the tenant's lease, the tenant's employer offered her the chance to live and work abroad for twelve months, at the company's expense. The tenant happily accepted, and found a friend to take over the next twelve months of her lease. While the tenant was out of the country, the friend hosted a small party at the apartment. One of the friend's guests tripped over an area rug on the floor and badly injured her knee. The lease was silent as to both assignments and subleases.

If the guest sues for damages related to her knee injury, from whom can she properly recover?

(A) The landlord or the tenant
(B) The landlord, the tenant, or the friend
(C) The tenant or the friend
(D) The landlord

45. A patient sued her physician for malpractice due to the physician's failure to timely diagnosis the patient's diabetes. At trial, the patient offered testimony from a national expert that the physician's failure to give the patient a newly developed test constituted a breach of the national standard of care. The physician countered this testimony with his own expert testimony that no physician within the local area utilized the new test. Consequently, the physician's expert concluded that the required standard of care was not breached.

The physician moved for summary judgment. How should the court rule on the motion?

(A) Deny the motion, because the court may determine that the local medical standards are negligent.

(B) Deny the motion, because physicians are generally held to a national standard of care.

(C) Grant the motion, because the physician's proffered expert testimony established that his medical practices fell within the standard of care observed within the community.

(D) Grant the motion, because a physician is normally held to a local standard of care.

46. Through a local community-based charitable organization, an athlete offered a recreational program for pre-school children during the summer. One day, the athlete noticed abrasions and bruises on a child that the athlete had reasonable cause to suspect were due to child abuse. Unknown to the athlete, state law required the athlete to report this matter to the appropriate state agency and made failure to report suspected child abuse a misdemeanor. The athlete discussed the matter with her supervisor, who was aware of the law. Concerned because the child's father was a substantial contributor to the charity, the supervisor advised the athlete to ignore the matter. Ten days later, the child in question was killed by her father. The athlete has been charged as an accomplice to the murder of the child.

Of the following, which is the athlete's best defense to this charge?

(A) The athlete did not possess the culpability necessary for this crime.

(B) The athlete reported the matter to her supervisor.

(C) The athlete's failure to act cannot be a basis for criminal liability.

(D) The athlete was not aware of the reporting statute.

47. A store purchased a truck from a dealer and took delivery of the truck. Under the terms of the contract, the store was to make monthly payments for three years. After the store made monthly payments for one year, the truck was involved in an accident that resulted in a fire which totally destroyed the truck. The store, having let its insurance on the truck lapse, refused to make any more payments to the dealer. Six months later, the dealer brought suit against the store.

How much can the dealer recover?

(A) Nothing, because the truck was destroyed.
(B) The payments due for six months, because only those payments are currently due and owing.
(C) The full amount remaining under the contract, because the dealer fully performed its contractual obligation.
(D) The full amount remaining under the contract, because the store repudiated its contractual obligation.

48. As designed by the manufacturer, an electric beater contained parts that could not safely handle the electric current over an extended period. The manufacturer used the parts, which were defective, in order to marginally lower the cost of the beater below that of a competitor's beater. On the plastic body of the beater, the manufacturer placed a label clearly warning that the beater should not be run at its highest speed for more than five minutes and that failure to do so could result in the beater overheating and catching fire. A consumer purchased a beater that was manufactured in conformity with the design. The consumer failed to read the warning label, and used the beater on several occasions in the preparation of food without incident. On one occasion, however, the consumer used the beater to prepare a mix at high speed for more than seven minutes. The beater caught fire, badly burning the consumer's hands and resulting in damage to the consumer's kitchen. The consumer filed a strict products liability action against the manufacturer for personal injury and property damages.

Will the consumer prevail?

(A) Yes, because the beater was defectively designed.
(B) Yes, because the beater had a manufacturing defect.
(C) No, because the manufacturer warned the consumer about prolonged use of the blender at its highest speed.
(D) No, because the consumer failed to read the warning.

49. The president of a corporation, erroneously thinking that the corporation owned a parcel of land, sold the parcel to a partnership. In reality, the corporation did not own the parcel, which contained valuable copper deposits. The partnership promptly and properly recorded the corporation's general warranty deed, but, due to a sudden drop in the price of copper, otherwise did nothing with respect to the land. Subsequently, the president retired and a new president assumed control of the corporation. Thereafter, the corporation acquired ownership of the parcel with the copper deposits in fee simple. The corporation sold the land at its fair market value to an individual who was unaware of the prior conveyance. The individual properly conducted a search of the land records. The jurisdiction in which the land was located required that the records only be searched for conveyances by the grantor during the time that the grantor owned the property. The individual promptly and properly recorded the corporation's general warranty deed. When a rise in the price of copper made recovery economically practicable, the partnership entered the land and began to set up mining operations. The individual, learning of the partnership's activities, brought an action to oust the partnership from the property. The applicable recording act reads: No conveyance or mortgage of real property shall be good against subsequent purchasers for value and without notice unless the same be recorded according to law.

Who will prevail in this action?

(A) The partnership, because the partnership recorded its property interest before the individual.
(B) The partnership, because, upon the corporation's acquisition of the land, ownership of the land automatically transferred to the partnership under the estoppel by deed doctrine.
(C) The individual, because the individual purchased the land without notice of the prior conveyance.
(D) The individual, because the partnership failed to conduct mining activities until after the conveyance to the individual.

50. A landowner devised real property to his three children, a daughter and two sons. The children were given equal joint interests in the property and upon the death of any child, that child's interest was to pass automatically to any surviving joint interest holders. Two years later, the daughter sold her interest in the property to a cousin. A year after that, one of the sons died. Under the terms of his will, his interest in the property passed to a friend.

Who has an interest in the land and what interests do they hold?

(A) The cousin and the surviving son each own an equal share as tenants in common.
(B) The cousin and the surviving son each own a share as tenants in common; the cousin owns a one-third share and the surviving son a two-thirds share.
(C) The cousin, friend, and surviving son each own an equal share as tenants in common.
(D) The cousin, friend, and surviving son each own an equal share as joint tenants.

51. A sister wanted to buy a special birthday gift for her brother's 40th birthday. Because he was a beer aficionado, she decided get him a one-year subscription to a beer-of-the-month club. Per the agreement between the parties, the sister paid $200 to the beer club and the beer club agreed to send a dozen different beers on the 15th day of each month to the brother. The agreement further stated that each of the 12 beers would be different in type and region from the others. For 11 months, the beer club sent 12 different types of beers from different regions to the brother on the 15th of each month. However, prior to the final shipment, the beer club had a dispute with its current beer distributor. As a result, the beer club was unable to provide 12 different types of beers from different regions to the brother.

If the brother brings legal action against the beer club, will he succeed?

(A) No, because the sister intended the beer-of-the-month club to be a gift for her brother.
(B) No, because the brother's rights had not yet vested.
(C) Yes, because the first 11 beer shipments were of different types and from different regions.
(D) Yes, because the sister and the beer club intended for the brother to benefit from the contract.

52. A psychologist was the host of a very popular radio talk show. In addition to offering general self-help advice to her listeners, the psychologist was also well known for the conversations she had with people who would call her while she was on air. One morning during the psychologist's radio show, a caller told the psychologist that he was embarrassed to be around his friends and co-workers because he had recently gotten a DUI. He also told the psychologist that he especially wanted the psychologist's advice because he had searched the public records and found out that the psychologist had also gotten three DUIs in the past year. In fact, the court record that the caller had seen was for another woman with the exact same name as that of the psychologist. Although the psychologist truthfully denied that she had any DUIs, the ratings for her radio show immediately plummeted as a result of the caller's statement.

If the psychologist sues the caller for defamation, will she succeed?

(A) No, because the caller did not act with actual malice.
(B) No, because the psychologist will be unable to prove actual damages.
(C) Yes, because the caller negligently assumed that the court record referenced the psychologist.
(D) Yes, because the psychologist did not have any DUIs.

53.   A residence was assessed annual county property taxes of $5,000. The residence was occupied by a life tenant who lived on the premises rent-free. The residence could have been rented to a third party for $2,000 a month. The life tenant did not pay the property taxes. Instead, the holder of the remainder interest paid them to prevent the county from imposing a lien on the property or possibly foreclosing on the property. The fair market value of the life estate was 10 percent of the fair market value of the property held in fee simple absolute.

Can the holder of the remainder interest recover the tax payment from the life tenant?

   (A)   No, because the property taxes are
         the responsibility of the holder of the
         remainder interest rather than the
         life tenant.
   (B)   No, because the holder of the
         remainder interest paid the property
         taxes in order to protect his own
         interest in the property.
   (C)   Yes, because the life tenant owes
         the holder of a remainder interest a
         duty to pay the property taxes.
   (D)   Yes, but only to the extent of the life
         estate's share of the property taxes
         based on the fair market value of the
         life estate.

54.   Two siblings, a brother and a sister, inherited the family residence as equal tenants in common upon the death of their mother. The brother lived out of state, so both siblings agreed that the sister would live in the residence. While the sister lived on the land, she paid all of the taxes. She also added a studio to the residence, which greatly improved its value.   Being a professional yoga instructor, she held yoga classes in the studio. The sister's classes proved profitable. The brother told his sister that she owed him a portion of the profits from the yoga studio.   The sister denied owing her brother a share of the profits, and retorted that the brother had to reimburse her for half of the costs of the studio.

Neither sibling has yet requested a partition or accounting.   Do either of the siblings owe the other money with respect to residence?

   (A)   The sister owes her brother a share
         of profits from the studio, and the
         brother owes his sister half the cost
         of the studio.
   (B)   The sister owes her brother a share
         of profits from the studio, but the
         brother does not owe his sister half
         the cost of the studio.
   (C)   The sister does not owe her brother
         a share of profits from the studio,
         but the brother does owe his sister
         half the cost of the studio.
   (D)   Neither sibling owes the other with
         regard to income from the yoga
         classes or the cost of the studio.

55. A builder entered into a written contract with a business owner to construct an addition to the owner's place of business. The builder was to supply all materials for the job, and was to be paid a total of $200,000. The builder anticipated that his profit would be 10 percent of that amount. Before construction began, the builder received a $25,000 payment from the business owner. The business owner, due to a downturn in his business, failed to make the first progress payment and ordered the builder to stop working on the project. At this time, the builder had expended $55,000 and it would have cost the builder $125,000 to continue the project to completion. The work completed added $35,000 in value to the building. The builder retained $10,000 of construction materials purchased but not used in the project, and used them in another construction job. The builder sued the business owner for breach of contract.

What is maximum amount of damages to which the builder is entitled?

(A) $20,000
(B) $35,000
(C) $40,000
(D) $55,000

56. A cleaning service advertised, "We'll clean your whole house for $99!" A hoarder's ex-wife, excited about the possibility of cleaning out her house and attached garage for such a low price, telephoned the cleaning service and asked, "You can really clean my whole house for $99?" The owner of the cleaning service replied, "Yes, absolutely!" The ex-wife said, "It's a deal!" The owner faxed her a contract that said, "Cleaning service agrees to clean the entire house located at 123 Maple Street. Home owner agrees to pay cleaning service $99." The ex-wife signed the contract and returned it. The cleaning service cleaned out the house so well that the ex-wife could eat off the floors. However, it did not touch the attached garage. When the ex-wife contacted the owner to complain, he said, "The contract was only for the house, not the garage." The ex-wife sued, claiming the cleaning service had failed to perform.

Upon the cleaning service's motion, will the court admit evidence of trade usage to support their argument that the contract did not included the attached garage?

(A) Yes, because there are no prior or contemporaneous documents to introduce.
(B) Yes, because the term "entire house" is ambiguous.
(C) No, because the trade usage is not admissible against a non-merchant.
(D) No, because such evidence is inadmissible under the "four corners" rule.

57. A federal act that provided funds to fight HIV/AIDS includes two relevant provisions. The first provision prohibits the use of funds to promote or advocate the legalization or practice of prostitution. The second provision requires a recipient of the funds to expressly adopt and espouse a policy against prostitution. In adopting this act, Congress specifically found that prostitution was a factor in the spread of HIV/AIDS. Prior to the adoption of this act, a private organization that received substantial funding from private sources did not have such a policy because the organization feared that such a policy would hinder its work with prostitutes, making its programs less effective in addressing the HIV/AIDS problem. Although the private organization otherwise qualified as a recipient of federal funds through the act, because the private organization refused to adopt and espouse the policy against prostitution, the organization's application for such funds was rejected. The organization has filed an action in federal court for a declaratory judgment that the act's anti-prostitution policy requirement violates the organization's First Amendment free speech rights.

How should the court rule?

(A) For the federal government, because Congress can place conditions on recipients of federal grants pursuant to the Spending Power of Article I, Section 8 of the U.S. Constitution.

(B) For the federal government, because of the government speech doctrine.

(C) For the private organization, because a federal grant cannot be contingent on a condition that limits a recipient's freedom of speech.

(D) For the private organization, because the First Amendment free speech rights include the right not to be forced by the government to adopt and espouse the government's views.

58. A woman erroneously believes that her boyfriend has stolen a valuable bracelet from her. She calls his cell phone and, after identifying him by name, leaves the following message, "You thief! Give me back my bracelet." Unknown to the woman, the boyfriend has another girlfriend. That girlfriend has access to the boyfriend's cell phone and listens to the message.

In a suit for slander by the boyfriend brought against the woman, will the boyfriend prevail?

(A) Yes, because the statement was false.

(B) Yes, because the statement was slander per se.

(C) No, because the woman was a private person and the matter was not one of public concern.

(D) No, because the statement was not published negligently or intentionally.

59. A buyer executed a contract with a seller to purchase the seller's house. The buyer granted a mortgage on the property to a bank in exchange for a loan with which to purchase the house. The terms of the loan stated that in the event of a default, the buyer had the right to redeem the property before the foreclosure sale. The buyer made regular payments for six months before renegotiating new terms with the bank. In exchange for a lowered interest rate, the buyer agreed to strike the redemption language from the mortgage and waive her right of redemption. Six months later, the buyer defaulted on the mortgage and the bank brought foreclosure proceedings. Before the foreclosure sale, the buyer attempted to redeem the property, but the bank refused to accept the buyer's payment. The buyer filed suit to prevent the foreclosure sale.

The applicable jurisdiction has enacted a statute giving the mortgagor the right to redeem the mortgaged property for six months after the foreclosure sale.

How should the court rule?

(A) The court should find for the buyer, because the waiver clogged the buyer's equity of redemption.
(B) The court should find for the buyer, because the mortgage was a purchase-money mortgage.
(C) The court should find for the bank, because the waiver was provided after the execution of the mortgage in exchange for a lowered interest rate.
(D) The court should find for the bank, because the buyer has a statutory right to redeem the property after the foreclosure sale.

60. An elderly patient received public aid benefits in her home state and voluntarily entered a nursing home to facilitate her care. The public aid benefits covered the cost of her nursing home care as well as medical treatment and living expenses. The nursing home was located in a small rural town where the patient had lived all her life, and where all of the patient's family and friends lived. Unbeknownst to the patient, the state conducted an investigation of the nursing home and disqualified the home from receiving any further state benefit payments. Due to the disqualification, the patient was told she would have to move to the nearest state-qualified nursing home, which was located seventy miles away, in order to continue using her benefits. The patient immediately filed a suit against the state, claiming that her due process rights were violated.

Will the patient prevail in her suit against the state?

(A) Yes, because the patient has a cognizable property interest in continuing to live in her nursing home and was denied fair notice.
(B) Yes, because the administrative burden of contacting the patient and holding a hearing is outweighed by the patient's interest in staying in her hometown.
(C) No, because the patient has no protected property or liberty interest that has been violated.
(D) No, because the patient is entitled only to a post-decision evidentiary hearing and has not pursued the hearing.

61. A customer at a restaurant ordered a dessert from the menu, which stated that the desserts were made by an independent third party. The restaurant had priced the dessert below its cost in order to attract customers to the restaurant. The dessert contained small slivers of glass. The glass was not detected by the restaurant, even though the restaurant conducted a reasonable inspection of the dessert and otherwise had no reason to suspect that the dessert contained the glass. The customer ate the dessert and incurred serious injuries from the glass slivers.

If the customer brings suit against the restaurant based on strict products liability for injuries suffered from eating the dessert, who will prevail?

(A) The customer, because the restaurant was a commercial supplier of the dessert.
(B) The customer, because the restaurant failed to warn the customer of the glass in the dessert.
(C) The restaurant, because the dessert was not produced by the restaurant.
(D) The restaurant, because the restaurant did not make a profit from the sale of the dessert.

62. A jurisdiction defines statutory rape as "sexual intercourse with a person under 16 with the knowledge that the person is underage." The jurisdiction also defines rape as "unlawful sexual intercourse with a female against her will." In all other applicable law, the jurisdiction follows the majority rule. A man who knew that his female coworker was 15, overheard the coworker making plans to go to a house party over the weekend. The man then encouraged his friend to go to the party and have sex with the coworker. He even gave his friend a drug to put in the coworker's drink, in case the coworker "needed encouragement." The friend went to the party and had sexual intercourse with the coworker. The coworker admitted that she was 15, but because she said she was consenting to sexual intercourse, the friend had sex with her anyway. The friend did not drug her.

The friend was charged and convicted of statutory rape. The man has been charged as an accomplice to statutory rape. Should he be convicted?

(A) Yes, because he encouraged and assisted his friend in having sex with a female he knew to be underage.
(B) Yes, because the friend was ultimately convicted of statutory rape as the principal actor.
(C) No, because mere knowledge that a crime will occur is not enough to create accomplice liability.
(D) No, because the friend did not actually use the drug provided by the man.

63. A woman was hit by a pizza delivery driver and suffered serious injury. The woman sued the driver for negligence, arguing that he was far exceeding the speed limit in a residential area. She also sued the driver's employer under a respondeat superior theory. At trial, the woman sought to introduce against the employer evidence that the driver had received five traffic violations during the previous year.

Is the evidence of the driver's traffic tickets admissible against the employer?

(A) No, because the woman may not introduce evidence of the driver's character trait of bad driving.

(B) No, because character may not be proved by evidence of prior bad acts in a civil case.

(C) Yes, because character evidence is generally admissible in civil cases.

(D) Yes, because the driver's character is an essential element of the woman's claim.

64. A commercial building owner entered into a contract with a painter to paint each of the units in the owner's building for a total price of $5,000. The painter instructed the owner to pay the $5,000 to the painter's friend. The friend had recently lost his job and his wife was pregnant. The painter thought the $5,000 would be a nice gesture and would help the friend with all of his upcoming expenses. The painter informed the friend that he should expect the $5,000 once the painter finished painting the units in the owner's building. After the painting was completed, the owner paid the $5,000 directly to the painter, despite being fully aware of the painter's request for the money to be paid to the friend. The painter, however, decided to keep the $5,000 because he had recently learned that the friend was using drugs and thought the money would be used for that purpose.

Can the friend recover the $5,000 from the painter?

(A) No, because an effective assignment requires consideration.

(B) No, because the painter validly revoked the assignment to the friend.

(C) Yes, because the assignment to the friend was irrevocable.

(D) Yes, because the friend was an intended beneficiary of the contract.

65. A wealthy widower hosted a dinner on his yacht for his son and the son's friend. The son, to induce his friend to marry him, told her that, if she would marry him, he would buy her a new car. After the son's friend accepted his proposal, the widower offered to transfer ownership of the yacht to her when she married his son if she agreed to wear the gown that his deceased wife had worn at her wedding to him. The woman readily agreed. The woman and the son married and at the wedding the woman wore the gown, but, due to incompatibility, they separated shortly thereafter and subsequently divorced.

Is the woman entitled to either the car from the son or the yacht from the widower?

(A) Yes, both the car and the yacht.
(B) Yes, but only the car.
(C) Yes, but only the yacht.
(D) No, neither the car nor the yacht.

66. Acting pursuant to its general power to tax and spend, Congress enacted a federal statute appropriating funds for the construction of religious schools in areas that (i) meet certain population requirements and (ii) are not within 50 miles of an existing public school. No such schools have yet been built, as no communities currently in existence meet both of these requirements. An organization aimed at preserving public education sued in federal court to enjoin the construction of any such schools, arguing that government funding for the construction violates the Establishment of Religion Clause.

Which of the following best describes how the district court should dispose of the suit?

(A) Hear the case, and issue the injunction if the government cannot show that the construction of the schools is rationally related to a legitimate government interest.
(B) Hear the case, and issue an injunction if the statute does not have a secular purpose.
(C) Dismiss the case, because there is no organizational standing to challenge appropriation of federal funds.
(D) Dismiss the case, because it does not involve a justiciable case or controversy.

67. Over the years, homeowners on a street have engaged in a friendly competition over decorating the outside of their houses for Halloween. Finding that the favorable publicity about the competition has increased the value of their homes, the homeowners enter into a signed written agreement that each will decorate the outside of his house for Halloween. The agreement, which is not recorded, specifically indicates an intent that successors in interest be bound by the agreement. One elderly homeowner moved away and sold her house to a young, childless couple. The couple was informed of the agreement before they entered into the contract to purchase the house in fee simple absolute. For aesthetic reasons, the couple refuses to decorate their house. The applicable jurisdiction follows the traditional rules with regard to the enforceability of a real covenant.

Can the couple's neighbor, who was a party to the agreement, enforce the agreement as a real covenant against the couple?

(A) No, because of a lack of privity.
(B) No, because the agreement was not recorded.
(C) Yes, because the covenant "touches and concerns" the property.
(D) Yes, because the couple had actual notice of the agreement.

68. There is a federal policy to encourage local recycling. A municipality passed an ordinance to enhance the processing of solid waste and improve recycling within its jurisdiction. The municipality required all solid waste to be brought to a transfer station owned by the municipality. Anyone who brought solid waste to the transfer station was charged a "tipping fee." In addition, the municipality required each commercial trash hauler to purchase a permit in order to collect solid waste in the municipality. The combined cost of the "tipping fee" and the permit was fixed at an amount to ensure that the municipality did not lose money in operating the transfer station.

Prior to the enactment of the ordinance, a local corporation had collected solid waste in the municipality and delivered it to an out-of-state facility, which charged much less than the combined cost of the fee and permit. The corporation filed a lawsuit challenging the constitutionality of the municipal ordinance. The court ruled in favor of the municipality.

Is the court's ruling correct?

(A) Yes, because the ordinance furthers the federal policy of encouraging recycling.
(B) Yes, because the transfer station is owned by the municipality.
(C) No, because the ordinance discriminates against interstate commerce.
(D) No, because the ordinance violates the Comity Clause of Article IV, Section 2.

69. A parking garage attendant found a necklace beside a car in the garage. Both the owner of the car and the owner of the garage claim ownership of the necklace, which has been valued at $73,000. The car owner has filed an action to gain possession of the necklace in state court naming the attendant as defendant. The attendant filed a federal statutory interpleader action in federal district court. The garage owner and the car owner are citizens of the same state and the attendant is a citizen of a neighboring state. The attendant has posted a bond with the federal court, but retains possession of the necklace. The car owner has filed a motion to dismiss the interpleader action for lack of subject matter jurisdiction.

For which of the following reasons should the court grant the car owner's motion?

(A) The garage owner and the car owner are citizens of the same state.
(B) The value of the necklace does not exceed $75,000.
(C) The attendant has retained possession of the necklace.
(D) The car owner had already filed an action in state court.

70. A private individual offered to purchase a large stone monument to display passages from the Koran if the city council would permit the monument to be erected in a public park located in a neighborhood that was composed largely of people of Arab descent. The council, viewing this offer as an opportunity to reach out to this ethnic group, accepted the offer on the condition that the council would have final approval regarding the passages to be displayed. A city resident has objected to the placement of the monument in the park, which has no other monuments.

Is a court likely to permit the display of the monument in the public park?

(A) No, because the display of the religious monument in a public park violates the Establishment Clause.
(B) No, because the council must maintain viewpoint neutrality in selecting donated monuments.
(C) Yes, because the council's choice to display the monument in a public park constitutes governmental speech.
(D) Yes, because the monument was purchased by a private individual.

71.   A shareholder brought a derivative action in federal district court on behalf of a closely-held corporation. At the time that the action was filed, the corporation had a total of nine shareholders. The complaint alleged that two of the three members of the board of directors had colluded to breach their duty of loyalty by usurping a corporate business opportunity prior to the shareholder's purchase of her shares. The complaint also alleged that a demand to take corrective action had not been made upon the board since such a demand would have been futile. The shareholder did not plead that she suffered special harm as a shareholder as a consequence of the directors' collusion.

Of the following, which is a ground on which the court may dismiss the complaint for failure to state a claim upon which relief may be granted?

(A)   The class of shareholders is not so numerous that joinder of all shareholders is impracticable.
(B)   The shareholder failed to make a demand upon the board of directors to take corrective action.
(C)   The shareholder did not own stock in the corporation at the time of the alleged wrong.
(D)   The shareholder did not plead that she suffered special harm as shareholder.

72.   A rancher, on retiring, conveyed her ranch in fee simple to her two children, a son and a daughter, equally. After this conveyance, the two children continued to live and work together on the ranch. Over the years, the rancher's son incurred charges on his credit card for personal expenses unrelated to the operation of the ranch. After the unpaid charges mounted up, the credit card company won a money judgment against the son and properly filed the judgment in the land records for the county in which the ranch is located. The daughter offered to buy her brother's interest in the ranch, but he refused. The son subsequently pursued an action for an involuntary partition. While this action was pending, the rancher died. In her will, she left all of her estate to a charity. Because division of the ranch was not practicable, the court sold the property at a public auction.

What claim does the judgment lien obtained by the credit card company have against the proceeds received from this sale?

(A)   The lien will have priority to the sale proceeds due to the rancher's son.
(B)   The lien will have priority to the sale proceeds due to the rancher's daughter.
(C)   The lien will have priority to the sale proceeds due to both of the rancher's children.
(D)   The lien is not entitled to the sale proceeds because they are payable to the charity.

73. Stockholders in a publicly-traded corporation brought suit against executives of the corporation for securities fraud. The stockholders requested that the judge take judicial notice of the price of the corporation's stock on specific dates, providing the judge with those prices as listed on a respected online financial news service. The prices were not generally known in the public at large, nor even among sophisticated investors without reference to a source such as the reliable news service. Nevertheless, the judge took judicial notice of the stock price on those dates. Since the executives did not make a request as to the propriety of taking judicial notice, the judge did not provide them with the opportunity to be heard on this issue.

Was the judge's taking judicial notice proper?

(A) Yes, because the stock prices were adjudicative facts subject to judicial notice.
(B) Yes, because a judge is generally free to rely on legislative facts.
(C) No, because the prices were not generally known to the public at large or by sophisticated investors without reference to a reliance source.
(D) No, because the judge failed to provide the executives with the opportunity to be heard on the propriety of taking judicial notice.

74. An art collector placed a painting up for auction, alongside a number of other works of art. There was no indication as to whether the painting was being auctioned with or without reserve. After the auctioneer had gaveled the highest bid for the collector's painting, the collector had seller's remorse. Before the conclusion of the auction and before the highest bidder, a public museum, paid for the painting, the collector notified the museum that she could not bring herself to part with the painting.

Is the collector entitled to keep the painting?

(A) Yes, because, by default, the painting was sold with reserve and the auction had not concluded.
(B) Yes, because the museum had not paid for the painting.
(C) No, because the auctioneer had accepted the museum's bid.
(D) No, because, by default, the painting was sold without reserve.

75. A defendant charged with murder timely and properly notified the prosecution of his intent to raise an insanity defense. The state follows the Model Penal Code test for insanity, and the initial burden of producing evidence of the defendant's insanity is on the defense. If the defense meets this burden, the prosecution bears the burden of persuasion that, beyond a reasonable doubt, the defendant is sane. At trial before a jury, the defense presented lay witnesses who testified as to the defendant's lack of self-control at the time of the murder due to his mental state, but did not present any expert witnesses. The prosecution called several expert witnesses who presented evidence, including opinion testimony, that the defendant's mental state did not prevent him from appreciating the wrongfulness of the murder or from conforming his conduct to the law. At the conclusion of the presentation of all evidence, both the prosecution and the defense moved for judgment as a matter of law. The judge granted the prosecution's motion and denied the defense's motion.

On appeal, should the appellate court sustain the judge's ruling?

(A) Yes, because the defense did not present any expert witnesses on the issue of the defendant's sanity.

(B) Yes, because the prosecution established the defendant's sanity beyond a reasonable doubt.

(C) No, because the judge may not direct a verdict in favor of the prosecution in a jury trial.

(D) No, because the defense presented evidence of the defendant's insanity at the time of the murder.

76. During a criminal trial for a federal racketeering charge, the prosecution would like to call the wife of one of the defendant's co-conspirators to the stand. The wife has knowledge of the defendant's and her husband's criminal activities, having discovered some incriminating paperwork in her husband's office. The wife's husband is on trial for the same charges, though the trials have been severed. The wife is willing to testify against the defendant and her husband in the defendant's trial. The husband is unwilling to waive the marital privilege, and the defendant objects to the wife's testifying.

Should the prosecutor be allowed to put the wife on the stand?

(A) Yes, because the wife will testify in the trial of the defendant, not of her husband.

(B) Yes, because the wife is willing to testify.

(C) No, because the husband refuses to waive the privilege.

(D) No, because the husband and wife are still married.

77. A police officer, seeing an automobile with an expired registration sticker on its license plate, stopped the car. As the officer walked to the car, the officer noticed that a valid temporary registration permit was properly affixed to the car. The officer continued to the driver's door and asked the driver for her license. In doing so, the officer recognized the passenger in the car as an individual who had a prior police record. After running a check for outstanding warrants, the officer arrested the passenger pursuant to a valid outstanding arrest warrant. The officer then searched the passenger. Burglary tools were found on the passenger's person. The passenger was charged with the possession of burglary tools. The passenger's attorney filed a suppression motion with regard to the burglary tools, asserting that their seizure was unconstitutional.

Should the court grant the motion?

(A) No, because the passenger of car was not seized by police until she was arrested.

(B) No, because a valid outstanding arrest warrant justified the police officer's arrest of the passenger.

(C) Yes, because the police may not arrest a passenger for a traffic or car-related offense.

(D) Yes, because the police lacked reasonable suspicion to approach the driver and ask for her license.

78. A membership-only warehouse club that sells a wide selection of merchandise contracted with a manufacturer of pool toys to purchase 20,000 bundles of pool toys for $3 per unit on May 1. The written agreement between the parties stated that the manufacturer was responsible for delivery of the toys to the club on or before May 15. The agreement did not include a "time is of the essence" clause. On May 16, the manufacturer delivered 20,000 bundles of pool toys to the warehouse club. The manufacturer did not notify the club with regard to this minor delay. The warehouse refused to accept the toys or make payment of $60,000.

In a suit for breach of contract against the warehouse club, will the manufacturer succeed?

(A) No, because the manufacturer failed to notify the club of the one-day delay.

(B) No, because the pool toys were not delivered on May 15.

(C) Yes, because the contract did not contain a "time is of the essence" clause.

(D) Yes, because a one-day delay in delivery did not constitute a material breach.

79. In a civil action being tried before a jury, a party objected to the introduction of evidence on the grounds that disclosure of the evidence was protected by the psychotherapist-patient privilege. In ruling on this objection, the court considered evidence protected by the attorney-client privilege.

Has the court acted properly in making its ruling?

(A) No, because the court considered privileged evidence in making its ruling.

(B) No, because the issue of the existence of a privilege is a matter for the jury, not the court to decide.

(C) Yes, because the court is not bound by the rules of evidence when making determinations as to admissibility.

(D) Yes, because the action was a civil action, not a criminal action.

80. A plaintiff was severely injured when he slipped while shopping at the defendant's department store. As a result, the plaintiff brought a state law negligence action against the defendant in federal district court under diversity jurisdiction. The defendant was properly served on January 1 and filed his answer on January 15. Discovery for the matter concluded on June 1. On June 25, three weeks prior to trial, the plaintiff filed a motion for summary judgment.

Was the plaintiff's motion for summary judgment timely?

(A) Yes, because it was filed within 30 days of trial.

(B) Yes, because it was filed within 30 days after the close of all discovery.

(C) No, because the motion must be filed prior to the close of all discovery.

(D) No, because the motion must be filed within 15 days after the close of all discovery.

81. After consuming a six pack of beer, a man decided to drive to the local bar to have a few more beers. At the bar, the man ordered a beer. The bartender initially refused to serve him because the man was already intoxicated. However, after some persuasion, the bartender agreed to serve the man. After consuming four additional beers, the man left the bar and drove home. On his way home, the man accidentally hit a pedestrian who was jaywalking across a part of the street without street lamps. The pedestrian sustained severe injuries and subsequently sued both the man and the bartender to recover damages. The jurisdiction has adopted a dram shop act and a pure comparative negligence system of recovery. The pedestrian obtained a judgment in her favor against both defendants for $200,000. The jury determined that the bartender was 20% at fault, the driver was 70% at fault, and the pedestrian was 10% at fault.

What is the total amount of damages that the pedestrian can recover from the bartender?

(A) $20,000
(B) $40,000
(C) $180,000
(D) $200,000

82. The owner of undeveloped land entered into a fully-integrated written contract to sell the land to a buyer for $500,000. The contract contained a description that accurately set out the boundaries of the land, but did not make reference to the specific acreage. Both the owner and the buyer mistakenly thought that the property encompassed 500 acres, on the basis of a negligent miscalculation made by a surveyor employed by the owner and contained in the surveyor's report. In fact the property encompassed 550 acres. The owner had sought, but the buyer had rejected, the inclusion of a provision in the contract that, in the event of a material error in the surveyor's report, the adversely affected party could cancel the contract.

Can the owner cancel the contract?

(A) Yes, because both the owner and seller were mistaken as to the land's acreage.
(B) Yes, because the parol evidence rule does not prevent the introduction of evidence of mistake.
(C) No, because the mistake was made by a surveyor employed by the owner.
(D) No, because the owner assumed the risk of the mistake.

83. Congress enacted a law making it a federal crime "to transport, or cause to be transported, one's spouse across state lines for the purpose of murder." A wife paid a third party $10,000 to take her husband on a hunting trip to another state and kill him there. The third party did so. The wife was indicted for violating this criminal provision. Her defense is that this criminal provision exceeds Congress's constitutional powers.

Will her defense likely succeed?

(A) Yes, because federalism prohibits Congress from interfering in an area of traditional state concern, the crime of murder.

(B) Yes, because the activity in question, murder, does not substantially affect interstate commerce.

(C) No, because Congress can protect the instrumentalities of interstate commerce.

(D) No, because Congress can keep the channels of interstate commerce free of immoral and injurious uses.

84. A witness in a civil action initiated for damages suffered as a result of a car accident testified that the defendant improperly failed to yield the right-of-way. The defendant impeached the witness's testimony by showing her long-time friendship with the plaintiff. The plaintiff sought to rehabilitate the witness by introducing a statement made by the witness several days after the accident to a neighbor that the defendant failed to yield the right-of-way. The defendant objected to the introduction of this statement.

May the court permit the plaintiff to introduce the witness's prior statement?

(A) Yes, because, as a prior consistent statement, it is not hearsay.

(B) Yes, because it is offered to rehabilitate the witness.

(C) No, because the prior statement was not made under oath.

(D) No, because the prior statement was made after the witness and plaintiff became friends.

85. The owner of an apartment building leased an apartment to a tenant at a fixed monthly rent for one year. Seven months later, the tenant informed the owner of her intent to leave the premises. The tenant vacated the premises and did not pay rent for the remaining five months of the lease. The owner did not enter the premises during those five months and made no effort to rent the unoccupied space to someone else. Subsequently, the owner sued the tenant for the five months of unpaid rent.

According to majority rule, is the owner entitled to recover the full amount of this unpaid rent from the tenant?

(A) Yes, because the owner did not retake possession of the leased premises.

(B) Yes, because the tenant abandoned her leasehold interest.

(C) No, because the owner made no effort to rent the apartment to someone else.

(D) No, because the owner accepted the tenant's surrender of her leasehold interest.

86. A local zoning board placed special restrictions on bookstores that primarily sell publications that appeal to prurient interests, depict sexual conduct in a patently offensive way, and are without serious literary, artistic, political, or scientific value. These "adult" bookstores are prohibited from all residential zones but are permitted in some commercial zones in order to limit their established secondary effects, such as increased crime. A corporation that owns and operates a chain of "adult" bookstores nationwide had plans to open such a bookstore in a community subject to the zoning board's restrictions. The corporation has filed an action in federal court seeking a declaratory judgment that the restrictions violate the First Amendment.

Should the court render this declaratory judgment?

(A) No, because the First Amendment guarantee of freedom of speech does not apply to corporations.

(B) No, because the zoning restrictions are valid time, place, and manner restrictions.

(C) Yes, because restrictions on commercial speech must be narrowly tailored to directly advance a substantial government interest.

(D) Yes, because the restrictions are based on the content of the books that would be sold in the corporation's bookstore.

87. Four men were bow-and-arrow hunting in a thickly wooded area. Each man was wearing brightly-colored apparel to minimize the risk of an accident. However, midway through the day, one hunter was struck in the leg by an arrow. The wounded man collapsed in agony, and eventually required several surgical procedures and months of rehabilitation in order to walk again. None of the other three men admitted responsibility for the accident. The injured man sued the other three hunters, claiming negligence. The injured man (i.e., the plaintiff) introduced evidence tending to show that no other hunting parties were within a five-mile radius at the time of the incident, but he was unable to show conclusively which of the three defendants fired the arrow that caused his injury. At the conclusion of the plaintiff's case, one of the defendants filed a motion for summary judgment.

How should the court rule on the motion?

(A) Deny the motion, because the defendant had not yet exonerated himself from responsibility.

(B) Deny the motion, because res ipsa loquitur applies.

(C) Grant the motion, because the plaintiff has failed to meet his burden of proof.

(D) Grant the motion, because the defendant was not a substantial factor in plaintiff's injury.

88. Twenty years ago, the owner of a residence died, devising it to the trusted caretaker of the owner's physically and mentally incapacitated son for the son's life with the remainder interest in the owner's only grandchild. The caretaker lived in the residence and cared for the owner's son until the caretaker died eight years later. The caretaker's property was inherited by her daughter who continued to live in the residence and care for the son. Five years ago, the son died. The caretaker's daughter has continued to live in the residence since his death.

The owner's grandchild has brought an action for possession of the residence against the caretaker's daughter. The applicable statute states: "Within 10 years from the date the cause of action accrues, a person shall file an action for recovery of possession of a freehold estate in real property."

For whom should the court rule?

(A) The owner's grandchild, because the owner's son was under a disability at the time that the caretaker's daughter took possession of the residence.

(B) The owner's grandchild, because less than 10 years have passed since the owner's son died.

(C) The caretaker's daughter, because the interest of the owner's grandchild existed at the time that the daughter took legal possession of the residence.

(D) The caretaker's daughter, because more than 10 years have passed since she inherited the caretaker's property.

89. A police detective saw a notorious convicted felon who had been released from prison at a local mall. The detective contacted the local police department office to see if there were any outstanding arrest warrants for the felon. A clerk in the office correctly stated that the police database revealed an outstanding arrest warrant for the felon. Unbeknownst to either the detective or the clerk, another police officer had intentionally altered the expiration date of the arrest warrant in the police database, extending the date in order to lay the groundwork for a future arrest of the felon. Acting on the clerk's statement, the detective arrested the felon. A search of the felon uncovered a gun. The felon was charged with possession of a weapon by a felon. The felon's attorney sought to dismiss the charge against his client, contending that the seizure of the gun was unconstitutional and therefore had to be excluded as evidence.

Should the court exclude the gun as evidence and dismiss the charges?

(A) No, because the gun was seized during a search incident to an arrest.

(B) No, because the detective acted in good faith reliance on the clerk's information that a valid arrest warrant existed.

(C) Yes, because a violation of the Fourth Amendment prohibition against unreasonable searches and seizures requires the suppression of the seized evidence.

(D) Yes, because the arrest warrant had expired.

90. A police officer received an anonymous tip that a teenager who lived in an apartment complex with his mother was the perpetrator of a recent rash of burglaries in the complex. The officer, together with another officer, went to the teenager's apartment in order to speak with him. After seeing the officers' uniforms and badges, the teenager, indicating that his mother was at work, invited the officers into the apartment. Once inside, one of the officers gave the teenager, who had a low IQ, a Miranda warning. The teenager responded that he didn't need an attorney and that the police could ask him all the questions they wanted. After almost an hour of questioning, the teenager confessed to the burglaries. The teenager was charged with the burglaries. Prior to trial, his attorney filed a motion to suppress the confession, contending that the teenager's waiver of his Miranda rights was invalid.

On which party is the burden to establish the validity of the waiver and what is that burden?

(A) The burden is on the prosecution to establish the validity of the defendant's waiver beyond a reasonable doubt.

(B) The burden is on the prosecution to establish the validity of the defendant's waiver by clear and convincing evidence.

(C) The burden is on the prosecution to establish the validity of the defendant's waiver by a preponderance of the evidence.

(D) The burden is on the defendant to establish that the waiver was invalid by a preponderance of the evidence.

91. A recently enacted city ordinance prohibited any "inflammatory" discussion or demonstrations regarding abortions on public sidewalks in front of churches located in the city at all times. A violation of the ordinance would result in a criminal misdemeanor. After learning of the ordinance, an individual rights activist planned to demonstrate in front of each of the churches in the city. The activist went to the first church on his list and stood on the public sidewalk in front of the church with signs indicating his "pro-choice" position. He then proceeded to discuss the importance of the right to choose. The police soon arrived and arrested the activist for violating the ordinance. The activist filed suit in federal court claiming that the ordinance violated his constitutional rights.

Which of the following would LEAST support the activist's challenge?

(A) The Establishment Clause
(B) The Due Process Clause
(C) The Equal Protection Clause
(D) Freedom of speech

92. A restaurant was poorly managed. The owner failed to ensure that the kitchen complied with the applicable health and safety regulations, including the regular clearing of the exhaust system. Due to the buildup of grease in the exhaust system, a fire started in the kitchen late one night. Responding to the fire alarm, a firefighter, searching the premises for individuals, sustained injuries due to smoke inhalation. The firefighter filed a negligence action against the owner of the restaurant to recover for his injuries.

Is the firefighter likely to prevail in his claim?

(A) No, because the doctrine of res ipsa loquitor would not apply.
(B) No, because the firefighter was an emergency professional.
(C) Yes, because the restaurant did not comply with the health and safety regulations.
(D) Yes, because the firefighter was a foreseeable plaintiff.

93. A plaintiff sued a defendant for driving through a red light and crashing into the plaintiff's truck. At trial, the plaintiff called a witness, who testified that as the defendant was speeding down the street toward the red light the witness called out to the defendant, whose car window was open, "Watch out, that light is red!"

Which of the following provides the best basis for overruling a hearsay objection by defendant's counsel?

(A) The statement is not hearsay, as it is not offered for its truth.
(B) The statement is not hearsay, as the declarant is available to testify.
(C) The statement constitutes an adoptive admission.
(D) The statement falls within the residual hearsay exception.

94. A plaintiff was involved in a serious car accident with a defendant. The plaintiff sustained damages to her vehicle and significant personal injuries. Two months after the accident, the plaintiff filed a complaint against the defendant in federal district court with subject matter jurisdiction, alleging that the defendant's negligent conduct in failing to stop at a stop sign caused the plaintiff's damages. Twenty days after the defendant served his answer specifically denying the plaintiff's allegations as to the defendant's negligence, the plaintiff moved for summary judgment on the issue of liability. In support of her motion, the plaintiff submitted an affidavit from an eyewitness, stating that he saw the defendant drive through a stop sign immediately before striking the plaintiff's car. This affidavit would be inadmissible at trial as hearsay. The defendant responded to the plaintiff's motion by repeating the denials in his answer.

Can the court grant the plaintiff's motion?

(A) No, because the defendant has specifically denied negligent conduct with regard to the accident.
(B) No, because the plaintiff relied on an affidavit that would not be admissible at trial.
(C) Yes, because there is not a genuine dispute as to the facts.
(D) Yes, because the plaintiff's motion was filed within 21 days of service of the answer.

95. A man's wife wanted to remarry. Though her husband had not been seen for five years, there was no evidence that he had died. The wife wanted the court to declare that her husband was deceased. An applicable statute provided that there is a rebuttable presumption that a person who had not been seen or heard from in five years, after a diligent search for that person, was presumed to have died. One of the husband's family members did not want the court to declare him dead, and she sought to introduce the testimony of a witness who claimed to have seen the husband alive at a gas station. The witness believed that the man had a similar build to the husband. Additionally, she heard him speak to the gas station attendant in an accent similar to the husband's, and she saw him get into a car with license plates from the husband's home state. However, as the witness did not see the man's face or speak to him herself, she could not be sure.

The wife opposes the introduction of the witness's testimony. Is the witness's testimony admissible?

(A) No, because the matter is governed by a presumption that the husband, who has not been heard from in five years, is dead.

(B) No, because the witness is not certain that the man she saw is actually the husband.

(C) Yes, because the Dead Man's Statute expressly permits this type of testimony.

(D) Yes, because it is relevant and not otherwise prohibited.

96. After obtaining a valid search warrant, the police searched a woman's home and discovered a new computer sitting in its original box in the middle of the woman's basement. The police traced the serial number of the computer and learned that it had been stolen from a local electronics shop earlier in the month. On proper questioning by the police, the woman asserted that she had been given the computer by a friend. At trial, the woman testified honestly that she had no idea that the computer was stolen. The jury finds that the woman's belief that the computer was not stolen was honestly held, but was nonetheless unreasonable.

Should they convict the woman of receiving stolen goods?

(A) No, because mistake of law is a valid defense to the crime of receiving stolen goods.

(B) No, because the jury concluded that the woman's belief was honest, even though it was unreasonable.

(C) Yes, because jury concluded that the woman's belief was unreasonable, even though it was honest.

(D) Yes, because receiving stolen goods is a strict liability crime.

97. A woman was attending a baby shower for her sister who was eight months pregnant. At one point during the shower, the woman became engaged in a conversation with her aunt in the kitchen. After taking a careful look around the area to ensure that her sister was not nearby, the woman told her aunt that her sister was not the "mothering type," and that she felt very sorry for the baby because she believed her sister would be a terrible mother. Although the woman believed her sister was not in earshot, the sister was in fact in a bathroom right off the kitchen, where she heard the entire conversation. The sister, who was so upset by the woman's comments that she went into early labor, has sued the woman for intentional infliction of emotional distress.

Is the sister likely to succeed in her claim?

(A) No, because the woman did not owe her sister a duty of care.

(B) No, because the sister cannot satisfy the intent element of the claim.

(C) Yes, because the sister is a member of a group with heightened sensitivity.

(D) Yes, because the woman's conduct is extreme and outrageous.

98. A state legislature enacted a statute providing that punitive damages were recoverable against an employer in a claim filed by an employee only if the employee waived the right to receive unemployment benefits. After the statute was enacted, many employees challenged the law and the state's lower appellate courts all ruled that the statute was valid under state constitutional law. A claim was then filed in federal district court in the state in which the statute had been enacted. The state supreme court had not yet addressed the constitutional issue. When determining whether to award punitive damages to the employee who had brought the claim, the federal district court followed the state court's intermediate appellate rulings. After the federal court's decision, but before a final appeal in the federal-court matter had been disposed of by the court of appeals, the state supreme court held that the statute was unconstitutional under state law.

Which of the following is a correct statement?

(A) The court of appeals must apply what it believes is the proper legal interpretation of state law on the issue.

(B) The court of appeals must defer to the ruling of the district court that followed the state court's intermediate appellate rulings on the issue.

(C) The court of appeals must apply the state supreme court's ruling on the issue.

(D) The court of appeals may, but need not, follow the state supreme court's ruling on the issue.

99. The purchaser of a free-standing heater brought a products liability action against the retailer who sold her the heater and the manufacturer of the heater, for personal injuries and property damages allegedly caused by a defect in the heater, totaling more than $100,000 in damages. The purchaser filed the action in the federal district court located in the state of which the purchaser was a citizen. The retailer was a corporation with its principal place of business located in an adjoining state. Both the manufacturer and the retailer were incorporated in a third state and the manufacturer's principal place of business was in a fourth state. The retailer filed a cross-claim against the manufacturer seeking indemnification pursuant to their contract of sale for any damages awarded to the purchaser. The manufacturer has moved to dismiss the cross-claim for lack of subject matter jurisdiction.

Should the court grant the manufacturer's motion?

(A) Yes, because the diversity-of-citizenship requirement is not met for the cross-claim.
(B) Yes, because the cross-claim is based on state law.
(C) No, because the cross-claim satisfies the requirements for diversity jurisdiction.
(D) No, because the court can exercise supplemental jurisdiction over the cross-claim.

100. The plaintiff sued the defendant after a car accident that occurred on a summer evening. The plaintiff produced evidence that the defendant suffered from night blindness and had trouble seeing in the dark. The plaintiff also produced evidence showing that the time of sunset on the evening of the accident was 8:41 p.m. Without a request from either party, the judge took judicial notice of the time of sunset. At the conclusion of the case, the judge instructed the jury that it was bound to accept as conclusive all judicially noticed facts, including the time of sunset on the evening of the accident.

Was the judge's instruction proper?

(A) No, because jury members may not be instructed that they are required to accept a judicially noticed fact.
(B) No, because a judge may take judicial notice of a fact only when so requested by a party.
(C) Yes, because a judge has discretion whether to instruct a civil jury that it is bound to accept as conclusive any judicially noticed fact.
(D) Yes, because a civil jury must be instructed that it is bound to accept as conclusive any judicially noticed fact.

ANSWER KEY

Remember to log in to your course to submit your answers and view detailed answer explanations.

Question	Answer	Subject	Chapter	Section	ID
1	C	Evidence	Witnesses	Competence	5833
2	B	Real Property	Disputes About Ownership In Land	Delivery and Recording of Deed	1625
3	A	Contracts & Sales	Formation Of Contracts	Mutual Assent	3181
4	B	Constitutional Law	Substantive Due Process	Fundamental Rights	1438
5	A	Contracts & Sales	Formation Of Contracts	Consideration	2403
6	D	Torts	Harms To Personal Property And Land	Trespass to Land	2969
7	A	Criminal Procedure	Trial	Jury Trial	394
8	B	Criminal Law	Inchoate Crimes	Attempt	189
9	D	Evidence	Relevance	Bad Acts	4322
10	D	Criminal Procedure	Fifth Amendment Rights And Privileges	The Fifth Amendment in a Police Interrogation Context	354
11	B	Real Property	Disputes About Ownership In Land	The Land Sale Contract	2008
12	D	Civil Procedure	Venue	General Venue Rule	4954
13	C	Evidence	Relevance	General Considerations	3020
14	C	Constitutional Law	Substantive Due Process	Fundamental Rights	3223
15	C	Torts	Intentional Torts Involving Personal Injury	Battery	6003
16	D	Civil Procedure	Post-Trial Procedure	Appeals	5158
17	A	Civil Procedure	Pleadings	Motions Against the Complaint	6305
18	D	Criminal Law	Homicide	Types of Homicide	169
19	D	Torts	Negligence	Defenses to Negligence	4300
20	A	Real Property	Disputes About The Use Of Land	Easements	4392
21	D	Civil Procedure	Pleadings	Amendments and Supplemental Pleadings	5166
22	C	Criminal Law	Homicide	Types of Homicide	4341
23	A	Civil Procedure	Trial Procedure	Jury Trial	4944
24	C	Torts	Negligence	The Standard of Care	1417
25	A	Criminal Law	Other Crimes	Crimes Against Property	184
26	A	Constitutional Law	Equal Protection	Suspect Classifications	4358
27	B	Civil Procedure	Pleadings	Motions Against the Complaint	5147
28	B	Contracts & Sales	Parol Evidence Rule	When the Parol Evidence Rule Is Inapplicable	6371
29	A	Contracts & Sales	Parol Evidence Rule	Integration	6034
30	A	Constitutional Law	The Powers Of Congress	Taxation and Spending	5853

Question	Answer	Subject	Chapter	Section	ID
31	C	Criminal Procedure	Sixth Amendment	Applicability: Right to Counsel	400
32	B	Civil Procedure	Trial Procedure	Jury Trial	5748
33	C	Constitutional Law	Federal Preemption Of State Law	Express Preemption	3202
34	D	Torts	Negligence	The Standard of Care	5974
35	C	Evidence	Hearsay Exceptions	Declarant's Availability Immaterial	4199
36	A	Evidence	Relevance	Character Evidence	7192
37	A	Real Property	Disputes About Ownership In Land	The Land Sale Contract	2012
38	C	Contracts & Sales	Third-Party Beneficiary Contracts	Vesting of Beneficiary's Rights	6345
39	D	Contracts & Sales	Formation Of Contracts	Mutual Assent	2794
40	B	Evidence	Hearsay	What Is Not Hearsay	5905
41	C	Civil Procedure	Post-Trial Procedure	Appeals	5157
42	B	Real Property	Disputes About The Use Of Land	Easements	3109
43	A	Constitutional Law	Judicial Power	Jurisdiction of the Supreme Court	6290
44	C	Real Property	Landlord And Tenant	Tort Liabilities	3117
45	B	Torts	Negligence	The Standard of Care	1496
46	A	Criminal Law	General Principles	Parties to a Crime	6687
47	B	Contracts & Sales	Breach Of Contract And Remedies	Remedies: Damages for Breach of Contract	3179
48	A	Torts	Products Liability	Strict Products Liability	1351
49	C	Real Property	Disputes About Ownership In Land	Delivery and Recording of Deed	2003
50	B	Real Property	Ownership	Concurrent Estates	1890
51	D	Contracts & Sales	Third-Party Beneficiary Contracts	Intended and Incidental Beneficiaries	6393
52	A	Torts	Defamation, Invasion Of Privacy, And Business Torts	Defamation	6541
53	C	Real Property	Ownership	Present Estates	3134
54	D	Real Property	Ownership	Concurrent Estates	3108
55	C	Contracts & Sales	Breach Of Contract And Remedies	Remedies: Damages for Breach of Contract	2792
56	B	Contracts & Sales	Parol Evidence Rule	When the Parol Evidence Rule Is Inapplicable	6035
57	D	Constitutional Law	Freedom Of Expression And Association	Regulation of Speech	6595
58	D	Torts	Defamation, Invasion Of Privacy, And Business Torts	Defamation	1354
59	D	Real Property	Mortgages and Security Interests	Pre-Foreclosure Rights and Duties	4388
60	C	Constitutional Law	Procedural Due Process	Procedural Due Process Applied	4181

Question	Answer	Subject	Chapter	Section	ID
61	A	Torts	Products Liability	Strict Products Liability	1346
62	A	Criminal Law	General Principles	Parties to a Crime	6238
63	A	Evidence	Relevance	Character Evidence	4317
64	B	Contracts & Sales	Assignment Of Rights And Delegation Of Duties	Assignment of Rights	6367
65	C	Contracts & Sales	Statute Of Frauds	Types of Contracts Within the Statute of Frauds	3194
66	D	Constitutional Law	Judicial Power	Judicial Review in Operation	3247
67	A	Real Property	Disputes About The Use Of Land	Covenants Running With the Land	6512
68	B	Constitutional Law	State Regulation And Taxation Of Commerce	The Dormant Commerce Clause	3261
69	A	Civil Procedure	Multiple Parties And Claims	Interpleader	5123
70	A	Constitutional Law	Freedom Of Religion	Establishment	3269
71	C	Civil Procedure	Multiple Parties And Claims	Class Actions	5127
72	A	Real Property	Ownership	Concurrent Estates	6223
73	A	Evidence	Presentation Of Evidence	Introduction of Evidence	3005
74	C	Contracts & Sales	Formation Of Contracts	Mutual Assent	4222
75	C	Criminal Procedure	Trial	Due Process	6709
76	B	Evidence	Privileges And Other Policy Exclusions	Privileges	636
77	B	Criminal Procedure	Fourth Amendment: Application To Arrest, Search And Seizure	Search and Seizure	411
78	B	Contracts & Sales	Conditions And Performance	Performance	6408
79	A	Evidence	Presentation Of Evidence	Introduction of Evidence	3002
80	B	Civil Procedure	Pretrial Procedure And Discovery	Adjudication Without Trial	5027
81	C	Torts	Negligence	Sharing Liability Among Multiple Defendants	6537
82	D	Contracts & Sales	Formation Of Contracts	Defenses to Formation	3169
83	D	Constitutional Law	The Powers Of Congress	Commerce	1458
84	D	Evidence	Hearsay	What Is Not Hearsay	4316
85	C	Real Property	Landlord And Tenant	Duties of Tenant	3149
86	B	Constitutional Law	Freedom Of Expression And Association	Regulation of Content	6611
87	C	Torts	Negligence	Causation	1446
88	B	Real Property	Titles	Adverse Possession	7402
89	D	Criminal Procedure	Fourth Amendment: Application To Arrest, Search And Seizure	Search and Seizure	410
90	C	Criminal Procedure	Fifth Amendment Rights And Privileges	The Fifth Amendment in a Police Interrogation Context	407
91	C	Constitutional Law	Equal Protection	General Considerations	7181
92	B	Torts	Negligence	Duty	4262

Question	Answer	Subject	Chapter	Section	ID
93	A	Evidence	Hearsay	What Is Hearsay	2996
94	C	Civil Procedure	Pretrial Procedure And Discovery	Adjudication Without Trial	5028
95	D	Evidence	Relevance	General Considerations	631
96	B	Criminal Law	Other Crimes	Crimes Against Property	3071
97	B	Torts	Intentional Torts Involving Personal Injury	Intentional Infliction of Emotional Distress	2967
98	C	Civil Procedure	Choice Of Law: The Erie Doctrine	Determining Applicable State Law	5189
99	D	Civil Procedure	Subject Matter Jurisdiction	Supplemental Jurisdiction	5110
100	D	Evidence	Presentation Of Evidence	Introduction of Evidence	3006